The Seventh Beggar

÷

The Seventh Beggar

÷

PEARL ABRAHAM

RIVERHEAD BOOKS

a member of Penguin Group (USA) Inc.

New York

2005

RIVERHEAD BOOKS
Published by the Penguin Group
Penguin Group (USA) Inc., 375 Hudson Street, New York, New York 10014, USA ·
Penguin Group (Canada), 10 Alcorn Avenue, Toronto, Ontario, Canada M4V 3B2 (a division
of Pearson Penguin Canada Inc.) · Penguin Books Ltd, 80 Strand, London WC2R 0RL,
England · Penguin Ireland, 25 St Stephen's Green, Dublin 2, Ireland (a division of Penguin
Books Ltd) · Penguin Group (Australia), 250 Camberwell Road, Camberwell, Victoria 3124,
Australia (a division of Pearson Australia Group Pty Ltd) · Penguin Books India Pvt Ltd,
11 Community Centre, Panchsheel Park, New Delhi—110 017, India · Penguin Group (NZ),
Cnr Airborne and Rosedale Roads, Albany, Auckland 1310, New Zealand (a division of Pearson
New Zealand Ltd) · Penguin Books (South Africa) (Pty) Ltd, 24 Sturdee Avenue,
Rosebank, Johannesburg 2196, South Africa

Penguin Books Ltd, Registered Offices:
80 Strand, London WC2R 0RL, England

A list of permissions can be found on page 355.

Library of Congress Cataloging-in-Publication Data

Abraham, Pearl, date.
The seventh beggar / Pearl Abraham.
p.   cm.
ISBN 1-57322-285-2
1. Nachman of Bratslav, 1772–1811—Influence—Fiction.   2. Jewish families—
Fiction.   3. Young men—Fiction.   I. Title.

PS3551.B615S47   2005   2004042187
813'.54—dc22

Printed in the United States of America
1   3   5   7   9   10   8   6   4   2

This book is printed on acid-free paper. ∞

BOOK DESIGN BY AMANDA DEWEY

To Stephen

and

to my brother Chaim

"I tell you my dreams also because a dream is but the story of a dream; yet the story of a dream is more than a dream."

—NACHMAN OF BRATSLAV

The inconsistencies in this novel of the English transliteration from Yiddish and Hebrew are not in error. You will find, for example, that in the excerpts of the biography and in the translation of the tale, Nachman's name is spelled without the "c"; in other sources the name is spelled with a "kh." The YIVO Institute for Jewish Research lists at least three different systems for phonetic transliteration from the Hebrew alphabet to the English one. In addition, the conventions differ for Yiddish and Hebrew. In Yiddish, for example, both the *chet* and *chaf* are transliterated as "kh"; in Hebrew the *chet* becomes an "h," the *chaf* a "kh." I arbitrarily use "ch" because it best represents the actual sound, formed farther back in the throat than the "kh." Since the characters in this book are predominantly Yiddish speakers for whom the "ch" sound is entirely natural, the choice of "ch," rather than the "h" or "kh," seems appropriate.

In using "R.," the abbreviated form of Rabbi and Reb, I adopt Arthur Green's usage.

PART

÷

One

I t begins with a stumble.

Joel Jakob stumbled and dropped his keys, which fell into a rain gutter. He hovered over the grating to see how far they had fallen and whether he could retrieve them. On his knees he wasted a precious quarter of an hour, then abruptly abandoned the effort. Inaccessible to him, the keys were also unavailable to others, thieves and murderers, God forbid. They were Medecos; therefore replicas would be costly, which was unfortunate—he would rather have spent the money at the bookstore—but it was almost eight and prayers were beginning in the synagogue. He hurried forward while debating whether to turn back. After another hour of sleep, he could get up again, this time on the right side of the bed, step out the door on his right foot, and begin the day the right way. But his craving for his pillow and the dream he'd left behind made him suspicious. Such seduction resembled the snake's forked tongue.

He picked up where he'd left off in the alphabet.

Nun-mem-lamed—to remember what came before the letter *lamed*, he had to pause and begin again. *Alef-beis-gimel-dalet-heh-vav-zayin-ches-tes-yud-kaf-lamed*—that was it, *nun-mem-lamed-kaf-yud*. Then he started again from the bottom, *taf-shin, resh, kuf, tzaddiq*, paused, at a loss again for the preceding letter. He mouthed the letters from the top, retrieved the *peh-ayin-samach-nun-mem-lamed-kaf*, and stumbled again.

He knew several alphabets, *a* to *z*, *alpha* to *omega*, *alef* to *taf*. He read Hebrew, Aramaic, and Rashi script, with and without vowels, studied the Babylonian and Jerusalem Talmud, the Mishnah, and other commentaries. Between sessions, he read Prophets and Writings. Late nights, he read the notebooks of great men. Early mornings, he started the day with a page from the Book of Creation. What he didn't know, and this astonished him, was *z* to *a*, or *taf* to *alef*.

Why was it so difficult to simply reverse what one knew so well forward? To know anything well is to know it forward and back. Memory is drawn to song; therefore the alphabet is learned in chant. Having learned the alphabetic chant, he was limited to only the forward direction. But he desired the agility to move back and forth with ease. To this end, he practiced.

taf-shin-resh-kuf-tzaddiq-peh-ayin-samach-nun-mem-lamed-kaf-yud-tes-ches-zayin-vav-heh-dalet-gimmel-beis-alef

taf-shin-resh-kuf-tzaddiq-peh-ayin-samach-nun-mem-lamed-kaf-yud-tes-ches-zayin-vav-heh-dalet-gimmel-beis-alef

taf-shin-resh-kuf-tzaddiq-peh-ayin-samach-nun-mem-lamed-kaf-yud-tes-ches-zayin-vav-heh-dalet-gimmel-beis-alef

In the synagogue it was noted that Joel Jakob, son of R. Moshele, grandson of Berditchev, was late to prayers.

During study session, he kept an eye on the time, but though he looked at his watch no less than five times during that hour, he didn't realize until it was too late that the hands remained too long at ten before ten, that on this unlucky day his watch had stopped. As a result he arrived late to his morning lecture.

After this second lateness, Joel felt eyes on the back of his head and fumbled the passage he was called on to elucidate. If only his teachers and colleagues could have looked the other way, pretended he wasn't there that day, or at least not judged him so severely. This was just one day. Never before had anyone found a blemish on him, not as a student, a scholar, or a son.

Considering himself as a son, Joel remembered that without permission from his father he'd purchased and read the Zeitlin biography of Nachman of Bratslav. Not that his reading normally required permission—however, every yeshiva boy was aware of the interdiction against Bratslaver books. Reading about Nachman's childhood concentration on the letters had gotten him started on his own alphabetic project, which had kept him awake later than usual. In the morning he'd been overtired, which had led to the dropped keys. That his watch had stopped on this particular day, Joel put down to retribution.

A stopped watch without a reenactment of the miracle in Joshua. The sun didn't remain high in the sky until the day's work was complete. Earth continued turning. To the modern mind, a stopped watch seems a matter of chance, the timing bad luck, but even as bright a young man as Joel, with a tendency toward freethinking, couldn't entirely escape the concepts of sin and salvation with which he'd been raised.

What had driven him to Nachman's story was a desire to know. Not much wrong with that, you might say, but that's also the reason Adam and Eve ate the forbidden fruit. With the episode of the forbidden fruit, the story of Creation escapes day-to-day sequence, E. M. Forster's "and then and then," and enters the more meaningful "because." Because God warned against eating the fruit, they ate. Which means God provoked the sin. He could have placed the forbidden tree out of reach, outside the garden, or if that was unacceptable to Him, in an obscure corner or thorny thicket. Simply refraining from designating the tree as forbidden might have at least delayed the sin, if not prevented it, but then the story would have remained a primitive one, satisfying only the urge to know what happens next. With the addition of the snake as Eve's seducer, and then Eve as Adam's, intrigue is added and the story becomes psychologically complex.

The forbidden fruit taught Adam and Eve. They learned self-consciousness; they discovered that they were naked and donned fig leaves. According to the Spanish Kabbalists, from the leaves of the tree of knowledge Adam and Eve learned the ingredients of man, that man is made of dust and returns to dust. What did Joel learn from the forbidden?

6

•

Despite this extraordinary day, Joel stopped at the bookstore on his way home. He edged past the towers of yarmulkes at the entrance, nodded his usual greeting to the owner behind the counter, and noted that R. Mendel Moshkovitz was paying for seven new psalters, most likely for his seven daughters, who according to Joel's sister would need prayer.

They're the finest girls, Ada explained, fine and fat, and unfortunately no prospective mother-in-law, not even the most obese, wants a fat bride for her son. That the thinnest of brides will be fat houses within a year or so makes no difference. Mothers-in-law don't want fat girls, Ada pronounced, because they want the credit for fattening up the bride.

Joel offered to make amends for all the sons of these discriminating mothers and marry the fattest girl in Monsey.

Before Mrs. Jakob could finish warning the two jokers about the power of words, even or especially when spoken in jest, Ada was already naming candidates.

She herself was not thin and not fat; she was just right and had a reputation for dressing too elegantly, for knowing such mundane details as the first day of the Charles Jourdan sale.

Ada shrugged off these criticisms.

She was a sixteen-year-old girl comparable to other Chasidic sixteen-year-olds. She enjoyed eating, shopping, and talking on the telephone. Unlike some others, she decided early in life to pursue freely what brought joy, and she became a skilled and uninhibited shopper. And she was generous with her knowledge. When the first girl in her graduating class became engaged, Ada was called upon to advise. More engagements and calls followed.

It was generally acknowledged that Ada Jakob would have made a talented store buyer; that is, if Chasidic girls pursued such careers. As it turned out, a service she'd offered her friends—sketches of acceptable variations on designer clothes complete with alterations based on Chasidic rules of modesty—was in demand, and Ada found herself in the fashion business. Years later, Mrs. Jakob would refer to her daughter as the Marc Jacobs of the Chasidic world.

In partnership with her friend Malke, a talented pattern maker, Ada developed patterns from the sketches and, together, she and Malke sold them for twenty to thirty-five dollars apiece. Every season, color Xeroxes of Ada's sketches were bound and sold as a catalog for ten dollars. What made these patterns more desirable than *Vogue's* or *Butterick's* was not only their suitability for Chasidic girls; they were also current. Ada followed the industry's seasonal schedule and worked quickly. The Chasidic customer required extra lead time for cutting and sewing.

This career brought Ada more notoriety than was generally acceptable in the community, and as with anyone who becomes someone, friends loved and defended her, enemies criticized. The Jakob family, with its reputed rabbinic credentials, was more vulnerable to criticism than others.

For Joel and her father there was little Ada could do fashion-wise: Like all Chasidic men, they wore black and white every day of their lives. The only difference was that unlike the others, they wore starched one hundred percent cotton, not the more practical permanent-press shirts. Sunday evenings Ada starched and ironed fifteen white cotton shirts, seven each for her father and brother, and one for an unexpected event. As a result there were usually spares on the shelf, but conscious of the hours spent ironing, the men didn't avail themselves of more than one fresh shirt a day unless Ada deemed the event worthy.

On Friday nights Joel changed from his black wool coat to his satin caftan. Before his bar mitzvah there had been much debate in the family about whether he ought to wear a velvet collar, a mark of rabbinic stature. As a young man R. Moshele had worn the velvet collar, then rejected it when he became the administrator of the yeshiva. If Joel decided to wear the velvet, he would be following in the tradition of his grandfather, the Berditchever.

Ada declared that the velvet would be soft and luxurious next to Joel's pale skin. He needs something distinguishing, she said. He's too skinny and too pale.

Mrs. Jakob admitted that the velvet collar her husband had worn as a young man had been a mark of distinction, that her friends had envied her the boy's grandeur.

In the end, the Berditchever purchased the velvet fabric, had it sent to the house with the request that it be sewn onto the bar mitzvah boy's caftan, and Joel was dressed for greatness.

The velvet collar made a difference. Thirteen-year-old Joel began to comport himself differently. He remembered always whose grandson he was and what was expected of such a boy. He was conscious of the admiration he saw reflected in the eyes of the younger boys and of the responsibility this conferred on him. The question of whether he merited such distinction began to worry him and he looked for ways to prove himself worthy.

He was a good scholar, but good scholars were plentiful. Along with his colleagues, Joel entered the annual challenges available to capable students. He received high marks for memorizing forty pages of Talmud and reciting them flawlessly in front of an audience of colleagues, scholars, and teachers. But Joel knew that an ability to recite forty pages proved only that he was industrious and had a good memory—something inherited, therefore not entirely to his credit. And it was originality, not scholarship, that distinguished the greats in early Chasidism. The Ba'al Shem Tov (BeShT), the founder of Chasidism, was said to have been a weak scholar, though Joel thought this was mere hearsay; it had all the markings of legend. The BeShT's great-grandson, Nachman of Bratslav, argued against academic achievement, knowledge for the sake of knowledge, recommending instead a humble, worshipful mind. But from the biography Joel had recently read, it was clear that Nachman had read and known more than he'd recommended for others to read and know. And reading and knowing hadn't damaged him; if anything, it had encouraged his talents. Indeed, Nachman's legacy was his book of thirteen tales, masterpieces of the imagination, not scholarly achievements. It was for these tales that Joel had come to the bookstore.

Picture this religious bookstore, an antiquarian's delight. A small space crowded with floor-to-ceiling shelves, the smell of books and pamphlets, old and new, grouped not alphabetically but according to the old divisions of Torah, Prophets, and Writings; the Talmud; and the commentaries of each category shelved alongside in a hierarchy of most to least significant, an organizational plan only an insider could penetrate. A scene of Joel browsing in this nineteenth-century-style bookstore written by a nineteenth-century writer would have the full-blown drama of represented life. Under the author's guiding hand, the privileged reader would listen in, as if eavesdropping, on Joel's grumblings and pleasures, while he walked between the bookshelves, avoiding the aisle and book he had come for, as long as R. Mendel remained in the bookstore. Idling, he would run his fingers along a row of dusty spines, contemplating how quickly he'd sunk into dishonorable behavior. It wasn't in Joel's nature to dissemble and he despised himself for it. Great men like Nachman didn't sink so low.

In the twentieth century, when the technique of stream of consciousness was already common, Joel could have remained browsing in the bookstore for the next three hundred pages. In the meantime, his thoughts, feelings, and reactions, uninterrupted by conventional scene, dialogue, or description, could range far and wide, from Nachman's life to his early death, over the details and structures of Nachman's tales, all of it interleaved with the subjective particulars of Joel's experience. From within one mind at work, a whole world would emerge.

For the twenty-first century, the pretense of represented reality and the containment within one consciousness are too restrictive. Hence a straightforward insertion—an excerpt from *Tormented Master*, Arthur Green's definitive biography of Nachman:

A picture may be constructed of a child who is the object of high expectations, the offspring of two great families, and the heir apparent to the Medzhibozh dynasty. Nahman was probably constantly watched for signs of incipient greatness. For a child who took his own religious life seriously, of course, this brought about grave conflicts with the values of humility and pure devotion taught by his ethical tracts. A conflict developed between the grand public display of religious enthusiasm (or even occult powers) and expectations of himself in this regard, and the values of inwardness in which he was coming to believe. How does the favorite child of a great rabbinic court, ever crowded about by hundreds of admiring *hasidim*, dare to disappoint their expectations? At the same time, how does one who allows himself to participate in the public display of virtuoso piety live with himself when the crowds are gone? This conflict came to manifest itself in Nahman as an increasing shyness about any show of piety or learning, a shyness that forced him to learn that he must hold a great deal within himself, sharing it with no one. *Inwardness* and *loneliness* go hand in hand in the descriptions of Nahman's early years; it seems that he dared not share his religious strivings with those around him, lest they only be used as further public confirmation of the image that would-be admirers sought in him, one which he felt a deepening need to avoid. The more such a child felt that the secrets of his inner life might be betrayed by those he trusted, including those proud and well-intentioned adults to whom he felt closest, the more deeply within himself he might feel a need to hide, and the thicker the wall of loneliness he might construct.

For books there had never been a budget. Joel and Ada had been encouraged to purchase books from R. Yidel on account ever since they could read. Although Nachman's book of tales was an unusual choice for a yeshiva boy, it wasn't Joel's first deviation. He'd read books on philosophy, science, and computer science. He'd read histories and secular analyses of Chasidism and found the perspective of outsiders illuminating in ways that insiders' couldn't be. Bratslav writings, however, were considered dangerous because Nachman's messianic ambitions were secreted within them. And a reputation as a Bratslav follower would do great harm, not only to himself, but to Ada and to his father, whose position at the yeshiva was important. Since Joel had no intention of becoming a Bratslaver—he simply wanted to know the tales and see for himself whether they were truly unusual—it would be prudent to keep his readings private. The tongues that wagged could make something of the smallest crumbs.

To avoid unnecessary talk, he delayed.

When R. Mendel had paid for the seven psalters and departed, Joel hurried over to the Bratslav corner, located an edition of the book of tales, slipped it between two innocuous titles he'd picked up, and brought the three books to the counter.

I'm certain your father has several copies of the *Maharal* at home, R. Yidel said. Probably also this edition of the *Rambam* (Maimonides), but definitely the *Maharal*.

Joel returned the two books to their respective places on the shelves. He wished his father were less renowned, or that this community wasn't so insular. Wherever he went, people knew who he was; whatever he did, people would talk. Then he reminded himself that this was only an issue when he was doing what he shouldn't.

When he returned to the counter, the book was already in a brown bag. As a Bratslav chasid, R. Yidel had firsthand knowledge of the prejudices against Bratslav and knew what the other books were for.

Joel slipped the book into the bosom pocket of his overcoat and prepared to hurry home for the evening meal, but without his keys he would have to ring to enter his father's house. With the book against his guilty heart, he couldn't bring himself to put his finger on the doorbell. To retrieve the keys he needed the miracle of an outstretched arm. For want of a miracle, he stopped at the hardware store and purchased a magnet and several feet of twine. Then he hurried from Main Street to Maple to Suzanne Drive, took the shortcut on Leon directly to the rain drain on Ida Road. Out of habit he looked at his watch, which remained uninformative. It had to be close to seven, he calculated, less than half an hour of light left. He placed his hat on the ground beside him and set to work, conscious that the image of a yeshiva boy in the street on all fours was less than dignified.

If the contraption had succeeded in retrieving the keys, science would have provided the answer that God had not. This wasn't, however, a day for easy resolutions. After half a dozen attempts, Joel managed to lift the keys from the corner in which they were lodged, but the magnet wasn't powerful enough to hold them, and the keys fell farther into the watery abyss.

Twenty minutes passed. At home, Joel knew, they were at dinner, wondering about his delay. It would be his third lateness on this exceptional day in which things had gone from bad to worse. He transferred the book of tales to the outer pocket of his coat, moving the weakness to his left hip, and walked home.

Joel was grateful that it was Ada, not his father, who opened the door. His explanations about the lost keys and stopped watch amused her; his father frowned, then smiled. After dinner, Mrs. Jakob gave him the extra set kept for such emergencies along with money for a new watch battery, and then Joel was on the street again, on his way to evening prayers, pondering the practical solutions that both did and didn't solve problems: The keys to his father's house had been restored to him, but that didn't make it right for him to enter freely, as if there had been no violation. But not returning home at all would cause pain. What could he do? What he wanted to do was find a quiet place to read the tales, but evening prayers were beginning in fifteen minutes, and after prayers, he would attend his two-hour study session. Out of habit he turned his wrist to see the time. The hands were still pointing at ten to ten. If only all hands on all watches of the world had miraculously remained pointing at ten to ten, he could have escaped time, escaped the demands of his schedule, read and reread the tales, and satisfied his interest in these strange writings. But the rigors of a Talmudic student's life required that he pray at certain times, study between such and such a time, eat, pray again, study. A full schedule made it impossible to concentrate on any subject long enough to reach a degree of knowledge that could count for something. Which was why, Joel concluded, there was no longer true greatness in the Chasidic world. To achieve unusual heights in anything, a certain amount of freedom is necessary, even if the result is a failure to fulfill the commandments.

A failure to fulfill the commandments? Joel justified this transgressive idea with a detail he'd come across in his reading of Nachman's biography. When held captive on a Turkish ship, Nachman had said that it was possible to fulfill the commandments spiritually, with concentrated mind rather than ritualistic activity. A similarly dangerous idea, Joel knew, had arisen a century before Nachman from Shabbatai Zevi, the false messiah of the seventeenth century, and had inspired Joseph Frank, another messianic figure, who led the Frankist rebellion and finally broke with Judaism, taking thousands of Jews with him. Impatient with restrictive law and seeking to make contact with the primal source of life, these mystics rejected authority, neglected law and order, and descended into the cauldron of freedom.

But where were these ideas taking him? Joel asked himself. He had wasted the day's walks, morning and evening, for a set of lost keys. He took a deep breath and attempted his first set of alphabetic combinations as described in the Book of Creation—*alef with them all and all of them with alef*—an exercise said to increase concentration.

alef-alef, alef-beis, alef-gimmel, alef-dalet, alef-heh, alef-vav, alef-zayin, alef-ches, alef-tes, alef-yud, alef-kaf, alef-lamed, alef-mem, alef-nun, alef-samach, alef-ayin, alef-peh, alef-tzaddiq, alef-kuf, alef-resh, alef-shin, alef-taf

Indeed, the concentration required for the exercise cleared his head. As soon as he started, he felt strangely enlarged, as if his mind had grown more spacious; he had the odd sensation of his mind as a room in which he could move about. He took on the second letter, *beis*, also known as the house, inhaled again—

beis-alef, beis-beis, beis-gimmel, beis-dalet, beis-heh, beis-vav, beis-zayin, beis-ches, beis-tes, beis-yud—

On the upper half of Suzanne Drive, his friend Aaron caught up with him, and Joel ceased reciting. Without much of a greeting—they spent so much of their day together, at the synagogue, in classrooms and study halls, and walking back and forth, to and fro, the intervals between their time together mere eyeblinks—Aaron resumed where they'd left off earlier:

We are required to recite along with our fathers that *We ourselves went out from Egypt, and not only our ancestors,* but how could all the generations—past, present, and future—have stood together at Sinai, as if they were all alive at once, as if time didn't exist? This is a modern idea.

Yes and but, Joel said, without missing a beat. The midrash binds the generations together for the sake of tradition and continuity, while modernism intends to destroy what came before. Tradition and modernism conflate time for entirely different reasons. The evil son of the Haggadah who says, What was this miracle wrought for you—for you and not for him—is a modern. He wants to have nothing to do with his ancestors' stories. The son wants to break the old vessel of tradition. That's why his father must knock out his teeth.

Early Chasidism broke the old vessel, Aaron pointed out. We now live to gather the shards and bring about a correction, but we broke the vessel in the first place.

And that's when we were most innovative, Joel said. We had true purpose in the world. As soon as we established ourselves, and lived by another version of the old vessel, we were nothing. And the Vilna Gaon saw through us. He suspected us of idol worship because we worshipped not God but the vessel: our Chasidic courts and our wonder rebbes.

If, Aaron said, tracing an arc with his thumb as though arguing a difficult Talmudic passage. If, he thumbed again, we failed to heed the second commandment, it was only in order to fulfill the first one. We worshipped the wonder rebbes because they helped us come closer to God and know Him as the One and Only.

But, Joel said, and stopped. If, then, and but. All their conversations adhered to the structure and chant of the Talmud. As always he found himself arguing the other side only because someone had to. The people who built the tower of Babel also wanted to know God, he could have said, but didn't. He had other things on his mind. He considered discussing with Aaron the difficulty of knowing the alphabet backward, to see if he too would find it difficult, but Aaron would want to know why such knowledge was desirable. He would accuse him of trying to break the vessel of the old alphabet.

They were good friends, they'd studied together since childhood, covered the same subjects at school then as yeshiva scholars, challenged themselves to the same extracurricular work, argued over every topic and remained friends, but his recent off-track reading and interests, Joel knew, were not what anyone would recommend for young scholars.

His course of studies as a child was more or less typical of the curriculum for the hasidic elite of his time. In addition to Talmud and codes, the mainstays of any traditional Jewish education, emphasis was placed upon mystical and ethical literature: he studied the *Zohar* and the *Tiqquney Zohar*, the entire corpus of the Lurianic writings (with particular emphasis on the *Peri'Eẓ Hayyim*), *Reshit Hokhmah*, and various other ethical tracts. It is also noteworthy and somewhat surprising that the Bible (*TeNaKH*) is listed as an item of his curriculum; Nahman had a thorough knowledge, unusual for his day, of even the more obscure parts of the Hebrew Bible, a knowledge which greatly aided his skill as a preacher. In addition to the regular diet of Talmudic subjects, special mention is also made of the study of *'Eyn Ya'aqov*, a popular selection of the Aggadic passages in the Talmud. The legends of the *'Eyn Ya'aqov* and the *Zohar* must have provided rich sustenance for Nahman's fertile imagination, an imagination already weaving together the strands of fantasy that were to emerge later with startling originality in his *Sippurey Ma'asiyot*.

It was after midnight when Joel finally had an opportunity to look at the book. He'd been carrying it around all evening, he'd even forgotten about it for moments at a time, until he felt again the hard right angles against the bone of his left hip.

He washed, undressed, and only when he was in bed did he take the book into his hands. He hesitated, held it closed. There were enough transgressions one committed in bed; in the best case they were involuntary. Reading the tales in bed in his father's house was a deliberate act. Joel wasn't concerned about the effect of the reading on his mind; he'd read Spinoza and Leibniz and recently a work of fiction by a secular Jew, and he felt capable of judging the quality of the writing and ideas without falling under undue influence. For example, he'd found the modern form of the fiction intriguing in that within several hundred pages, a whole world was created. And while reading he hadn't paused to doubt the existence of this man-made world or the characters that resided in it. Afterward he'd marveled at how small a universe it was, how much was missing from it, how many pages were required to contain it, and how much effort and time the writer must have expended in its creation. The creation of the real and infinite world took seven days, but man isn't God. Since Joel was only a man, he was intrigued by the lesser achievement, which he thought the more extraordinary, given the limited powers. Man, created in the image of his Maker, turns around and attempts the Maker's work, complete with creatures in His own image. But the man-made is never perfect, Joel reminded himself.

Though he would have liked not to sin against his blameless father, Joel was eager to begin reading. If he were a better person, if he'd had an ounce of patience, he would have taken his time, searched the shelves in the study halls and his grandfather's collection of ancient books and manuscripts, and with a bit of fortune, come upon the book of tales. Or he could have asked his father to buy the book for him.

But he wasn't that person. He'd recently turned seventeen and nothing was more urgent than to know and become. Hillel Zeitlin, Nachman's biographer, wrote that microcosms of the otherworldly exist within Nachman's tales. That a mere man could create such otherness, it seemed to Joel, was indeed miraculous. He would read to know the unknown.

Joel had a restless tendency to thumb through books from front to back and back to front before he settled in to read. He resisted entering into the writer's spell; he read the titles of Nachman's tales first, tried to predict their contents, then scanned the pages for character names. He found no names, only identifiers, labels. There were rabbis and rabbis' sons, as expected in Chasidic tales, but also kings, emperors, princes and princesses, burghers, cripples, and paupers. The last and longest tale,

"The Seven Beggars," was considered Nachman's greatest, and Joel was impatient to get to it. He wanted to start with the best, worried that it was the wrong thing to do, then dismissed his concern as mere rigidity. In machine logic, he knew, it was most efficient to process what comes in last first; however, since the human brain isn't limited to any organizational systems, it ought to be free to retrieve its information in any or no order. What the human brain does share with the machine: a dependence on incoming information. Therefore an if-then construction: If the sequence of tales in the book corresponds to the order in which they were written, then the last tale ought to bear the experience and knowledge of what was learned in the composition of the first twelve. However, since the human brain is unpredictable, there remains a but; a writer's final work is not always his best. With this back-and-forth reasoning, Joel justified reading the final achievement first. In the morning, he would begin at the beginning, and follow the growth curve, presuming there had been one.

Another Extraordinary Day

In Joel's life, day usually followed day without much differentiation, and if not for the change in the reading at the synagogue he wouldn't know Tuesday from Wednesday. Thursday mornings his mother had to remind him of what day it was, because on Thursday evenings, in honor of the Sabbath, he ran an errand: he picked up the fish for the Sabbath meals.

On this particular Thursday, feeling a need for personal penance, he had refrained from food and drink and felt weak, but the fish had to be brought home. He walked toward Main Street, newly crowded with shoppers after a long, quiet summer. The New Year was two weeks away, and already apples, mangoes, kiwi, dates, and figs were piled high on fruit vendors' stands. Flyers announcing the availability of kosher and organic honey from beehives in Kerhonkson, New York, were posted everywhere, and suddenly the demand for organic honey was great, though Joel wondered how organic honey differed from the usual kosher honey. Wasn't all honey produced by bees? But no one begrudged the extra dollar to help celebrate the new year, and the standard jars of golden honey accumulated dust on grocery shelves.

A large fish, red mouth gaping, stared out at Joel from the display window at Klein's fish store. He looked away quickly. Those glassy eyes, or perhaps it was the teeth, made him dizzy. Inside, he acknowledged the familiar nod from Mrs. Klein, who personally packaged the Jakobs' fish every week and kept the bag in the refrigerator until Joel arrived. As soon as she saw him at the door, she went to retrieve the bag and then placed it on the counter so that R. Moshele's son, grandson of Berditchev, wouldn't have to commit the sin of accepting something from the hand of a woman. Joel acknowledged her thoughtfulness with a nod of thanks. Not so long ago, before his bar mitzvah, Mrs. Klein would pinch his cheek and call him a *nagyon szép*, and perhaps he was a nice boy, but then he'd smell of fish. Now she wished him a peaceful Shabbos but her words were strangely garbled, as if she were underwater. Joel smiled in response and turned to leave, too quickly, because his head spun. The blurred door was only a few steps away, but though he walked toward it, it maintained its distance. Waves of water arose in front of him. He would have to swim, though he'd never learned how. The air was thick. There was no air. He'd sinned and now he would drown. It was dark and he couldn't see. He was afloat in the belly of a fish and deep inside was a flicker of light and Joel thought he saw a man. He inched closer, groped the air, not wanting to touch the mucous walls. He struggled to breathe. Again the flame flickered and Joel made out a face with only the beginning of a beard. The man's hair was red and he wore the black-and-gold-striped caftan of the Chasidim of the Ukraine.

Nachman, Joel knew.

Joel had often wished he'd lived in another era, but he'd been inconstant about which one. At one time he'd wanted to have come into the world in the days of Moses; at other times, in the grand court of King

Solomon; more recently he'd focused on the small group of mystic initiates in Safed who were renowned for their intuitive depths of knowledge and for the bond they formed with Bar Yochai, their teacher, the second-century Tannaite credited with authorship of the *Zohar*. It was possible, Joel thought, that his soul had lived in other eras, but clothed in a different body, which would have made all the difference. And he had no memory of another life. Like all newborns, Joel had suffered the angel's indelible flick beneath his nose, which dented his upper lip and erased all former knowledge. His task in life was to learn again.

He moved forward gropingly, and when he was only a few feet away, Nachman of Bratslav stepped forward and stood before him. When he saw Joel, an unnatural shudder began in the man's shoulders and traveled down his back, rattling every vertebra in the most inhuman way.

Joel put his hand out to reassure, to explain that he wanted merely to know him, but his voice wouldn't emerge. The veins in Nachman's neck bulged, and his hands struck out, slapped the humid air, and resounded on Joel's face.

Joel opened his eyes to a smeared white apron hovering above him, and strangely he was lying on the ground. He reached for his hat. His head hurt and his cheeks were warm. What had he done? Why had they slapped him?

You fainted, Mrs. Klein explained.

Mr. Klein helped Joel up and led him to a chair. Your father is on his way, he said.

Joel shook his head. His inner ear itched terribly, he wanted a Q-tip, but he was fine otherwise. He could wait outside. He'd caused enough trouble already. He looked around. How many customers had witnessed his faint? The news would be all over Monsey by morning. Every woman would go home and tell her husband and also a few friends, who would tell their husbands. In the synagogue the next day people would ask how he was.

What was the matter with him? He'd fasted often enough before. He remembered the fish in the window, but was afraid to look again. He was behaving like a pregnant woman.

Joel kept his eyes down and sipped water from the cup that had passed from Mrs. Klein to her husband to Joel, and then R. Moshele arrived, and he and Mrs. Klein spoke in Hungarian, of which Joel understood very little. R. Moshele offered his arm, but Joel stood alone. I'm quite fine, he insisted. It was nothing, and it's passed.

Outside, Joel avoided the fish in the window and hurried toward his father's parked car. What's the rush? R. Moshele asked.

I'm perfectly fine, Joel said. I've wasted enough time already.

Mrs. Klein says it wasn't a mere faint. She describes something more unusual. Can you remember what happened just before you fell?

I couldn't breathe. And the smell of fish was strong. But it's probably just lack of sleep. I didn't sleep well last night.

Mrs. Jakob came to the door, put her wrist, which smelled of chicken, on Joel's forehead, and he remembered the Sabbath fish. When he looked down, the handles of the brown bag were still looped over his wrist, and he delivered the fish to his mother, who handed the bag to Ada without looking at it. Joel looked at Ada, who was dressed, it seemed to him, for a wedding. He sniffed. It was Ada, she smelled of waxy crayons.

His mother led the way to the kitchen table. Sit, sit, she said, as if he were about to topple over.

She put in front of him a steaming bowl of soup with yellow soup nuts afloat, Osem's, his favorite, but his head hurt.

I'm not hungry, he said. Maybe in a little while.

What do you mean, not hungry? You're white as a sheet. Have you eaten anything today? You didn't stop for breakfast or lunch. All day no food has passed those blue lips. No wonder you fainted. I keep begging you to take something with you, an apple, some crackers. Mrs. Jakob paused for breath. If for no other reason than to honor your mother, you must eat the soup, she declared.

Joel ate the soup.

The telephone rang. Ada answered and, seeing her roll her eyes heavenward, Joel understood that it was their grandmother, the Berditchever rebbetzin, and that the local grapevine, the most efficient newswire worldwide, was in full operation.

He's fine, Ada said, he's right here. . . . No, he was tired and hadn't eaten. . . . He'll be fine . . . yes, people . . . unfortunately . . . yes, I know it runs on your side of the family, but it's never happened to Joel before, and, God willing, it won't happen again. . . . Yes, I'll be late, but I'm already dressed.

R. Moshele thought it would be better—that is if Joel felt well enough—to appear in public sooner rather than later. Ada agreed with her father. Except for a headache, Joel said he felt fine and had no good reason not to attend prayers at the synagogue. Mrs. Jakob disagreed. She would rather Joel stay home all evening. To reassure his mother, Joel agreed to remain beside his father and forgo his evening walks to and fro. On this night, he would ride.

As expected, Joel felt eyes on the back of his head. Friends, classmates with whom he sat at yeshiva every day, that very day, walked up to him, shook hands, and asked how he was, as if he'd crossed a desert.

Late that evening, alone in his room, Joel held the book of Nachman's tales in his hands. What powers did these writings have? He'd experienced two strange days, stranger than he would admit to anyone. Fainting at the fish store was the culmination of an evil forty-eight hours and now he found himself afraid of the book, though at this point, he asked himself, what choice did he have? He had to continue his search for meaning, try to understand it better. Why had Nachman left his final tale incomplete? Why didn't the seventh beggar arrive? The story was so packed with stories, it was hard to keep the details separate. It seemed to Joel that one story converged on the other. They gave him vertigo. To counter the dizziness, to recapture the stories and organize them in his head, he borrowed from Ada's room a large sketch pad, a pencil, and a ruler, and sketched an outline.

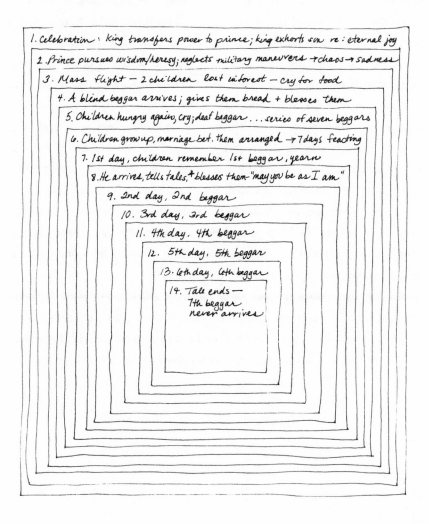

1. Celebration: King transfers power to prince; king exhorts son re: eternal joy
2. Prince pursues wisdom/heresy; neglects military maneuvers → chaos → sadness
3. Mass flight — 2 children lost in forest — cry for food
4. A blind beggar arrives; gives them bread + blesses them
5. Children hungry again, cry; deaf beggar . . . series of seven beggars
6. Children grow up, marriage bet. them arranged → 7 days feasting
7. 1st day, children remember 1st beggar, yearn
8. He arrives, tells tales, + blesses them "may you be as I am"
9. 2nd day, 2nd beggar
10. 3rd day, 3rd beggar
11. 4th day, 4th beggar
12. 5th day, 5th beggar
13. 6th day, 6th beggar
14. Tale ends — 7th beggar never arrives

.   .   .

It was late when he was finished. The house was silent. He folded the sheet of paper into the book and placed it under his pillow—he'd read somewhere that this was conducive to dreaming—and hoped that in the morning he would understand.

Not quite a faint, his father had said. Mrs. Klein had described something more violent, with thrashing and choking and gasping for air. The word they were avoiding was seizure. Joel remembered a strange sinking, hard to resist. It had drawn him toward nothingness, a *tohu va-vohu*. He'd resisted at first and that had been painful. When he'd relinquished control, it became easy, and he'd felt himself spiraling downward into the deep dark. He'd heard his name called—Joel, Joel, Joel—and he'd struggled to respond but it hurt. And then his eyes were open and he'd expected a new day, a different year. Months had passed. He'd lived what seemed to him a long time and he felt older. Which couldn't quite be because he'd traveled backward in time. The man he'd met was about seventeen, Joel's age, which would place the scene in Medvedevka in the year 1788, when Nachman was newly married. But was there such a thing as past, present, and future in the next world, Joel wondered, or was it all one, an embracing of all time at once?

Asking the question, Joel once again smelled fish. He'd bathed, brushed his teeth, and still. The smell came from within, fish breath, as if he'd swallowed the Leviathan. He could get up and gargle with Listerine, but his mother would hear him and worry. Instead, he closed his eyes.

The Seven Fat Brides

It came to pass that Joel's father stood waiting beside his son's bed, basin and pitcher in his hands. Joel gave his fingertips to the splash of cold water without lifting his head, one-two-three, and mouthed the "I admit before thee, O live and lasting King, who has returned to me my soul . . ."

Then he remembered what day it was. He would be meeting for a second time with R. Mendel's seventh daughter. Before she would agree to marry him, there was a detail to work out, and she wanted to be sure it was acceptable to Joel. It was unusual for a young girl to make such a demand, and he wondered what she had in mind. He'd seen her once, and had decided right away that she was very acceptable to him.

The meeting was set for ten that morning, which meant that he would miss his nine o'clock study session, and wouldn't have an opportunity to review yesterday's lecture. Which was why he'd asked his father to wake him early.

Traditionally the boy is expected to begin talking, Joel knew, but since this second meeting was arranged at the girl's request, he thought she might begin. When she didn't, he smiled, she smiled shyly in return, and he thought her smiling face immensely pleasing. He asked how she'd been.

The seventh daughter looked up into his eyes, nodded, and said fine, then looked down. Probably not so fine, Joel thought.

She hesitated, maybe it was just shyness, then spoke. I wanted to see you again because there is something I must explain to you. It was decided that such intimate information would be most acceptable to you coming from me.

Joel smiled encouragement. She seemed so serious, he thought the knowledge she was about to impart must be very intimate indeed. And who was it who had decided? Her parents?

You see, she said, you don't know my other sisters, but if you did, and God willing you soon will, you would see that I owe everything I have to them. When you see them it will become clear to you that every one of my parts that has been called beautiful is a copy of one of theirs, that I am altogether made up of my sisters' parts. I have my eldest sister's deep blue eyes, my second sister's shapely ears, my third sister's fluid voice, my fourth sister's slender, long neck, my fifth sister's straight shoulders, and my sixth sister's pale long fingers. The best of each is in me, which is perhaps why I am fattest. So you see, in marrying me, you acquire also them, and therefore I must propose that you marry each of us separately, in the order in which we were born. You seem shocked. Perhaps you are thinking of the edict of Rabeinu Gershom against multiple wives. That shouldn't be a concern. Our father has received an allowance signed by forty elders. I have been told to advise you to think of this as Jacob's seven years of labor.

Joel nodded to acknowledge the reference. Although he was amazed at the request, he was conscious enough to register the girl's words and how well they'd been put together. She must have rehearsed them.

My sisters are here to meet you, she said, and stood.

He watched her walk to the door quickly, rather lightly, he thought, for someone carrying so much weight. Her six sisters came in and took seats at the table, leaving the chair on his immediate right for the youngest, and this too seemed significant.

The eldest sister

cleared her throat, and when Joel turned toward her, he felt himself transfixed. She spoke.

I have been blessed with what others agree are the most beautiful, bluest eyes. Seeing through this deep blue makes everything appear more attractive and leaves me in a highly receptive state. Since I am always in this state, I will see you with utmost tenderness at all times. You will always be certain of the friendliest, kindest reception. Never will a harsh word pass between us. Never will you have to waste a moment thinking about what I said, or what I may have intended. Your mind will be free to think only of Torah, twelve hours a day. However, before I can agree to be your bride, there is something you must do. You must prove yourself worthy by fulfilling one of the seven tasks practiced by the great ascetics of Safed. The choice of the task is yours and I hope you will accomplish it with great joy.

Joel looked into her eyes as she spoke. It was true they were beautiful, deeply blue with a kind and deep black center. They held his own eyes. He couldn't turn away until she closed her eyes for a long blink, and then he was able to look into the seventh daughter's eyes for comparison. They were similar, but the younger eyes didn't hold him as her sister's had, didn't contain the same depths. About the girl's request that he perform an ascetic task, he didn't know what to think. Wasn't marrying all seven of them enough of a challenge?

The second sister

shifted her weight and Joel turned toward her.

I have been blessed with the most intricately formed ears, which provide me with a level of hearing rarely attained by humans. I have the ability to detect the softest breaths and sighs. With such ears, I will be attuned to your every mood, your every discontent, however minor. I will understand what you are experiencing even before you are fully conscious of it. With every discomfort acknowledged and attended to, you will be free for only the highest thoughts. However, there is one thing you must do for me, and that is to take upon yourself the challenge of a daily recital of Psalms.

When Joel compared the ears of the youngest sister with those of her sister's, he saw the difference and acquired a new appreciation for ears. These ears were livelier, attentive and expressive in a way other ears merely imitated. The challenge of a daily recital of Psalms, though not an impossible task, was unusual, the kind of burden a man ought to take upon himself only on personal impulse.

Joel heard the sound of a smooth, clear voice, fluid and sweet as milk and honey, and he turned toward

the third sister

who was merely speaking but with so much melody it occurred to Joel that although a woman's voice is illicit to men only in song, this woman's plain speech was more beautiful than most singing. He was hearing the sound of her voice and not what she said, but it didn't matter. He knew that what she had to say was convincing, that her voice would inspire him to great prayer and song. And he was certain she had requested something difficult of him, too. He would have to ask about that later because already she was finished and the fourth sister had begun.

Joel turned toward her. Her neck was wrapped in a silk cloth spun of gold. Joel watched as she slowly untied it and looked into his eyes, but it was hard for him to take his own eyes from her pale, slender, and impossibly long neck, so delicate, you were afraid for it. He wanted to tell her to keep it wrapped, to protect it, but then he wouldn't see it. She was sitting down, but still he could see that the thinness of her neck was in great contrast to the rest of her, which made her appear more vulnerable.

She spoke softly and Joel had to crane his own neck to hear her.

The fragility of my exposed neck creates in men a great empathy for the weak and vulnerable. Seeing it on a daily basis will make of you a better person, a considerate being whose desire will be to help the weak. In helping others you will feel yourself most generous, and with such a feeling, every day of your life will be worthwhile. You will not experience a moment of despair, of wondering why you have been placed on earth. However, before I can become your bride, there is a difficult task I must ask of you. That you commit one day of every week to fasting for the first seven years of our married life.

Joel nodded. Fasting was a standard ascetic practice and he'd been expecting such a request from one of the sisters.

He turned toward

the fifth sister

whose posture was perfect. Without a trace of a slouch, she spoke.

I am blessedly noted for the straightest shoulders among women. These are shoulders that inspire men to take on the great burdens of the world, and such men, as you know, become eligible for a position among the thirty-six just men whose goodness maintains cosmic equilibrium. Much has been asked of you today, and therefore I will refrain from adding my own request. I choose rather merely to second those of the others.

Joel thought the girl's humility in the face of her sisters' demands quite fine and also clever. And he found much to admire in her shoulders, which were covered in a pretty yellow crocheted shawl whose

31

◆

loose stitches provided glimpses of the fine flesh beneath. He nodded to show his appreciation, and turned to the next sister.

The sixth sister

put her hands, which were beautifully pale and slender, on the table, but before she could speak, the door opened and there was his mother, and behind her, the girls' mother, carrying the seven plates to be broken. He and the seven sisters watched as his mother broke the first plate and said *mazel tov* and then reached for the next plate, and the next. He tried to stop her, to make himself heard above the clattering sound of porcelain breaking. He tried to shout, Wait, but no sound emerged. His throat was dry and hoarse.

Moving his legs, he felt the dampness of his undergarments and his heart sank. He'd released spirits without bodies, demons who would work against man, and set back the redemption of the world. And these demons would attend his funeral, follow him to his grave, complaining of their bodiless state, and weigh in against him just as he entered the next world, with Judgment Day upon him.

He would have to attempt a correction, refrain from food and drink all day. He looked at his watch. It was late, he was tired, if only he could get to bed, but already his wedding to the eldest of the seven sisters was in full swing; he was sitting beside the bride, along with the wedding guests, waiting for Yankel Yankevitch, the first of the seven wedding rhymers to begin. The bride's father was talking to him, and Yankel nodded in agreement. Then, in the traditional *badkhn*'s chant, Yankel began, and Joel knew that whether he kept his eyes open or closed, whether conscious or not, the next six weddings would take place, the story would continue.

Yankel Yankevitch began with a preface, explaining that the father of the bride, R. Mendel, had begged him to keep the performance short, seeing as it was close to midnight and there were six more weddings scheduled to follow. And since he, Yankel, had always been a reasonable man, he had agreed, especially since there was good reason to keep things short: The family was tired, and marrying off one daughter required difficult and multitudinous preparations; multiplied seven times, the work would be without end, especially since each daughter had been promised a wedding unique to her. After all, Yankel pointed out, Reb Mendel's daughters are fine Jewish girls, they deserve proper Jewish weddings, no Sun Mung Moon orgy of sameness. To persuade the guests of the enormity of R. Mendel's burden, Yankel proposed to take a few moments to reflect on the preparations seven weddings might entail.

First
    the purchase of forty-five to fifty yards of heavy white satin, and plenty of yards of lace and several pounds of glistening pearls and other beads, and then some of that sheer fabric, what is it called, the women here ought to know—organza, thank you—and how many spools of thread, and packets of hooks and eyes, and don't forget the satin-covered buttons, and the stiff white tulle for the underlayers of the skirts. And I'm sure, being only a man and ignorant of such womanly things, I've managed to leave out some significant items.

    Then the measuring, cutting, pinning, and stitching of seven bridal dresses must begin, each bride with her own style; and the question of whether to hire one seamstress for all the dresses, or seven different ones, has to be debated; however, my wife informs me that good seamstresses aren't easy to come by, the name of a good seamstress is entered into the family vault of secrets.

    Then the fittings. The seamstress finds that one daughter has gained five pounds (she runs out of the room crying), the other has shed a few (she tries and fails to hide her feeling of triumph), and you can't blame the girls, it's how things are before a wedding, some eat more when they're nervous, others don't eat at all; and so one dress is taken in, another let out, and the seamstress begs the girls to be certain there are no more changes in their figures. And then on the third fitting, it's discovered that the youngest daughter, who's still growing, has shot up two inches, and the dress has to be lengthened. After much discussion and debate, a band of lace is added. In the making of a bridal dress, every woman will inform you, traces of the miracles of Creation can be found. Since in this world every creative act features aspects of God's work, you have to agree that there's some truth in the claim. And if even God needed rest on the seventh day, how tired must this family be. Is it any wonder then that R. Mendel wants to keep things short. And I've only given you a taste of things. Listen further:

Of course every bride must have a pair of white shoes, and even if R. Mendel's virtuous daughters wanted to save their dear father some hard-earned money, as fate would have it, the feet of these sisters happen to be like a set of Russian dolls, each pair a half size larger than the one before her. And so seven pairs of white shoes had to be purchased, and as we all know, in September, white shoes aren't easy to come by. The girls would have spent hours searching the sale racks of last season's shoes. In a dusty store on the Lower East Side, which has become a kind of open-air discount mall, the eldest sister found a pair of shoes made by Ralph Lauren, formerly Lipschutz, called a slingback. The second sister purchased a pair that raised her off the floor several inches, and since she was already an inch or two taller than the others, she would stand out even more, which she didn't mind. Several more shopping trips, and a third shoe was found, this one so pointed and narrow that to wear it comfortably, a full size larger was necessary. The fourth sister came home one evening with a famous square-toed, square-heeled shoe. Her mother and sisters stared. The shoe was all corners, not a single note of grace. That's the whole point, the girl explained. It breaks out of the traditional ideas of what makes a shoe beautiful. That's what this designer is known for. Their mother shrugged. If you love it, I love it. The fifth sister decided to do what none of the others would: she purchased the traditional bridal pump from a traditional bridal shop, the renowned Kleinfeld's of Bay Ridge, and what brought amazed looks to the faces of her sisters: she paid more for this plain shoe than any of the others had. The sixth sister then broke all the rules and purchased an open-toe, open-heel, open-everywhere shoe. The youngest sister went to her favorite shoe store, Buster Brown, and bought a pair of white patent-leather Mary Janes that previously she'd owned only in black. The cost: a mere forty-five dollars, which meant that she hadn't cut so deeply into her bridal budget. The others fell in love with the innocence of the shoe, with the originality of the idea, and especially the cost, which had left their youngest sister with the most spending power. Also, she would be the only one who would dance comfortably at her own wedding.

The sisters decided that one bridal crown and veil could be used by all, which meant that all of them would have something to say about the design of this crown, the fabrics used, the length, the style, until their dear, exhausted mother put her foot down and said there will be seven different crowns and veils.

In the design and writing of the invitations, R. Mendel was consulted. A single invitation for all seven weddings was considered and ruled out. First the paper had to be selected, the stock and color, the shape and fold. Then the typeface, script or block type, traditional serif or modern sans serif, raised or not, and in which color—black, brown, gold, or silver. One daughter insisted on white ink on linen white card stock, a style called white-on-white, and R. Mendel feared for the attendance at her wedding. Another decision he had to make: whether or not to feature an English-language version of the invitation on the facing side, as had become common even in Williamsburg. R. Mendel went back and forth on this, pointing out that each and every person on the guest list was perfectly fluent in Hebrew. In the end, though, he gave in to what his daughters wanted, and English-language versions were featured on all seven invitations.

And when the printed invitations finally arrived, and were carefully examined and proofread for errors, the next seven evenings had to be spent addressing the envelopes, stuffing, stamping, and finally mailing them, and not all from the same mailbox, since mailmen have been known to dump too-large batches of the same envelope in the trash.

In the addressing of the envelopes, more decisions had to be made. The color of the ink to be used. One daughter took great pride in her handwriting, she'd always excelled in penmanship, and so insisted on personally addressing all her invitations. Another daughter had studied calligraphy, and all her envelopes had to feature the flourishes of a fountain pen fitted with a half-inch nib. Not to be outdone, the other sisters devised their own solutions to the task of addressing invitations. The youngest sister, who worked on the computer at the office of the Beth Rachel School for Girls and had experience with mass mailings, entered the guest list into the computer and printed the addresses in Matura MT Script capitals on transparent labels. When R. Mendel saw the labels, he was inclined to grab and kiss his smartest of daughters, but not wanting to start something among the sisters—every father knows what Joseph's robe of many colors led to—satisfied himself with patting her on the back. Since the guest lists were identical for each sister, she offered to print several sets of labels. After showing samples of the various choices available, she brought home one set of labels in Brush Script, another in Arial Black, a third in Times New Roman, and a fourth in Bookman Old Style, and the remaining invitations were in the mail in a matter of hours.

Yankel held his hand up and counted off the next series of tasks on his fingers. There was the hiring of seven caterers, the planning of seven meals, the designing of seven centerpieces, the selecting of seven different wines, the writing of seven marriage contracts, the distributing of honors to the various rabbis and relatives of personage, seven per wedding, which adds up to forty-nine difficult decisions.

He paused to sip water, and in the audience someone shouted,

Enough is enough. You call yourself a wedding *badkhn*. Where are the promised rhymes? Not one word you've uttered has rhymed with another. I've been doing this work for only a year and I can do better than that.

Yankel faced the man. You're obviously still wet behind the ears, he said. I haven't begun. This has all been a preface. But since you ask, I'll show you how an experienced *badkhn* works. Novices rhyme the last words, and that's fine, but child's play. In my work, every word rhymes with the one above it. In poetry this difficult technique is known as internal rhyming. If you and your colleagues agree to give up this evening's earnings to me, I'll show you how it's done.

The younger man looked to his five colleagues, and when he had a nod from each, shook hands on the agreement.

Listen closely and you'll learn a thing or two. He pressed the young man back into the throng, took three strides toward center stage, twirled his mustache, inhaled deeply, and delivered his first line:

The holy groom, Reb Joel, son of Reb Moshe, is a heightened soul. . . .

The audience filled in the missing notes: yaididaididaidaidai . . .

Joel closed his eyes. When he opened them again, the second daughter was sitting beside him and Yankel Yankevitch was preparing to deliver the second internally rhyming line, as promised. Expectations were high. Various people had come up with various rhyming words for each of the words in the first line, but to conceive of the right combination of words and put them together in a meaningful sentence seemed impossible.

Yankel lifted his arms and there was silence. He twirled the ends of his mustache once again, put his hands behind his back, and delivered the second line:

The holy groom, Reb Joel, son of Reb Moshe, is a heightened soul. . . .

The audience filled in the missing notes. After which there was a hush in the room of held breaths as they listened for the next line. But Yankel merely retired to his seat to wait for the next wedding.

Joel opened and closed his eyes, a reverse eyeblink, since in the scheme of cosmogonic time, everything in this world, including our dreams, is only as long as an eyeblink. And then his third bride was beside him, and Yankel Yankevitch was preparing to deliver his third line.

The room was silent; all eyes were on Yankel, who was in no hurry. He made a great show of putting his hands behind his back, of pacing to the right, then left. He paused at stage center, raised his hands as if in an appeal to the muses, and chanted:

The holy groom, Reb Joel, son of Reb Moshe, is a heightened soul. . . .

The audience roared.

Before Joel opened and closed his eyes again, he saw the six rivals surround Yankel.

In the morning, Joel had another seizure, this time in bed.

He'd been awake and in pain. He'd felt cramps in his arms and legs, in his stomach, as if he'd been poisoned. He'd closed his eyes and recognized the blackness pulling him in. He struggled against it briefly and felt himself going in circles, a painful repetition in his head, and the passing of what seemed hours. From a distance, he heard his name called, Joel, Joel, and wanted to answer, but he was drawn toward the dark and spiraling deeper. Continuing the descent, he understood, meant annihilation, but to interrupt the plunge required enormous effort and it hurt.

When Joel opened his eyes, his mother and Ada were leaning over him. Mrs. Jakob breathed in relief, and went to call her husband and the doctor.

Joel's head throbbed. He also felt strangely rested, as if he'd been sleeping for days, though Ada informed him that only minutes could have passed, because she'd looked in on him seconds before. Then from my room I heard hoarse choking sounds, as if you were trying to talk and couldn't. I came in and your eyes were rolled back into your head. I shouted for Mother. It was frightening.

My throat does feel sore, Joel said, and swallowed.

I'll put up water for tea, Ada said.

Joel took the Bratslav book from under his pillow. He'd started something and now he would have to keep going, to find out what it was about. He would begin at the beginning. He would understand what was in these tales. Each one seemed a separate, dangerous dream.

When his mother came in, Joel set the book on the chair beside his bed. He wouldn't hide it. Exposure, he felt, would help diminish its powers.

Dr. Levine says it's not a faint if you're already lying down, Mrs. Jakob explained. He says it was probably a grand mal seizure. He wants to examine you. Your father is coming home at noon and then we'll go.

She wiped her hands on her apron and put her cool wrist on his forehead. How do you feel?

My head hurts, Joel said. But otherwise fine.

Mrs. Jakob nodded. I'll be in the kitchen. I must cook the fish, skim the soup. Ada can take over from there. By the time we get back, it will be close to sundown. Call if you feel anything.

Ada remained with him while he sipped tea with milk and ate a coddled egg and toast. She sat at the foot of his bed and looked at him.

Levine, Joel grumbled.

He was being childish, he knew, but he hated Levine's prodding, and the way he showed off his knowledge of Yiddish, all dirty words. Besides, Levine wouldn't find anything wrong with him; externally he was perfectly fine. It was internally that there was confusion. He was certain that these faints or seizures had something to do with the tales, and what could Levine possibly know about them?

He sought, and at times felt he found, various miraculous signs proving to him that God was present in his life and showed some special concern for him.

The choices of two of these signs are rather revealing in psychological terms, each of them showing a different face of Nahman's ongoing fascination and struggle with the idea of death. The young Nahman would row a small boat out into the middle of the nearby river in order there to be alone with God. Not knowing very well how to handle the boat, Nahman would sometimes stop rowing when he was at the place farthest from shore and nearly allow the boat to capsize. At that moment he would call out to God to save him from drowning.

Another account of Nahman's search for such "signs" tells us that "he wanted to see a dead man. He pressed for this until it happened: once, while he was sitting in the attic room of his father-in-law's house, a dead person came to him. Our master became very frightened, for this was the first time he had seen a dead man with his own eyes; this was in his early youth. Afterwards our master said that this dead man had been a particularly wicked one, and that was why he had become so overwhelmed by terrible boundless fear in his presence. He began to cry out in a most awful way, and everyone in the house came running and tried to get into his room. They were unable to do so, however, since he had already locked the door from the inside. They had to resort to some trick in order to get into the room; I don't remember if they broke through a wall or climbed over the partition. After they got to him his fears were eased."

Everything off, Levine demanded, waving his hand from head to toe. Joel cringed. From experience, he knew that in the waiting room every word could be heard. Levine was a man who had only one vocal note and it registered as a shout.

Joel removed his shoes and socks. He delayed, hoping the nurse would leave the room. His mother should have insisted when she made the appointment. He shouldn't be undressing in front of a woman. He removed his shirt, then his pants, and waited.

Those too, Levine shouted, whatever it is you call them. Shirley, do those rags qualify as underwear?

Shirley laughed and pushed open the sliding partition.

While you're out there, Levine shouted, ask the rabbi what those strings are called. He wears them, too, they all do.

Joel quickly removed everything else. Now he wanted to get through the exam quickly.

Levine pinched, pressed, prodded, and pricked. He struck Joel's knobby knee with a rubber hammer, and Joel's long leg shot out. On the second knee, Joel tried to control the movement and failed.

Now let me see your *tuches*, Levine roared, and Joel buried his flaming face in the tissue paper lining the table.

You're too skinny, Levine said. You have zero muscle tone. Look at this, he said to Shirley, who'd returned. No fatty tissue for the needle to enter. The boy does nothing but sit on his bony *tuches* all day.

Joel felt a woman's fingers pinch his flesh, then the prick of the needle, and the cool sting of alcohol.

He hated Levine. Better to die of disease than submit to this man.

He joined his parents in Levine's office, which was furnished in leather and dark wood, pomp and pomposity.

Levine told them what Joel already knew: that all his nerve synapses were fine. To be absolutely certain that nothing was out of order, he pre-scribed an EEG. He explained that he'd ministered a shot of vitamin B-12 for an immediate boost, and prescribed a daily dose of B-complex. And plenty of water. Extreme dehydration, Levine said, can cause a seizure. And stay home for a day or two.

. . .

With the door to her room open—she was keeping an eye on Joel, who was in his own room across the hall—Ada sat at her drafting table and looked at the pile of tear sheets she'd accumulated. As always, something from Calvin Klein and Ralph Lauren. This year, Agnès B., Perry Ellis, and Michael Kors. These were the designers who would translate well to Chasidic variation. Hardest to tame were the ones who excelled at elegant evening wear, Galanos, de la Renta, Saint Laurent. Something to do with the subtlety of their immodesty: unlike the plunging neckline and deep slits of a Versace, which could be raised and dropped as needed, their work depended on every line, the final design emerging as an organic and unchangeable thing.

She would begin with Calvin Klein, who posed a particular problem. The purity and simplicity of his designs easily turned dowdy. Once the sleeves were lengthened, necklines and hemlines brought up or down, as needed, there wasn't much of the marvelous left. This year, his white-with-tan windowpane ensembles were promising. He'd shown it in a knee-length skirt, which made adding the necessary inch or two easy. And the collar line of the top had a placket with buttons, which was modest already. The Chasidic girl could wear it buttoned up. Which meant the only necessary modifications were sleeve extensions—she would extend them to three-quarters rather than full length to keep it seasonal. This was mere tweaking, something designers did regularly before sending their merchandise off to the stores. As she worked, it occurred to her that it was possible the fabric would be available for purchase by spring and she made a note to call Zarin's on Fifty-seventh.

She eyed her sketch. Where the top ended could make all the difference. She added a note for Malke. Three to four inches below the waist, definitely above the hips. Since the wearer's height affected the length, pattern adjustments would have to be offered.

She moved on to the Michael Kors. Navy pants, a striped shirt, and red sweater. Very like early Ralph. The pants would have to be replaced by a skirt, but in what style? Skirts were never quite as casual or modern as pants, still there were skirts and skirts. Pleats had the right classic note, but they weren't modern enough. But maybe fewer pleats. If there were only one or two pleats in the front, and none in the back. Or maybe two and two, which would make it preppy. With no pleats in the back, it edged into ladylike. Ada kneaded her eraser. Preppy might be a good exchange for the modern ease of pants. And the added pleats would make the skirt easier to wear.

She moved on to consider the classic trenches popular for spring. The Chasidic girl could sew one, if only to keep costs down. And it was an excellent light cover-up for these classic styles. She ought to recommend a particular one. She looked at the Burberry, the Perry Ellis, the Agnès B. If you were going to have one, should it be the classic Burberry? She sketched the coat, then looked at the Agnès B. shirtdress she'd circled. It was wonderful, completely right, a long, lean shape. If she selected it as one of the final patterns for spring, there'd be only two slots left for evening. A dress and a two-piece. And the quota of six patterns a season would be fulfilled, and still no evening coat. But the trench could be worn anytime. She sharpened her pencil and continued sketching. For an evening dress, she took the shape of a sleeveless Armani and added to it. But with long sleeves, the dress lost its magic. She gave the right sleeve a slight bell and at the cuff inserted a slit in the bell to reveal the wrist bone. Then brought the collar line up to a funnel neck to balance the bell in the sleeve. Still it needed more. Ada paused, then inserted a short slit on the right side of the funnel at the neck and it worked. The dress had asymmetry. There was magic in sketching. She heard Joel at the door, turned around, and said, Abracadabra, I create as I sketch.

Show me, Joel said. I'll tell you if it's truly magical. Though he knew that when it came to dress design Ada didn't need his opinion, he welcomed the pretense and fulfilled the role of admiring critic.

She showed him her sketch of the evening dress. Joel looked at it silently, then smiled. His finger followed the collar line and cuffs. Repetition of the form, he said, the bell and the slit. Just enough repetition for resonance.

Ada laughed. He'd overheard her conversations with Malke, had learned a few words, and now he was imitating her. She reached up to straighten the collar of his shirt.

You know, she said. Since Chasidic men don't wear ties, why do they need pointed collars?

She flipped some pages of her sketch pad and showed Joel the Calvin Klein top, with its three-button placket and Nehru collar.

Why not a shirt like this? she asked.

Because men don't change styles. We wear the same thing from birth to death. It simplifies things.

It's also boring, Ada said.

The following Monday, R. Moshele made a point of consulting Joel's teachers.

It's difficult to put a finger on it, R. Moshele's brother, R. Chatzkel, said. The boy seems distracted, as if troubled. Also, he was late to morning prayer and then to lecture, which is unlike him. As it turned out, he wasn't well that day. I wouldn't make too much of it. With Joel, one word can be one too many.

R. Moshele went home and did what he'd promised never to do to a son of his, because he'd resented his own parents for similar intrusions, especially his meddlesome mother—he investigated Joel's room and found the two Bratslaver books, not recommended reading for any yeshiva boy, and certainly not for a boy of Joel's temperament. R. Moshele knew that his son was more temperamental than he had been at that age; in this, as in other things, Joel resembled his grandfather, the Berditchever. Even as a schoolboy, Joel had impressed his rebbes. The boy was able to memorize a page of Talmud after looking at it. And his mind was sharper and quicker than most. R. Moshele had admitted long ago that genius had skipped a generation; unlike himself, Joel had the ability to become a scholar of note, with God's help, a great one. But he was also a nervous child, chewing on his lip till it bled. At the age of two he'd pulled out most of his own hair, and a specialist had suggested that he would turn out either brilliant or crazy. R. Moshele and his wife had raised the child with silken gloves. And as far as was possible, they'd kept an overbearing grandmother at a distance. With time and age, he'd settled into schoolboy routines and was classifiable as average in emotional range. These recent events were an aberration, therefore all the more disturbing. It was important to find a cause, to set things right, but how best to go about it, that would be difficult to determine. Even as a child, Joel hadn't required much reprimanding. As a young adult, he was certainly beyond that.

R. Moshele sat on Joel's bed. Confronting his son with accusations was out of the question. The boy had never been denied intellectual freedom and R. Moshele didn't want to begin now. Even when there hadn't been money for new shoes or a hat, there'd always been enough for books. Joel had known since he was a bar mitzvah boy that he could purchase any book on account. Of one thing R. Moshele was glad. Joel had left the Bratslav books on his nightstand, unhidden. That was a good sign.

He was reading it when I came in, his wife confirmed. He put it aside calmly and I thought nothing of it.

She sat on the chair beside the bed and looked at her husband. What are you thinking? she asked.

I don't know what to think. It could be simple curiosity and there's not much wrong with that. The sudden illness may have nothing to do with it, a mere coincidence. Still what I'd like to do is take him to the Satmar rebbe for a blessing.

. . .

During the EEG the doctors were interested only in his brain, therefore Joel was required to bare only his head. He lay on the table fully clothed, and bareheaded.

The technician said that his hairstyle—Joel smiled at this choice of words used to refer to what was the Chasidic man's nonstyle—made things both easy and hard. Your shaved head makes for better contact; on the other hand, I can't use hair clips to keep the nodes in place. I'll have to use tape.

The man dabbed at Joel's scalp with what felt like sandpaper and then taped a cold disk to his head. A wire emanating from the disk attached him to another module, which was attached to another module, which led to the screen that displayed the reading.

The man dabbed and taped, dabbed and taped, dabbed and taped until Joel felt his entire head covered, and with the wires weighing him down, he thought of Samson. This is how it might've felt to have a full head of long hair.

There wasn't a blank centimeter left on his head and still the man dabbed. He finished finally with a disk on each side of Joel's temple.

What do these contacts do? Joel asked.

They provide a brain wave reading. We're looking for abnormal waves that would indicate seizure activity. In epileptics the brain waves are periodically erratic.

Joel nodded to indicate comprehension. But could brain waves reveal one's thoughts? When he looked to his right, at the hard copy of the reading, it seemed to him a continuous pattern of mathematical sine and cosine waves. And if the wave diverged from the usual pattern, what would that prove? The reading would provide a kind of knowledge, but whether the waves were erratic or continuous, what could be done to alter them?

Don't move, the man said. Look straight up at the ceiling and try not to blink.

On any given day Joel's ability to concentrate was remarkable. Today, concentrating on remaining still made not moving impossible. The problem was that under testing for seizure activity he suddenly felt he might have one. He realized that ever since the second seizure he'd lived in fear of a third. Evil comes in threes, and after a third, anything could follow. At lecture, trying to concentrate on what was said, it had suddenly seemed to him that he wasn't breathing well, and he had begun to feel afraid. He'd felt his heart racing, he'd become overheated. Once the panic started, it was hard to control. Worried about disrupting the lecture with a sudden seizure, right there in front of his colleagues and teachers, he'd tried deep breathing.

And what if he had disrupted the lecture? Joel asked himself afterward, in calmer moments. Everyone would see and know: something was wrong with Joel Jakob. How concerned did he have to be about that? He knew his parents wouldn't like it. Rumors of a mysterious ailment would cause irreversible damage on the marital front, not only for himself, but also for Ada. Unless of course she agreed to marry Aaron, in whom Joel felt confident. Aaron wouldn't allow the mundane to stand in his way. Aaron's parents, however, couldn't be counted on to look past questions of health. It was their responsibility to protect their son from impractical, potentially unhappy choices, and if they thought that Ada had some genetic frailty, they wouldn't agree to such a match.

Try not to think about anything in particular, the technician interrupted. We need as clear a reading as possible.

Is it possible not to think? Joel thought. It was hard enough to control voluntary nerves and muscles. He concentrated on alphabetic combinations as a way to clear his head.

You're still thinking or concentrating too hard. Relax your forehead, let go. That's better.

After what seemed empty hours, the reading was finished, the wires removed, and Joel was free to go.

Did the scan reveal anything unusual? he asked.

The technician studied the screen silently for what seemed long minutes, and Joel was certain the prognosis would be terrible.

From what I can see, the man said, everything looks quite regular. Still, a neurologist will look at it and write up a report.

Well? Ada asked, pausing to look at him. She was cleaning up, clearing her walls of drawings and fabric samples from the previous season to make way for the new one.

It seemed to Joel that they were all looking at him a bit too hard these days. He shrugged. Nothing, he said. A waste of time, as expected.

He sat on the edge of her bed. He liked Ada's surroundings, her work, and watching her work. She was always moving, bustling. He mostly sat still, or swayed. Their rooms were as night and day, hers as full and colorful as his was severe. In his room, other than a narrow bed and wooden chair that served as his nightstand, he had only books. Waist-high stacks of books running along every available wall, a wainscot built of books. Above the books, his walls were bare and white.

Ada had the largest bedroom in the house and her own bathroom. Two years earlier, their parents had exchanged their room for hers, and still it was crowded. Besides her narrow bed, night table, and dresser, the room contained a drawing table, a sewing machine on its own stand, a seamstress's dummy, an ironing board, and long shelves for bolts and swatches of fabric. All four walls were used for display purposes. Working sketches of women in dresses and coats were tacked up, unusual in a Chasidic home, where images are prohibited. Even the catalogs that served a specific purpose had provoked in the community murmurs of idol worship. It was to Mrs. Jakob's credit that R. Moshele hadn't put a stop to the whole design business. She'd argued that there was nothing wrong with a girl's putting her sewing skills and good eye for design to work, and pointed out that an ability to earn a living would help keep Ada's future husband in yeshiva. Proud of her daughter's talent, and ambitious for her in ways she hadn't been for herself, Mrs. Jakob convinced her husband that the gossip was a result purely of envy, that he could see for himself that the figures had no eyes, ears, or mouths, that they were mere silhouettes on which to hang the dress designs.

When he looked at the drawings, R. Moshele had to admit that his wife was right. And he preferred not to interfere with this activity that came to Ada so instinctively and brought her such joy. A parent's authority had to be used with discretion. His daughter had grown up with the knowledge of Abraham smashing his father's idols, as did every Chasidic girl, and understood at an early age that her dolls had to have the tips of their noses sliced off as a mark of their imperfection. At four, R. Moshele remembered, she'd brought him a new doll without waiting to be asked, and suggested that this time he nick the doll's earlobe instead of the nose, and although a sliced ear was a bit obscure as imperfections go, he'd complied.

R. Moshele listened to his wife and the business flourished. In his one concession to public opinion, he mounted a latch at the top corner of Ada's new bedroom door to prevent access when there were visitors to the house.

For the journey to the Satmar rebbe, R. Moshele hired a car and driver, thereby diminishing the chance of a pointless mechanical breakdown or a wrong turn that would make of a forty-five-minute ride a daylong trip. And R. Moshele didn't want to exhaust Joel, who was already complaining about all the interruptions. The old Chevrolet wagon, good enough in town, where help was always a few minutes away, wasn't reliable enough for longer distances. He advised Joel to bring along some reading. R. Moshele hoped that his son would bring the Bratslav tales and provide the opening for conversation about them.

The day would begin early. They'd have to attend a six-thirty service, then eat a quick breakfast. The car was scheduled to pick them up at the house at a quarter to eight; with God's will, they would arrive in Monroe before nine. Morning hours at the rebbe's house were from nine to eleven. If the lines were long and they didn't see the rebbe in the morning, they'd have to wait until three in the afternoon, when he was once again available to the public.

Life rarely conforms to plan. At the last minute, the Berditchever decided to join his son and grandson. With door-to-door service available, the trip provided an excellent opportunity to visit the rebbe. Besides, he wanted to introduce his eldest grandson.

On any given morning Joel was up and out of the house before his father. On this morning, when R. Moshele woke Joel at six, the boy mumbled, In a minute, and turned onto his other side. Ten minutes later he had to be awakened again.

When they pulled into the Berditchever's driveway, they waited ten minutes before he emerged, paused to kiss the mezuzah, took a careful step across the threshold right foot first, and finally folded up his caftan and entered the car. Behind him came his wife, R. Moshele's mother, saying, Go with *mazel* and come with *mazel*, as if, Joel thought, life were merely a matter of luck.

R. Moshele had to make an effort to repress the impulse to berate his father. The day would be trying enough without harsh words. Besides, he didn't want Joel to hear his own father rage against his grandfather, certainly not on this day. In his youth, R. Moshele had often found himself wishing he could take back words. He didn't come by patience and tolerance naturally; he had to work hard for them. In this as in other things he resembled his difficult mother. But though quick to anger, they were fortunately also quick to forget. His father, the Berditchever, was slow to anger and he didn't bear grudges, which sometimes made him seem more godly than God. Joel, who resembled his grandfather in so many other ways, seemed to have inherited the worst traits. He was quick to anger and slow to forget. But that was his innate temperament. With time, R. Moshele thought, the boy was developing greater patience, finding forgiveness more easily. He was sitting tall, pale, and silent, and R. Moshele wondered, as he often did, what exactly went on in his son's head. He tried to remember himself at that age, but his son, though of his own flesh and blood, was cut from different cloth.

The Berditchever took out of his pocket a book of Psalms, which went with him everywhere. At thirteen he'd set himself the task of a complete reading a day, which with some effort was possible then, though often he'd stayed up late to finish. These days he made do with one or two readings a week. His reward for so much prayer: complete lines of poetry came to him at various times of day, poetry in response to life's snares and snarls. If necessary, he could recite the psalms from memory. Without thinking about it, he often found himself reciting while walking from the study house and back. It had become habitual. This gift of prayer had come from his dear mother. Even near death, she'd insisted that he leave her bedside to attend services. He'd hurry to the nearest synagogue and then race back, afraid she wouldn't be there on his return. He'd sprint through the streets, mumbling the few psalms he knew then, repeating the same line when he was stuck for the next one, his heart pounding not as a result of the physical exertion but in fear. He'd begun reciting psalms to save his mother, but in the end the psalms had come to his own aid. One morning, she was no longer there. It was said that in the Russian gulag the Jews who remained sane were those who knew enough psalms and prayers to recite them from memory. The Berditchever had recommended the psalms to all his children, but none had made reciting a habit, and it seemed Joel wouldn't, either. A fine scholar and avid reader, he had no patience for mere reciting. He needed to read and know.

America isn't czarist or Communist Russia, the Berditchever told himself, and his children were fortunate to live in comfort and relative security. Still, in every life there are crises, and not having availed one-self of the Psalms in good times, one wouldn't know to regret its absence in times of need. It was possible some early crisis was necessary; perhaps Joel's illness, may God protect him, would bring with it some benefit. Though of the two, his son and grandson, it seemed to the Berditchever that it was R. Moshele who was most perturbed. Joel sat still and haughty as always. The young boys at the yeshiva were a little afraid to approach the boy, the Berditchever knew, and was pleased. He recognized himself in this grandson. He too had been pale and thin, quietly studious and not a little too sensitive. Life would change the boy as it had changed him. He would reach out to others when he discovered that man isn't an island. With age and experience, he'd grow less intensively himself, more comfortable within the larger community. For now, his exclusivity was a good thing; it allowed him to engage only in study, which is what a young man ought to focus on. Unlike the more outgoing boys, Joel didn't have time for chatter. He didn't gossip. His good friends were fine young men like himself, boys whose conversations were scholarly. Such a life was possible only at their age, before marriage and fatherhood, and it would be a shame to end such single-minded scholarship prematurely. He would advise his son not to think of marrying off Joel too soon. He was a scholar worth detaining from petty, everyday life. He ought to have a father-in-law who could shield him from the concerns of a family man. He looked at his eldest son, harried and overworked, a fine administrator at the yeshiva and an excellent family man, but also an example of what ought to be avoided for Joel. Unlike his son, R. Moshele had never had the makings of a scholar. He was a being who needed to move about, to do things, and for whom family life had brought a certain stature. Time and experience had rewarded R. Moshele with patience and tolerance, both attributes that served his work well. No one else at the yeshiva had the necessary forbearance to deal with parental concerns. As a child, what Moshele had wanted most was to be like others, to not stand out among the boys. The Berditchever was aware that the extraordinary in the father may have been responsible for the son's attraction to the ordinary. The sins of the father visit upon the son. To his credit, his son had raised a young scholar with a mind any grandfather could take pride in.

Joel tried not to hear the Berditchever's intakes of air, his whispered prayers, loud enough that anyone within two feet of him could make out which passage he was reciting, as if to force those around him to recite along. On Joel's left, R. Moshele sat silently studying a passage of *Gittin*. Joel had never been able to read in a moving vehicle, not without a feeling of nausea. He would rather have sat on one side or the other, beside either window. Or up front. He looked straight ahead, concentrated on the road, which was wide open. It was only September and already the leaves were turning, from the deep green of middle life to the oranges and burgundies of advanced age. Every autumn, Ada said, fashion falls in love with fall colors, as if discovering them for the first time. She brought in a variety of leaves from the backyard and taped them to a board. Joel thought the freshness of rediscovery in this low point of the natural life cycle an interesting incongruity in a world so enamored of youth, indicative perhaps of a greater complexity than Ada was willing to acknowledge. He thought that like Chasidism, the world of fashion wasn't as insular as it would seem, that its currents and trends were attached to events in the wider world. For example, nature and the individual were significant for Chasidim in the late eighteenth and early nineteenth centuries, when in literature and elsewhere Romanticism was taking hold. These days trees and leaves left no great impression on his father and grandfather, two contemporary examples. They'd become like other Jews, a people of the tent, not the wanderers of the forests, not the mystical, subscholarly miracle workers with greater intuitive powers than intellect.

Shortly after Nahman's Bar Mitzvah, at which his uncle the rabbi of Sudilkov addressed him in a way that he took very seriously, perhaps charging him with the responsibility of carrying on the family name, a marriage was arranged between Nahman and Sosia, the daughter of one Ephraim, a respected and somewhat wealthy tax-farmer who lived in the small village of Usyatin, near the town of Smela, on the western shores of the Dnieper some two hundred miles to the east of Medzhibozh. Following the custom of the times, the couple went to live at the home of the bride's father. Thus it was that sometime in early adolescence Nahman left Medzhibozh and the court of his uncle, moving from the deeply Jewish milieu of that town to the isolated life of a village, at some distance from even the smallest organized Jewish community.

In later years, Nahman was wont to look back with fondness upon his days in Usyatin. "Rabbi Simeon said that once, after our master had become a public figure, the two of them traveled together through the village of Usyatin . . . As they passed through the fields, our master was filled with longing and said: 'How good it was for me here; with every step I felt the taste of Eden . . .' At another time he said in my presence that when he had been alone somewhere in the woods or the fields, he would find on his return that he had come back to a completely new world. The world that he saw now, so he imagined, was completely different, not at all like that world which he had known before."

One could argue, Joel thought, that the Chasidic movement was dead even before its fragmented transplant to America, where assemblages of the various sects lived side by side in various boroughs and suburbs of New York, each one known by the name of the Eastern European city it came from. Satumare, Debrecen, Koln, Skvere, Lubavitch, Bratslav,

Berditchev, Vizhnitz, Kretchme. Renowned names, but their days of glory were long past. This trip was a good example of that. It was proceeding too smoothly, eerily trouble-free. A momentous voyage to a great rebbe should prove more eventful, with obstacles and delays, the workings of the other side preventing its success. Even post–horse-and-cart there were things that could go wrong. The engine could overheat, the tires could blow out, they could be held up in traffic. At the very least a carload of Chasidim ought to be stuck at the side of the road.

> And Samael (Satan) replied: Do you remember? When you traveled with your son, first the horse fell on the bridge, and you returned. Then the axles broke. Then you met me and I told you that the zadik was frivolous. And now that I have done away with your son you are allowed to go on. For your son was in the aspect of "the small light" and that zadik is in the aspect of "the great light," and if they had united the Messiah would have come. But now that I have done away with him, you are allowed to travel.
>
> FROM NACHMAN OF BRATSLAV, "The Rabbi's Son"

With nothing else to distract him Joel looked for the usual landmarks, the inn at the top of the mountain just past Suffern, New York, the lascivious Rolling Stones tongue painted on a rock, and on Route 17, the Lubavitch Moshiach Is Coming sign, which reminded Joel of Nachman's messianic claims and the unhappiness they'd brought. All his ambitious maneuvering had ended in nothing but enemies everywhere, and a break with his own uncle. After the death of his son, when he despaired of leaving behind a successor, Nachman turned to the composition of the tales, and these became his legacy. And the interrupted tale? It could be said to mirror Nachman's interrupted life, since he died at the age of thirty-eight.

·   ·   ·

When they entered Monroe Township, R. Moshele and his father closed their books and took up the subject of local politics. Kiryas Joel, as this relatively new Satmar community was named, had attempted to declare itself a separate township, which would entitle them to federal and state funds they could use to further community development. In court they had argued that the taxes paid, including school taxes, which went into the coffers of the Monroe Township, brought no benefit to the Chasidic community, since its children didn't attend public schools. Other town services were also not of much use to religious families living here. The issue had generated national press and Jews everywhere asked themselves whether such negative publicity wasn't a sin, even dangerous.

Though it wasn't his place to say so, Joel thought that such thinking was regressive, based in the Old World. This was the New World, with new ways where different methods were required and even Chasidism would have to adapt. The fear of anti-Semitism was an issue best expressed publicly. Keeping it behind closed doors only served the perpetrators' cause. If the residents of Monroe expressed publicly their misgivings about a Jewish township in their midst, thereby giving voice to their racist feelings, they'd be forced to confront what was within, which could only benefit Jews everywhere. It was the absence of self-knowledge that was dangerous.

They arrived in Kiryas Joel, which was much changed. Joel remembered it when it was newly settled, with only ten or so houses and the building of the main synagogue still in progress. Today it was not urban, like the communities in Brooklyn, and not small-mindedly suburban like Monsey. It was crowded and dusty, the grass too trodden to be green, and everywhere cars parked and double-parked. It was a shtetl out of old Europe, without the poverty.

The driver lost patience when children on Big Wheels and bicycles stared instead of getting out of the way. He beeped loud and long. A double-parked moving van had to be circumvented and then they fell behind a garbage truck making slow progress. Here were finally a few obstacles, Joel thought. Not from demons on the other side, but rather in the town of Kiryas Joel itself.

In the rebbe's house they didn't have to wait long. The beadle recognized the Berditchever and brought tea with lemon. Soon they were ushered into the rebbe's private chambers.

The first thing that impressed itself on Joel was how very small the rebbe was. Wizened was the word. He sat wrapped in a tallis behind a small writing table that appeared too high for his comfort. The beadle spoke the names of the visitors into the rebbe's ear and handshakes were exchanged. Joel brought the rebbe's hand to his lips as his father and grandfather had done. The Berditchever was offered a seat beside the rebbe, and then the rebbe asked about the yeshiva and how many students it accepted every year. The Berditchever deferred to his son for these details. R. Moshele spoke of the difficult compromises every yeshiva had to make these days. The Satmar schools weren't turning out outstanding scholars because they weren't turning anyone away. Though the elite students raised the general level of the student body, they themselves suffered. Some of the best Chasidic minds had recently been lost to Lakewood and Telz, both *Litvish* yeshivas. At Berditchev, R. Moshele explained, this fact had prompted a decision to keep the level of scholarship high by accepting only the most gifted minds. This was an important correction worthy of support, the rebbe said, and directed the beadle to write a check for $500. Then he turned to Joel and asked whether he was one of Berditchev's gifted scholars.

The Berditchever introduced Joel as his grandson, took from R. Moshele the folded paper on which was written Joel's name and the details of his recent illness, and handed it to the rebbe as a *kvitel*. The rebbe put hands on Joel's head, blessed him, and then the beadle ushered them out.

The drive home also was uneventful. No one had lifted a finger to prevent the visit or the return. Worse, Joel felt himself entirely unchanged. He'd stood before the rebbe, was looked over, spoken of, blessed, and felt nothing. Joel turned against himself. This absence of something, anything, was damning. There was only one possible conclusion: that he was unworthy of ecstatic experience. A man who prays hard and studies hard remains concentrated, in a receptive state. Greatness requires great effort. That's how the prophets came by their revelations. That's how Nachman composed his tales. Even God had to work to create.

The next day Joel remembered that in sleep and in his daytime descents into unconsciousness—perhaps they were one and the same— he had had worthwhile experiences. He also knew that dream, which requires interpretation, is the lesser form of prophecy because it provides a limited type of knowledge, a mere glimpse. Joel wanted more. He wanted the intuitive open-eyed understanding that prophets and mystics achieved. He wanted whole sight, not a fragmented, human perception. To that end, he unearthed his old *alef-beis* primer and thumbed through the much-abused, colorful pages. He'd forgotten that the alphabet, the source of creative knowledge and wisdom, had first come to him in primary colors, and he wondered about the effect of color on his early perception. Surely the generations before him, his father and grandfather, had experienced the letters in stark black on white, pure calligraphic lines and curves. Thinking about shape and form, Joel thought of the scribes who spent their days with ink and feather quills, scribing every precise crown and flourish, knowing every letter intimately, and he envied them this knowledge. Such knowledge, he thought, was the closest man could come to knowing God, for whom the letters served as tools. With these letters He made the words that made the world.

At dinner, Joel announced that he wanted to study the art of the scribe.

R. Moshele looked at Joel anxiously. At one time, he said, the scribes were holy men said to have known the great secrets of the alphabet. But that was then. Today a scribe works long hours for little pay. He writes ten mezuzahs a day and sells them for twenty dollars apiece. There's no glory in it.

Joel explained that he wasn't interested in becoming a scribe, he merely wanted to learn the art, and his father agreed to look into the matter.

To smooth the wrinkle in her father's brow, Ada launched into the story of a Sephardic woman newly arrived from Algiers via Jerusalem, whose long black hair was so tangled, the Women's Auxiliary had to organize a team effort to help comb out the mop. I'm told that not one strand of hair can be separated and identified as a strand, Ada said. Every evening, the Auxiliary sends a young girl to the house to work on the woman's head. In the morning, they're back where they started. Sleeping on this hair tangles it. The only way out of this recursive rut is to do the entire head in one night and put the hair in a tight braid to keep it from tangling again. Malke and I have agreed to work together all evening and get it done.

Why don't you simply cut it? Joel asked.

Ada shook her head. Her hair is this woman's pride. She believes that without it, her husband won't return. She's already depressed. Cutting off her hair would make her worse. She has three children with him, one a month-old newborn, which her husband hasn't yet seen. He left before she gave birth. She became distraught and let herself go.

Someone ought to have a talk with this barbarian of a husband, R. Moshele said.

Have spray conditioners and detanglers been tried? Mrs. Jakob asked.

Malke and I plan to stop at CVS on our way. We'll arrive armed with every variety of comb and spray. We'll each take one side of the woman's head. We're determined to get it done. I'm taking along a pair of nail scissors to cut out the worst knots. With so much hair, a bit of thinning won't hurt.

Mrs. Jakob shook her head. With a newborn, too. The poor woman. I'll send along a large slice of sponge cake. When you arrive, make a large cup of tea to go with it. Maybe it will help her relax while you tear away at the two sides of her head.

Joel borrowed a black Marks-A-Lot from Ada and covered his white walls and ceiling with the letters of the alphabet, in no particular order, and large enough to distinguish from anywhere in the room, particularly the head of his bed. He would go to sleep seeing the letters and wake up to them. He would concentrate on them so hard, they would become imprinted on his mind as images, shapes, and forms, rather than sounds and meanings. As images he could use them more abstractly, in combinations that formed no obvious meanings. As images they could impart a different knowledge.

He finished late, after two in the morning, and looked at what he'd done, nodded, and whispered that it was good. It was even interesting as a design, a kind of abstract pattern. Ada will like it, he knew. He fell asleep with letters dancing in his head, combining and recombining on the inner lids of his eyes. In the morning, when the sun came up and his eyes opened to the letters, he remained in bed an extra five minutes, opening and closing his eyes.

At dinner, when R. Moshele suggested talking to a distant cousin who worked as a scribe, Joel informed him that it was no longer necessary. R. Moshele raised an eyebrow.

Have you seen his room? Ada asked. It's insane and amazing at the same time.

R. Moshele's head turned from his son to his daughter and back to his son. What were they up to now? Joel looked down, hiding a self-pleased smile.

Do you know anything about this? R. Moshele asked his wife.

I've seen it, she said, but can't say I understand. I don't know what Ada sees in it. She seems to think it delightful.

It's mahd, Ada said, affecting an English accent. My dear brother is simply mahd.

Since when does madness deserve applause? R. Moshele asked.

You must see it, Ada said. She pushed her chair back, took her father's arm, and led him to Joel's room.

Joel and his mother looked at each other across the table, listening to the sound of R. Moshele clearing his throat, meaning he didn't know what to say.

Joel grinned.

You'll give your father gray hair, Mrs. Jakob said.

Joel shrugged. It's his life purpose to worry. He worries about every-thing and every boy at the yeshiva.

Mrs. Jakob nodded. She knew her husband. She also knew that Joel's health was indeed worrisome. Everything else, his strange readings, his decorating, was merely life, and she was prepared to be amused. Her husband took such things too seriously. Joel and Ada had always had a competitive relationship, they liked to outdo each other, not as rivals really, merely to impress. They'd always served as each other's best audi-ence. The new wall drawing, Mrs. Jakob thought, came out of this desire to astonish. Ada had been rearranging her room, hanging collages of fall colors, and the wall writing was Joel's response. He didn't rearrange his room every time Ada did, but when he did get around to doing some-thing, it always had an extremist edge. There was this difference between her children: Ada tended toward construction, bringing dis-parate objects or colors or styles together, forming collages. Joel moved against cohesion, he pulled things apart. It was no coincidence that his walls featured letters, not words, Mrs. Jakob mused. It was a kind of breakdown characteristic of her son, and it was this that his father found alarming. Several years before, when Ada moved into the master bed-room and threw herself into arranging her new space, Joel responded by ridding his room of bookcases—they didn't hold enough books anyway, he said. Instead, he stacked his books along the walls, taking care to establish some symmetry. Every stack ended at waist-level height, pro-viding the scheme with the appearance of an intended design.

Book paneling, Ada named it.

She'd thought it especially clever, something about books made of paper which was made of wood pulp, which meant that the books as paneling weren't so far from the real thing, namely a wood wainscot. Joel's room looked like a library, but an unnatural one, one you'd design for a stage. Since Joel spent enough time studying in the real thing, Mrs. Jakob thought her husband shouldn't protest.

When she was alone with R. Moshele she reminded him to take such things less anxiously. It doesn't help anyone to know that you're wor-ried, she pointed out.

R. Moshele shook his head. You're surely right, he said, still the boy has some strange whims.

They might be the passing whims of a young man; still, he resolved to keep an eye on his son. He hadn't discussed with Joel his Bratslav reading. Uncomfortable with the way in which he'd learned of it, R. Moshele decided not to disclose his knowledge, but to wait until Joel talked of it of his own free will. R. Moshele hoped that he wasn't speak-ing of it with anyone else. He was just at the age when inner stirrings and emotions are strong. Unfortunately, this is also the age when fathers with eligible daughters begin prospecting for sons-in-law. After years of great promise, the slightest word of Joel's misadventures could give pause to any father. R. Moshele understood how this worked. He would do the same for Ada, who was as fine and bright a young girl as there ever was. How often he found himself smiling at something she'd said the previous evening. She and Joel were a kind of team, wit matched with wit, and Ada, though younger by a year, more than held her own. She was also more pragmatic. R. Moshele frowned, thinking about the public setting of Joel's seizure at the fish store. Gossip would also affect Ada's prospects. Joel was likely to scoff at the effect of rumors in the community, but he would have to watch his step, if not for his own sake then for his sister's. If he felt ill on any given day, it would be better to miss classes and return home. And his extraordinary readings and interests would have to end. They were signs of restlessness. Such restlessness was often a sign of boredom, and a change of setting could help. In similar cases at the yeshiva, R. Moshele had recommended sending the boy to a Jerusalem yeshiva for a year or two. If Joel hadn't developed his strange illness, R. Moshele would have considered such a step. For now, he would keep Joel at home, keep a close watch, as the doctor had recommended. If the seizures continued, Dr. Levine had explained, Joel would have to be put on medication to avoid the possibility of brain damage. The medication would slow him down. In the meantime, he'd recommended no less than eight glasses of water a day. To make certain Joel drank enough water, Mrs. Jakob ordered several cases of bottled water and saw to it that her son didn't leave the house without a bottle in hand.

Like the models, Ada teased. With their tall skinny bottles of Evian.

Joel complained that the water was disrupting his studies. First it was a chore to drink so much of it. Worse, on its way out the water became altogether too demanding. It seemed to him that he was relieving himself every hour. Mrs. Jakob insisted. At dinner, she brought a pitcher of fresh water to the table, and took it upon herself to refill the glasses. To set a good example and soothe his wife, R. Moshele gulped down a full glass at a time. Mrs. Jakob and Ada followed suit. Joel looked at them in wonder, but the strategy worked. As a result they were all drinking more water, which couldn't hurt.

. . .

In bed, surrounded by the alphabet, Joel combined letters randomly, as his eyes registered them. After encountering certain combinations repeatedly, he understood that without a methodical system the same omissions and repetitions were likely. And there were also the vowels to consider: each letter could be permuted with any of the eight vowels. The number of possible permutations for any given combination could be calculated mathematically: x to the nth power, with x representing the number of available vowels and n the number of letters in the combination. If it were true that the name of God consists of the four letters *yud heh vav heh*, it could be pronounced any of 4,096 ways, a finite number of possibilities. Surely if you took the time to articulate each possibility you would know or feel when you'd arrived at the correct one.

But merely thinking of God's name as knowable was heresy. Moreover, in the attempt to discover God's name, he would have to take it in vain. But if he could visualize rather than speak the name, the transgression might be circumvented. To this end, Joel meditated, using the mind's eye.

During lecture one morning, Joel visualized and unintentionally mouthed a permutation. The rebbe, who saw Joel's lips move but didn't hear him, asked him to repeat himself, and Joel was forced to explain that he hadn't said anything at all, or hadn't meant to. His teacher looked at him quizzically, then resumed his lecture, glancing back from time to time to keep an eye on Joel. They'd all grown watchful and concerned, which made every ordinary twitch significant. Was it so abnormal for one's lips to occasionally mouth one's thoughts? Joel knew his thoughts weren't the kind his teachers would approve. He remembered Nachman's experience as a schoolboy and felt a kinship. He brimmed with this feeling of closeness; it filled him with joy and he wanted to share the pleasure with someone, and there was only one possible person. At the end of the day, he cut short his review session and hurried to the bookstore, hesitated, then entered.

R. Yidel looked up. Seeing the boy's hesitation, he stepped briskly around the counter and shook Joel's hand. You're well, thank the Lord. I heard something.

Joel nodded. It was a strange and sudden illness. I felt that it was related somehow to my reading. I still think so, though I can't explain it rationally. And I've been afraid to read more.

The rational has its limitations, R. Yidel said. When I first read the tales, I felt that I'd stepped into another world. At first I too thought the feeling was one of weakness or illness. Later I learned it was joy. The joy of boundless imagination, thirteen gems that reveal an immensity of a kind I hadn't encountered anywhere else in our world.

Joel nodded long and hard. Yes, he agreed, it was true, nothing was so true. Joy. Could joy stimulate a seizure?

Until today, he said, I was afraid. Today I had a feeling that R. Nachman was near me and I felt something so strange, I believe now that it was indeed joy, I didn't know what to do with myself. That's what brought me here.

R. Yidel tugged at his beard, looked at Joel as if weighing him, then spoke slowly. Every year a few of us make the voyage to Uman for Yom Kippur. I wonder whether this experience would be good for you. You'll have to discuss it with your father, for whom I have great love and respect. When the fact of my first trip to Uman became public knowledge and people boycotted the store, your virtuous father made it a point of stopping in every day. Not because he believed in Bratslav; he wanted to set an example for tolerance. For two weeks straight, he came in daily and purchased something. A *siddur*, a small book of Psalms, an alphabet primer, a braided candle, another yarmulke of which he probably already had a dozen. I understood what he was doing and didn't want to take his money. It was enough that he was seen coming and going. People saw R. Moshele here and understood that he didn't approve of the boycott. But your father insisted on paying. You may inform him that finances for the journey aren't an issue. We set aside funds for this trip every year and there is enough for an extra round-trip fare. However, you'll have to act quickly.

Joel grasped R. Yidel's hands. He was certain that a journey to Nachman would provide everything the trip to Monroe hadn't. Such an experience was bound to change his life.

He was in a hurry to leave, to go home and procure R. Moshele's permission. It wouldn't be easy to convince his father of the significance for him of this journey. If he mentioned the joy he'd experienced his father would think him feverish. He would have to begin at the beginning, explain about the readings, which led to the seizures, which led to the alphabet, which led to R. Yidel, which led to the idea of the journey. He would have to convince his father that the illness was related to the readings.

R. Yidel stopped him. Perhaps you'd better wait a day or two, think it over, sleep on it. You're young and impetuous, you want everything quickly. I know, because I was once your age. But you ought to weigh the dangers, consider what such a decision will do to your reputation, how it could shape your life. I warn you as a friend of your father's.

Joel walked home on air. He was willing to risk anything. Still he would listen to R. Yidel and wait a day or two, but only because he wanted recent episodes to subside from his father's memory. He greatly regretted mentioning his sudden interest in scribing and just as sudden lack of interest. It revealed an immaturity, and with such a record, R. Moshele would have good reason to dismiss yet another request. His father would consider it just another strange idea, a sign of his son's restlessness. Timing, Joel decided, could make the difference, and he recognized that for the first time in his life he was forcing himself to delay, bide his time, and that this was either a sign of maturity or an indication of the journey's significance.

Two days later, on the eve of the New Year, during the ritual request for forgiveness, Joel told his father about his recent readings.

R. Moshele exhaled in relief and nodded. It's good you told me. It would have been even better if you'd approached me before you did it. I might have questioned your interest in Bratslav, but I could also have acquired the books more discreetly. Reading them isn't the issue; most scholars end up reading at least some of it, but not at your age, not as a yeshiva boy. I would strongly have advised waiting. You surely know that the Kabbalah is limited to men past the age of forty.

Joel shook his head. This was precisely what he'd wanted to avoid. Delaying. These were things he wanted to know now, not at forty, when he would be a married family man, with his life already in place, when change would be near impossible. He took a deep breath. He wasn't finished.

R. Moshele looked at him. What else?

I want permission to make an important journey. I want to pray at Reb Nachman's grave on Yom Kippur. I have a feeling I can't explain that my illness is related to my readings and that I must pursue it.

R. Moshele scratched his beard. This was not good. The boy was taking things too far. It was unheard of for a young yeshiva boy to undertake such a voyage. His reputation would be beyond repair. And his recent illness made travel to the Ukraine, a difficult and not entirely safe destination, out of the question. In addition, Joel's language was too extreme. He related the illness to the readings, used the word *must*. He wasn't entreating, he was demanding. R. Moshele knew he would have to refuse Joel's request, but didn't want to seem arbitrary.

I'll give it some thought, he promised.

There isn't time for that, Joel said.

You'll have an answer right after Rosh Hashana. In the meantime, stay away from the bookstore.

At the ritual table that evening, Joel noted that his father was subdued. Though R. Moshele conducted the dippings of apple and honey, sampled the new fruits, recited the blessings aloud, he didn't perform them with his usual enthusiasm. Furthermore, R. Moshele seemed to have forgotten that Joel was sitting on his left. Usually, before he passed the platter of fruit or bread to his right, he took Joel's portion between thumb and forefinger, in rebbe-to-disciple style, dipped it in honey, and handed it directly to his son. Today Joel had to wait for the platter to make its way around the table, from guest to guest, to his mother and to Ada, then to more guests, until it arrived at his end; when R. Moshele recited the blessing, Joel didn't yet have his portion. And ever since he could remember, his father had honored Ada with the eye of the fish and Joel with a portion of the head and together they would say, *May we be as the head, and not the tail; leaders rather than followers.* On this night, Ada was awarded both the eye and portion of head, and a chastened Joel ate his regular slice of fish.

During the singing, Joel attempted to infuse enthusiasm into his own voice and hoped to help his father regain his usual rigor, but R. Moshele looked at him strangely, suspiciously, Joel thought. If it was merely that he'd fallen out of favor, he could accept it, but Joel knew his father wasn't a man who sent messages this way, certainly not consciously. R. Moshele must be troubled and his behavior was that of an aggrieved man. Joel suffered for his father.

Joel had grown up with the privileges of a young and free adult, without the constraints of a child. And after so much favor, he'd done what a son shouldn't: he'd strayed from the path of his father and grandfather, aligned himself with another rebbe, which no father relishes. But this alignment couldn't be what upset R. Moshele, Joel knew. He wasn't that kind of man. His father was worried. He was worried about Joel's health, and worried about the negative impression Joel's Bratslav readings and leanings would make, and knowing this galvanized Joel's adolescent-sharp sense of right and wrong. Against such pettiness, it was more than worth risking one's future. Such a world ought to be defied no matter the consequences; to do so was a noble attempt at world repair, but he wished not to hurt R. Moshele.

That night Joel remained sleepless. He remembered every advantage his father had provided, each of which now stood as a separate reproach to the son, and still he knew that he couldn't and wouldn't relinquish his interest in Nachman. He wished there were something he could say to his father that would give him ease, but R. Moshele was a man with experience of the world to whom fathers came for advice, and what could Joel tell him that he didn't already know?

Near dawn, finally asleep, Joel killed his father, and awoke knowing why he couldn't and shouldn't sleep. They were in a store of garden statuary, and it wasn't clear who owned the business, nor why Joel or his father would have anything to do with it. Stranger still, R. Moshele, who in life was the most nonviolent of men, took an ax and began smashing the inventory, beginning with the most valuable. To prevent more irreparable damage, Joel lifted a hammer and brought it down on his father's head.

In the morning, remembering what his father had said about visiting R. Yidel's store, Joel understood that permission for the journey to Uman would be denied, that he would have to go without it, and that this was the meaning of his dream.

Joel avoided his father, dreaded the decision. He hoped his father's language would remain mild. It would be terrible if his father used the word *forbid*. And it would be worse if his father prohibited R. Yidel any further contact with his son. R. Yidel would certainly respect R. Moshele's wishes, and Joel would have no access to the travelers or to the funds. That would be an insurmountable problem. He determined that his best course of action was to remain very quiet, to appear accepting of his father's decision. He would not protest, because if his father thought that Joel might disobey him, he would take action to ensure against it.

The answer when it came was as expected, with a difference. R. Moshele informed Joel that the journey to Uman would be reconsidered the following year, that they might even travel together, but that this year was impossible for practical and other reasons.

The next morning Joel mailed a note to R. Yidel in which he declared his commitment to the voyage and explained that he couldn't call on him personally because his father had asked him not to. Whenever possible, Joel explained, he would attempt to minimize the sin against his father. He had to take the trip to Uman because the journey was too important to pass up, but he would attempt to stay away from the bookstore. Joel ended the note by stressing again the significance for him of the journey, and the danger of postponement, reminding R. Yidel of Nachman's tale of "The Rabbi's Son."

In preparation for the journey, Joel took upon himself daily fasting, wondering every afternoon, when he was hungriest, why it had to be self-denial rather than self-indulgence that developed a heightened receptivity. He'd seen a photograph of an ascetic from India who'd sacrificed his right arm to God, which meant not using it. The picture, which was taken ten years after the sacrificial vow, showed the ossified arm flung over the ascetic's left shoulder, a long, limp shawl. On the man's face was a permanent grimace, almost a smile, and Joel found himself both attracted and repelled at once. There was violence in such self-mutilation, but also something strangely fascinating, and Joel wondered about the nature of ecstatic experience. Could this man have achieved the same ecstasy through overuse of the arm? If he had lifted the heaviest of weights, begged and carried with it alms to the poor until it was as swollen as Popeye's, would he arrive at the same place? For some reason not. For some reason, self-denial, breakdown, and finally loss were the steps required to achieve higher states of being.

Joel's daily fasting alarmed his mother, even though he ate every evening after sundown, and agreed to drink water throughout the day. R. Moshele didn't know what to make of this new impulse, and though it was worrisome, he advised his wife to let the boy be. Clearly their son was going through a phase and R. Moshele felt that it was best not to stand in the way. On the larger issues, he would insist; he couldn't, for example, permit the trip to Uman, but on lesser matters it was probably best to look the other way. Joel, he assured his wife, won't die of hunger.

A week went by and Joel was too jittery to eat or sleep. Yom Kippur was three days away and he hadn't yet heard from R. Yidel. It wasn't hard to find a yeshiva boy if you knew where he studied; still Joel regretted not providing more details. Or he could have suggested meeting elsewhere, somewhere other than the bookstore, and then he wouldn't be disregarding his father's injunction.

The next day, desperate, convinced that his father had spoken to R. Yidel, he felt as if he were going under. His head was stuffed with cotton, he could concentrate on nothing at yeshiva. During study session, he walked toward the bathroom, stopped there for a moment, and then slipped outdoors. He went out of his way to avoid the busy streets. And he worried. Had R. Moshele forbidden R. Yidel to speak with him? Would R. Yidel turn him away at the door?

Joel walked faster, and this time he didn't hesitate at the door. Inside, behind the table, sat a woman Joel hadn't seen before, but then he'd never stopped in during the day. Was this the wife who couldn't have children and whom R. Yidel wouldn't divorce? He must like her very much, Joel thought, trying not to look too hard. She was looking at him, a question in her face.

Is Reb Yidel at home? Joel asked.

She nodded. He's upstairs, studying. Is it very important?

Joel nodded.

She stood. I'll tell him.

She went through a curtain and Joel heard her light tread on stairs. He stood alone in the store, feeling the responsibility of a shopkeeper.

Moments later, he heard two sets of footsteps, one heavier. R. Yidel

stepped into the room briskly, shook Joel's hand, and told him him to
come upstairs.

Joel followed him up the steps into a room with a large table and
chairs, and on every wall, books. R. Yidel pulled out a chair and Joel sat.

I was beginning to think you wouldn't come. I couldn't come for
you. To defy your father's wishes, it was necessary that you come to me
and not the other way around. In any case, you came, but there isn't
much time. The group leaves tomorrow afternoon. Pack very little. Your
tefillin. A change of underclothes, two shirts. Something to eat, perhaps.
Do you have a small suitcase?

Joel shook his head and R. Yidel stepped into another room and
returned with a small black case. Your ticket, he said, and took a striped
blue KLM folder from his bosom pocket and handed it to Joel. We stop
in Antwerp and then continue east into the Ukraine from there. You
have your passport?

Joel nodded. This was the one significant thing he'd done during the
past week: searched his father's files and found and pocketed his passport. Now he pulled it out. R. Yidel took it from him, checked the expi-
ration date, and nodded.

We have a contact at the Ukrainian embassy who is arranging two
last-minute visas. I am also going, R. Yidel said. I realized that I couldn't
do such a thing to your father; I couldn't send you alone with people you
don't know. Be here tomorrow at four o'clock. The taxi arrives at four-
thirty. My wife will serve us a cooked meal before we leave. There won't
be another until we return.

That night Joel ate more than usual, which pleased his mother. In
another form of contrition, he agreed to play Ada one round of their
high-speed games of chess in which no time for thinking was allowed,
move followed move, and when for a moment, his concentration
lagged, Ada took his queen, and he lost. She was good, she knew, but

not that good, and feeling that Joel had somehow let her win, that he was distracted, she proposed another round, an opportunity for a tie.

He declined. He had little time and there were practical things to consider like when to pack his bag. He wished he could reveal his plan to Ada: telling her would be a relief, and she could help, but it would mean burdening her with his guilt. When R. Moshele grieved over his son's mischief, Ada would shoulder the blame for something she hadn't done. He would think this through by himself. He could leave with his packed bag early in the morning, and in the afternoon go directly from yeshiva to R. Yidel's. This was the most efficient way, leaving him least open to obstacles, especially those imposed by well-meaning family. He wanted little contact with his father right now.

Nahman saw the expected opposition of his family to the journey as a *meni'ah*, an obstacle in the path which had to be overcome.

When his daughter asked what would become of the family while he was away, he replied: "You will go to your in-laws. Someone will take your older sister as a household servant. Your younger sister will be taken into someone's home out of pity. Your mother can find work as a cook, and I shall sell everything in the house to cover expenses for the journey."

The Journey

Gray GTI telephones were embedded in the backs of all middle seats; with all lifelines to earth severed, you could still talk.

Joel waited until they were in the air, when there could be no turning back. It was eight o'clock. At home they would have finished the evening meal and wondered at Joel's lateness. There was no reason to cause more anguish than necessary.

An excellent idea, R. Yidel agreed. R. Moshele ought to know that his son was physically safe. Although a son's spiritual well-being was also a concern, and given a choice, no father would entrust this to a Bratslaver, it was too late to change that. Joel had found Bratslav on his own, he had developed an inner need, and at such times it was a great risk to place obstacles in the soul's way. And Joel had overcome enough personal obstacles to earn a helping hand.

He said that he was very happy to have merited to be in Erez Israel. For on the way to Erez Israel he had undergone many obstacles, confusing thoughts, delays, and struggles, including financial obstacles. But he had overcome them all and had brought the matter to completion by reaching Erez Israel. He further said this: I believe, and indeed I know well, that of all the movements, thoughts, and deeds that one undertakes in order to perform some holy act, not a single one is ever lost. For after all the obstacles have been broken through and the act has been completed, all those confusing thoughts and movements which had taken place while one was still weighing the act . . . are elevated to the highest state of holiness. Everything is recorded above for good, including every move one had to make along the way. Blessed are those who manage to overcome all the obstacles and to complete some good deed.

R. Yidel purchased from the flight attendant a prepaid phone card and Joel followed the directions on the handset to place the call. He hoped his father wouldn't pick up. He would rather talk to his mother, who would convey the unwelcome facts to her husband. It was cowardly, Joel knew, to want someone else to bear his bad news, but he couldn't help himself and he understood, as he hadn't before, that he was a little afraid. But of what? His father or himself?

With the phone pressed to his ear, he heard the lines connecting, he heard the familiar ringing, the noise of the receiver lifting off the cradle, but before he could hear a voice, the connection was severed. Joel looked at the handset, feeling inexplicably pained. Was this a sign?

Try again, R. Yidel advised.

The second time Ada answered and Joel was relieved. He told her where he was.

You're on a plane? The day before Yom Kippur? she asked without expecting an answer, and Joel could picture Ada rolling her eyes heavenward. Where are you going?

Joel told her in as few words as possible. He heard her intake of breath, a gasp, but she recovered quickly.

We were wondering what happened to you, why you were late again. Where did you get money? Weren't you afraid? Wait. Mother wants to talk to you.

Joel held his breath. Even from this distance he could read his sister. She was electrified by his daring. If his boldness was a little frightening, it was also thrilling. But his mother wouldn't be thrilled. And where was his father?

Your father will be beside himself, Mrs. Jakob said. I'm glad he's not here now. It will allow me to break the news to him at an opportune moment. He just left, wondering why you hadn't shown up for the evening meal. Have you eaten anything? Do you have water and fresh clothing?

Joel assured her that he'd eaten well and wasn't alone. This journey, he explained, was too important to postpone, too dangerous to delay.

Dangerous? Mrs. Jakob echoed. This was Joel in one of his extreme modes, she thought. But this wasn't the time to chastise. Joel asked for forgiveness, wished her an easy fast, left the same message for his father, and she responded with her own wishes and exhortations to drink plenty of water before and after the fast, to eat something hot, to stay warm.

Joel hung up, relieved not to have had to speak with his father.

Forty-eight hours later, on his return trip, Joel wished that his father had been home, that they'd already had their first conversation and were now onto the next one, whatever that might be. There would be a second one, he knew, in which R. Moshele would have more to say. After thinking things over, he would decide on a course of action, and once decided, he would inform his son. Joel tried to imagine what this course might be. If his father decided to send him to a yeshiva in Jerusalem, as he was known to have advised others, he would make it possible for Joel to follow Nachman's footsteps to Israel, to the caves of Safed and the grave of Simeon bar Yochai. Nachman had imagined himself the reincarnated soul of bar Yochai. From his readings, Joel knew that this kind of imagining was a useful technique. He knew that the Method actor dresses, talks, thinks, eats, sleeps, indeed lives the life of the character he wants to inhabit. This was one approach to knowing another, Joel thought. He would look for habitual tics or twitches, a particular turn of the nose or lips, anything that might get him closer.

> He took a bit of wax between his fingers, and began to roll it, absorbed in thought . . . He often did this toward the end of his days, rolling wax between his fingers as he thought. Even in this last hour of his life, his mind occupied with some unknown thought, he lay there skillfully and gracefully rolling the wax between his fingers . . .

Of course the attempt to replicate an eighteenth-century journey with one taken in a world of flight schedules and precise reports of departures and arrivals, and with the possibility of tracking a plane on its flight path across the Atlantic, was near impossible. But, Joel thought, even if the world has changed drastically, humans remain similar enough, therefore a spiritual replication of Nachman's journey ought to be feasible. But how to understand the journey? Nachman gave various explanations:

> I heard in his name that he said before his journey to Erez Israel that he wanted to go in order to attain supernal wisdom. There exist higher and lower forms of wisdom; the lower he had already acquired, but he was yet to attain the higher. For this he had to go to the Land of Israel.

> It was heard from his holy mouth during the Passover season that preceded his journey from Medvedevka to the Land of Israel that he wanted

to go to Erez Israel in order there to fulfill all of the six hundred and thirteen commandments, including those which are dependent upon the land together with those which may be fulfilled outside it, fulfilling them all spiritually so that afterward he would be able to fulfill them all physically.

He then told to R. Yudil . . . "I could fulfill that which I seek and desire to do in Erez Israel right here by means of prayer and supplication alone. Then I would not have to travel to Erez Israel. The difference is that if I merit to be in Erez Israel I will receive my understanding in 'garments,' whereas if I stay here I will receive it without the 'garments.' This is also the difference between the holiness of the Sabbath and that of the festival . . . on Sabbath the light is clothed in garments while on the festivals it does not have this garb."

When a certain scholar in the Holy Land pleaded with him to reveal the nature of his visit there, Nahman explained that he was sworn to secrecy on this matter. When pressed, he began to discourse on it indirectly. "But as he began to speak, blood came forth from his throat, and he said to the scholar: 'Now you see that God does not agree that I should reveal this to you.'"

The constant hum of the plane and the dry air gave him a headache. Joel leaned back, fingered the crease in his pants between his index finger and thumb, which always relaxed him, and closed his eyes. What had he gained from the journey? Eventually his father too would ask, and Joel wanted to say, Knowledge.

But knowledge of what?

Joel was certain that for fleeting moments, perhaps in the final moments of creation, when Nachman approached the end of each tale and could discern how it would complete the circle and arrive at meaning, he had known or come close to knowing the genius of God. Therefore, Joel reasoned, knowing Nachman was a way of approaching such knowledge, if only fleeting milliseconds of knowledge. As soon as a given tale was complete, Nachman was back at the beginning, not knowing. To achieve such heights again, he had to maneuver again in the dark, with only the letters of the alphabet, which were once again disparate and random.

Joel talked to himself, concentrated. What had he learned?

Nachman's burial site, situated within a housing complex designed for the proletariat, was unimpressive. All around, the comings and goings of Ukrainians, not a few of them attempting to earn a dollar off the tourists, though the men in long black gabardines didn't have a reputation as big spenders. One, a girl about Ada's age, but as slender and tall as a young tree, unlike any Chasidic girls he'd seen or dreamed, beckoned. She wanted to show him something, but what? Jew place, she said in her foreigner's English. She pointed at Joel, then at herself. She wanted him to come to her and he wanted to, if only this were a world in which such things were allowed, but surely she wasn't what he had come for.

When R. Yidel flung himself on the ground, on Nachman's headstone, and poured his heart out in Yiddish, admitting lapses in concentration, days of doubt, difficulty in study and prayer, all spiritual troubles, Joel attempted to look away. It was difficult not to notice what went unmentioned: a barren wife, no children. Not one of the men mentioned financial troubles, difficult wives, unhealthy children, and surely they had their share of difficulties, as does every human on earth. They cried, grown men crying real tears, and spoke of spiritual lapses and doubts, and they talked to Nachman as if he were there, fully alive. Though these Bratslaver were called the "dead Chasidim" because they prayed to a dead rebbe, Joel thought they might be more alive than any Chasid he'd known.

In life Nachman had refused to hear about anything but spiritual matters—for the magic of amulets, he'd said, there are charlatans.

How can one be a Chasid? Nachman asked.

Six abilities are necessary, he answered. The ability to kneel while standing, to scream while silent, to dance while sitting, to fast while slurping soup, to be most alone while in a roomful of people, and to roll in snow for bodily mortification while in bed under a warm eiderdown.

When Joel approached Nachman's gravestone the others turned aside to give him some privacy, but still he was self-conscious. He wanted to throw himself on the ground like the others, but all he could do was stand stiffly and mouth a prayer. R. Yidel assured him that the urge would come, that before the end of the visit, he would find himself capable of talking to Nachman, who could see through a man like no one else. He related the story of Yudil of Dashev, of his renowned arrogance, and of how Nachman broke through his hardened spirit. Joel had read of the Dashever, but of his own soul he remained uncertain because what he had come for was something altogether different. He lacked the humility of a true disciple, therefore it was possible that his quest would be denied.

Late that night, in the partial privacy of the room that he shared with R. Yidel, Joel contemplated slipping out to return to Nachman's grave in the dark. Then he asked himself whether it wasn't the girl who was the attraction, and he felt afraid. This, he told himself firmly, was what rules and fences are for, to prevent just such transgressions. Her beauty was Satan's lure. If, as in Nachman's tales, deformities turn out to be illusions, how much more so mere superficial beauty?

Still wakeful an hour later, he slipped out of his room and walked down the stairs. In the courtyard, it was dark, it was quiet, and he spoke softly. He said he wished to have known the rebbe, that he was trying to know him, then wondered aloud whether such knowledge had ever been possible. Even in life, disciples said Nachman was unknowable, and perhaps greatness always is.

He did not allow himself to be treated as one would treat another rebbe. When people came to him in search of help in worldly matters, he would at times dismiss them brusquely. "I don't know how you find it in yourself," he once said to such a visitor, "to confound me with the vanities of this world! I am like a man who digs in the desert, day and night, trying to build a settlement. Each of you has a heart like a desert, with no dwelling place in it for the Presence of God. I am constantly digging in your hearts, working to fashion that dwelling. Do you know how hard a person has to work, starting with an oak tree, in order to fashion from it vessels fit for use? First you have to chop the tree down, then saw the boards, make them smooth, and all the rest. I am doing all that for each of you. And you bother me with such trifles?"

Joel found himself asking questions.

To eliminate all doubt, why couldn't the facts of science and mathematics correspond more often to the Torah's version of the world? He wondered whether deprivation and self-denial in a man's life served any purpose; did God truly desire an ascetic lifestyle, or was this merely a man-made idea? And why was it necessary to so isolate oneself from the modern world? Was it indeed a terrible thing to gain secular knowledge, seeing as, in the writing of the tales, such exposure had proved useful to Nachman? And Joel wondered aloud about his own purpose on earth, what he was meant for, how he would leave his mark.

Before his final question, Joel hesitated. He knew it was sinful to know a stranger, a girl from a foreign nation, but then why was this desire keeping him awake, why was his own body working against him? He'd had a vision of his male organ as a withered, calcified arm tangled around his legs, making it difficult to walk. Its unceasing demand was torture. And too many mornings, he awoke to the knowledge that in sleep he'd committed the gravest sin.

When he looked up the girl was there, watching him, wearing what looked like a long nightdress, not the revealing pants she'd worn earlier. He closed and opened his eyes, thinking she was a vision, created by Satan. He pinched his wrist, to be sure he was awake, and still she stood there. And lifted the hem of her nightdress above her pale thighs, bent her knees to squat, and from the dark center a trickle, then a stream emerged. Joel didn't move, or blink.

Then she was finished and her dress fell back in place. She came forward.

Like old man, she said and pantomimed, disgust in her voice, you talk to dead.

I ask questions, Joel explained.

He answer?

Joel paused. Perhaps you are an answer, he said. Or a trial, he thought, to see what he would do.

She stood silhouetted in the moonlight, and he noticed when she spoke that she had unusually strong, white teeth, and that there were too many of them in her mouth, they were jumbled, they overlapped one another in their struggle to find space. In a Jewish mouth, Joel was convinced, too few teeth were more likely. Another mark of her foreign nature: a complete lack of shame. While he watched, she lifted her gown again and slipped her hand under it. And strangely he wasn't appalled. He found himself wanting to mirror her somehow, to touch himself. And he wanted her to lift her dress once again and stand with her legs apart and bent, and allow his hot water to mingle with hers. In the dark she wouldn't see its vitamin-B yellow, but she might smell it because he'd swallowed a capsule just before sundown.

Joel's pulse raced hard and loud. Before it was too late, before he could do something he would regret, he wished the girl good night, and crossed the courtyard.

Zhid, she shouted at his back.

Joel ran. He ran through the door from which he'd exited, took a left turn where he'd turned right, and a right where he'd gone left, went up fifteen flights of stairs, taking three steps at a time at first, then two, then, out of breath, he slowed down to a trudge, one tired step at a time. He walked down the hallway, looking for his room, number 1513. But he was already at 1519. He walked back, checked door numbers. He was on the fifteenth floor, that was certain because he passed room 1511 and 1512, even a 1514, but no 1513. He retraced his steps to the stairwell and walked down another hallway, also brown. He walked past the 1540s, then the 1550s. He went back again, took another corridor, and stopped halfway. There was an order in the numbering system: for the most part the fifties remained within the corridor for the fifties, with an occasional exception: a 1501 turned up inexplicably, then a 1521. He remembered that in his hallway the 1511 had been on the opposite side. Perhaps if he concentrated, he could figure out the key to this system and avoid walking the entire length of every corridor, of what seemed an endless number of corridors on this floor. The building was built around a court called the Skvere Nacionale, and encompassed a massive area, the length and width, Joel calculated, of two New York City blocks. He walked back to the stairs, where he'd started, to what he'd thought was the center, looked to his left and right, and realized there were other stairwells to his left and right. This is a tower of Babel, he thought, though the biblical allusion would probably not amuse the Communists who had built it.

He paused. Were there more stairwells leading to other corridors? Had he come up the right stairwell? Tired now, confused, and overheated, he leaned against a wall and slid to the ground. He closed his eyes. If he couldn't find the room, he'd have to spend the night in this hallway, and provide more proof of the strangeness of Chasidim, about whom the Ukrainians were already curious, if only to understand what it was that had made these people the targets of so many pogroms and libels, and why it had been necessary to isolate them within ghettos and camps, then usher them into their final chambers.

There were always reasons for hatred. In Western Europe, anti-Semitism had been blamed on Jewish-owned banks; in Germany, the troubles of the impoverished Weimar Republic. At home, when Joel felt the eyes of an elderly modern Jew on his black hat and coat, his *peyos*, he sensed skepticism and disgust in the gaze. But why should a modern Jew abhor a traditional one? Joel understood the scientific rationality that had shaped the Jew's skepticism, but the source of one Jew's hatred for another Jew was harder to comprehend. And the man's bitter knowledge that to Hitler the difference between modern and traditional Jews had meant nothing didn't help. University-educated, modern Jews had been forced to share the fate of the Chasidim from the Carpathian Mountains. From younger generations of American Jews, the skeptical Jew's children and grandchildren, Joel felt an interested empathy. The choices of their forward-looking parents, they knew, weren't entirely without error. But every generation perceives the shortcomings of the previous one. Nachman knew that his uncle's Chasidism had yielded to corrupt indulgence, that without stringent guidelines for individual struggle, there could be no great achievement, no world repair.

In his rejection of the popular Hasidism of his uncle and the "miracles" offered by the various wonder-workers to be found throughout the Ukraine, Nahman sought to present a renewed Hasidism, which would truly concern itself with a spiritual search and the creation of a new ideal type of Jew. His task was that of leading a revival within a waning Hasidism; the goal of such a revival would have to be to fashion each of his disciples into a *zaddiq*. No lesser definition of the master's task would do . . .

In the utter seriousness of the Bratslav revival there was no room for the often lighthearted gatherings common to other Hasidic courts . . . Nahman's path, based on the model of the suffering *zaddiq* rather than on the regal model, and seeking out deep religious conflict as the sign of spiritual growth, could never achieve broad-based popular support. The privilege of following Nahman was reserved for a spiritual elite.

And that, Joel calculated, was a hundred and ninety years ago. The attempt to breathe new life into Chasidism had failed, and the true spirit of the movement had died. According to the Kapuster rebbe, a great-grandfather of the recent Lubavitcher rebbe, Chasidism had been given to the Jews as a much-needed gift for only a hundred years. By Nachman's assessment, it hadn't survived in true form for even that long. These days nothing but clothing distinguished a Chasid from other Orthodox Jews. What was called Chasidism was mere orthodoxy under a different coat. And if this were true, why continue wearing the outer garments, his own black caftan?

Joel pulled himself together. Where was this thinking taking him? Modern Orthodox life didn't interest him. And in the meantime, he was a man without a bed, who had looked upon the nakedness of a woman on the eve of Yom Kippur. Another sin to confess.

And what if she were still there, waiting for him with her dress hitched up above her thighs? He couldn't dare walk downstairs to begin again at the beginning. He had to assume this was the right floor and the right staircase. Even if it wasn't the right staircase, there ought to be a 1513 on the fifteenth floor. He would count on some consistency in the use of numerics—why else number the doors?—and methodically walk up and down each corridor. He would find his room. In computerized searches, it was proven most efficient to cut the given search material in halves and quarters, look to one side, then the other. He would conduct such a Boolean search. Even though he'd already walked the farthest corridor twice, he decided not to skip it because, unlike God and machine, he was fallible. And tonight he was excessively fallible, weakened by his strange desires. As a machine he could avoid such weaknesses. In a modern rewrite of the liturgy, Joel imagined, machine terminology would replace the old agricultural linguistics and man would find himself chanting of abilities greater than human, of knowledge deeper and wider than any intelligence, of energies more powerful than the most advanced nuclear fission, of a being who could dispense with binary, Boolean, and bubble searches and solve problems faster than the speed of light. And we would sing of His control of the purest underground water and the largest oil-rich parcels of real estate, of an ability to mediate the most tortuous peace talks in history, and through everything remain more elusive than the most advanced of Teflons.

Joel walked the corridors again and felt that his waking hours were more dreamlike than his dreams. Fifteen minutes later, methodical persistence triumphed, and he found his room in the most unlikely of corridors, an anomaly amid the 1590s. Then, for an hour, he lay in bed wondering about this experience with numbers, numbers rather than letters, numbers that are infinite and mathematically beautiful in their own hard way.

When the plane prepared to land and passengers were asked to bring their seats forward, Joel emerged from his reverie on what the journey had provided; he sat up and in quick summary, ticked off on his fingers a list:

He'd seen with his own eyes and personally experienced the Bratslaver ability to be emotionally vulnerable, alive to pain.

He'd experienced shivering lawless desire for a foreign woman and seen the sinfully inexplicable.

In exile from his own room and bed, he'd spent an evening wandering hallways and stairwells, meditating on numerics.

In other words, he'd encountered obstacles.

None of which he would report to his father.

An experience that travelers since Creation have known: From a distance, away from home, one can contemplate one's life and achieve if not whole, at least more comprehensive sight. Before this journey, Joel had seen his life only up close, within the confines of family and community. For the first time he'd freed himself to see wider and farther, and he wondered: What was the significance of a man's experience in the world? What was the purpose of his journey on earth? And of the journeys within this larger journey? What had Nachman derived from his journey to Israel?

Biographers have speculated, disciples have proposed answers. It seemed clear that the journey itself, complete with its own set of Laistrygonians and Cyclops, its windy Poseidon, was the point, since immediately upon arrival Nachman was prepared to turn around and begin his return trip. Among other journeyers: Cain, for whom wandering was a life sentence; Joseph, who was sold down to Egypt; the Israelites in the desert; the Jews in exile. Thousands of years later, taking up the old motif of obstacles, temptations, and challenges, Joel had been awarded his own siren, the Ukrainian girl.

> While Nahman was in Haifa, another strange thing to which he attributed great significance occurred. It seems that a young Arab "discovered" Nahman and began to visit his quarters regularly. The young man took a great liking to Nahman, but in vain did he seek to transcend the language barrier which existed between them. Failing to make his affection for Nahman understood, he at one point became angry and challenged the *zaddiq* to a duel. Frightened by the prospect, Nahman hid himself in the home of his friend the rabbi of Charny-Ostrog, who had arrived in Haifa with him. The "Ishmaelite," however, was soon appeased, and again showed great affection for Nahman. This, too, Nahman found disquieting, and said that he "suffered more from the love of this Ishmaelite than from his hate or anger." He felt that some great danger might await him in this person, and he may have claimed that the young man was none other than Samael himself.

Coming through customs, Joel saw Ada first, striding toward him, sparkling as always, with a circlet of soft brown fur at her neck. Behind her were his mother and father, his sweet mother in her elegant dark skirt and belted coat. They had all come to greet him.

R. Moshele shook his son's hand, then held him, and Joel had to force himself to breathe. What was this? Why wasn't his father angry? This was too incredible, his father was smiling, his mother was fussing with his *peyos*, smoothing them, and Joel, pierced with guilt, couldn't help himself, he chattered nervously.

How did you know where to go and when I was arriving? he asked, and without waiting for an answer, continued: I'm so hungry, I could eat a house.

Mrs. Jakob produced a large red apple from the shiny black pocketbook she carried, and no apple had ever tasted better.

Then R. Yidel came through customs and R. Moshele stepped forward to greet him. Joel listened anxiously, but they were shaking hands, exchanging warm greetings, mouthing the usual New Year wishes. It was too perfect, Joel thought, even for a miracle.

In the evening, Ada informed her brother that he was right, it was too miraculous.

Their father, Ada reported, had grieved all Yom Kippur, and although tears were expected on such a day, people were noticing and wondering. It was the Berditchever's idea to put a good face on the whole thing, to let it be known that Joel had been sent to Uman to fulfill the will of a great-grandfather on his maternal side, a Bratslaver from Jerusalem, who requested that every male grandchild visit Nachman's gravesite before the age of eighteen. It was also the Berditchever's idea, Ada explained, to meet you at the airport, to welcome you home as the beloved son that you are.

You think people will fall for it? Joel asked.

Ada shrugged. If you repeat it often enough. The general stupidity in the world is truly amazing.

She took great pleasure in the wisdom of the Berditchever's strategy, of his ability to turn a thing on its head, she said. And on Yom Kippur yet, when the man had spent the day on his feet, praying and fasting. This was the kind of thing she could excel at, she knew. In this she took after her grandfather, not her straight-arrow father. She pointed to a poster on her wall, THE MASSES ARE ASSES. She'd come across the slogan years ago, had printed it in block type on a large board, added a cartoon line drawing of a donkey, and hung it above her sewing table. Whatever happened in her life, of one thing she was determined: She wouldn't live in fear of rumor and reputation. Whenever she heard the petty criticisms that she was altogether too fashionable for a Chasidic girl, she responded by purchasing or sewing something in the latest style. Gentle warnings from her grandmother only brought out Ada's fighting spirit, until Mrs. Jakob advised withholding such reports from her daughter altogether. She was committing no sin, after all. It was a young girl's prerogative to look good. If she managed better than others, talk was to be expected.

Joel shook his head. He understood that manipulations and contrived controversies were the ways in which men differentiated themselves and became leaders, and still he found such behavior disturbing. Nachman had also engaged in such questionable activities, but it was his late turn to storytelling that brought him the greatest satisfaction.

"All the zaddiqim reach whatever rung it is that they are to attain, and they just remain there. But I, praise God, in every single moment become another person." Thus he provided an explanation for the fact that others opposed him. The zaddiq is likened to a tree, having roots, branches, and so forth. Every zaddiq is controversial before he reaches his particular rung. Thus the sages have said: "Controversy is like a burst of water. Controversy is the water that makes the zaddiq grow tall. . . . Concerning me there must be constant controversy, for I keep moving, in every moment, from rung to rung. If I were to realize that I stand now at the same place where I stood an hour ago, I would be completely dissatisfied with myself."

Ada had more to tell. Though she remained at home, things happened to her, stories arrived. He'd flown halfway around the world and back and had little to show, a series of inexplicable stumbling blocks. There was some basic difference in their lives or in the workings of their minds, he wasn't sure which. In hers, every event, the smallest incident, formed a legitimate narrative. His experiences were impossible to recount. One event had nothing to do with the other, at least not logically. When he attempted to attach them, the connective tissue felt forced, false, a strained cohesion that was narrow-minded, all too weakly, subjectively human. For example, the episode of his nocturnal wandering in the corridors, lost in sameness, confused by numbers out of sequence. How did it relate to the temptation of the Ukrainian girl outside? In Ada's mind, Joel was certain, these disparate parts would add up to form a story.

What else could've happened here? he asked her.

The phone rang minutes before sunset, Ada began. We thought it was you calling a second time. Instead, on the phone was a schoolgirl, the younger Heller girl asking me for forgiveness. It was minutes before Yom Kippur, how could I refuse, but I wondered aloud what for, what could she possibly have done to me since we hardly know one another? Her oldest sister was in my graduating class.

She'd heard criticism of a dress I'd worn, she said, after someone's wedding.

I was speechless, Ada said. Momentarily anyway. Then I asked her whether she realized that informing me of this criticism hurt me more than the initial gossip. Furthermore, in the act of asking forgiveness she herself was reporting someone else's evildoings, which would require more requests for forgiveness than she could possibly accomplish in these last seconds before sundown.

Joel was amused. This was piety taken to a level of stupidity. How did she respond? Joel asked.

She asked to be forgiven a second time.

The next morning, when Joel found himself in his own bed, in his father's house, with his regular schedule ahead of him, he dreaded the day. Just yesterday he'd looked forward to the safety of regular life, to the day after his first meeting with his father, to a full day of study at the yeshiva. Now, with precisely this ahead of him, he felt no desire to rise.

He did rise, washed, dressed, and became Joel Jakob, the young scholar he was known as, a Berditchever grandson. With the mere act of waking, the half-conscious taking of the first and second steps of the morning ritual, he had re-created himself.

On his way to morning prayers, he inhaled the freshness of cut greens, the cattails and bamboo on the roofs of the neighborhood sukkot, the temporary houses Chasidim would live in for the next eight days of the holiday, and remembered that this was not after all a regular day; it was a day before the harvest festival, and yeshivas were closed for the month. As always during holiday vacations, he would spend the morning with Aaron. In the afternoon, he and R. Moshele would build their own hut. Indeed, they were late getting started this year, due to his own delinquency, and Joel was moved by the fact that no one at home, not even Ada, had sounded an impatient note.

Aaron was already at the table when Joel arrived. They shook hands.

I wish you'd asked me to join you, Aaron said.

Joel looked at Aaron. I wouldn't do such a thing to a friend, he said. You know what going there means.

If we'd gone together, two friends undertaking the journey, it would've been seen as a prank. Alone, taking off by yourself in secrecy, makes it seem significant.

I don't mind the talk, Joel said, though my father does. And your father would have.

Joel told Aaron about the gravesite, enclosed within the vast urban housing complex, with corridors as streets and lobbies as squares, not the forest of trees you'd imagine for R. Nachman, he finished.

Aaron wanted to know whether this visit had been more meaningful than the one to the Satmar rebbe.

I think so, Joel said, hesitatantly. Though I'm unable yet to say precisely how or why. At first I couldn't pray or speak, not thoroughly, emotionally, the way the Bratslaver do. Late that night I went out, and after a struggle I experienced a breakthrough. It seems my heart was hardened.

Hearing himself describe the event, Joel wondered whether his sudden ability to speak at Nachman's gravesite had come to him through the girl, whether it had been the sin itself that had humbled his hardened heart, a descent for the purpose of ascent. He had achieved something, he felt now, though he hadn't arrived at the state of humility of R. Yidel and the others. Unlike them, he'd questioned rather than confessed.

The account given of the first meeting between Nahman and Yudil of Dashev is highly revealing of the intense personal style in which Nahman conducted himself in his early years as *rebbe*. Yudil, who was surely the elder of the two by quite a few years, was a highly respected man in his own community. In addition to having studied with Pinhas of Korets, he was the son-in-law of the *zaddiq* Leib of Strestinits, and was reputed to be something of an authority on Kabbalah. He thus entered Nahman's room rather self-confidently and said: "Let our master show us a path in the service of God." Nahman, feeling a touch of arrogance in the other's tone, replied by quoting in a questioning voice: "To know Thy ways in the earth?" (Ps. 67:3), as though to say: Can one so filled with earthly concerns as you indeed be seeking a way to God? At this R. Yudil became so filled with awe and terror that he stepped back to the doorway and was afraid to come any closer to Nahman than that. Nahman then began to smile, lessening the tension in the room, and said: "Why should you be afraid of me? I'm only a human being, just like you—except that I am more clever than you." He continued to appease the visitor until R. Yudil drew near and stood right next to him. Then once again he let out with a word that shook the poor man to the core, and he again fled to the

threshold. Again Nahman began to smile and draw him near. This happened a number of times, until R. Yudil's spirit was so broken that Nahman could order him to confess to him all that had transpired in his life.
This moment of *widui* or confession to the *zaddiq* was apparently the
moment of initiation into the circle of Nahman's *hasidim*. So central was
this confession to Bratslav and so well known did it become that other
hasidim referred to the disciples of Nahman as *widuiniks* (confessors). . . .
This initiatory rite made it quite clear to the would-be joiner of the
community that a bond of unusual intensity was being forged here, and
therefore that becoming a part of this particular community was a matter
not to be taken lightly.

R. Moshele was one of several in the neighborhood who invested in a
prefabricated plywood hut sold by a Jewish entrepreneur catering to
specific holiday requirements with solutions that made their fulfillment
easier. Every hole in the hut was pre-stamped and pre-drilled; every
screw, nut, and bolt color-coded and matched. R. Moshele and Joel
began as always with the eastern wall, at first silently, tensely. With
Black & Decker's cordless screwdriver, newly purchased this year, the
walls went up quickly, and tensions eased, as if in building this eight-day
home, they were reconstructing the family circle; by the time the final
screw was sunk, the last wall secured, Joel felt himself restored to his
place as the good son, courtesy of Home Depot.

When the bamboo slats and cattails were in place overhead, Ada took
charge of decorating and Joel served as her assistant. R. Moshele went to
work designing this year's light fixture—the chandelier, he called it. How
light enters a room, he liked to say, makes all the difference.

In designer terminology, Ada explained, it's called ambience.

R. Moshele nodded. Of course. To celebrate the holiday appropriately, the proper ambience is necessary.

Mrs. Jakob smiled. Her husband knew little about design or ambience, but every year he took the opportunity to express himself through

his chandelier design. This year, he'd saved seven small amber-colored medicine bottles.

Glass reflects light, he announced, as if this were news. This is why most dining room chandeliers have crystal pendants.

His idea this year: he would fill each bottle with one of the seven crops of biblical Israel: wheat, barley, wine, figs, pomegranates, olive oil, and honey. The year before, he had included apples in the chandelier design. The previous year, plastic birds. Ever since the children had grown old enough to attend to the task of decorating the walls, R. Moshele had focused on the light fixture. Mrs. Jakob tended the pots on the stove in the kitchen, though R. Moshele liked it when she wiped her hands on her apron, stepped from the house into the late September light, walked into the grassy shade of the hut, and offered opinions and advice. Our best star ought to hang on the wall directly across the door, the first thing visitors see, she said. When they were young, Mrs. Jakob recalled, she and R. Moshele had decorated the hut together, usually late at night, after the children had been put to bed and they were both tired. Still they'd enjoyed the annual task of creating a temporary home. And now Joel and Ada found pleasure in it. In a few years, God willing, they would each have their own huts to decorate and soon after, there'd be grandchildren offering help.

Mrs. Jakob brought a stack of freshly laundered, starched, and pressed white sheets, placed them on the outdoor table, with some nostalgic pleasure; these old sheets had served as a clean white backdrop on the plywood walls all the years of her marriage.

There are holes and tears in some of them, she warned. Hang them where they won't be seen.

Joel stood on the ladder, stapler in hand. From below, Ada handed him the sheet's corner, and he stapled. She stepped back to eye the work critically. If she approved, they went on to the next sheet.

This was one of their favorite holidays. The experience of eating and sleeping outdoors in the fortifying autumn weather was a reminder of the agricultural life Jews once lived. They camped, and the change from the usual routine made even the discomforts of outdoor living welcome. At the sight or sound of rain it was Joel's task to climb up the ladder to the roof and spread the tarp, which provided good enough cover for the light variety of showers. Anything heavier and puddles collected on the plastic; the damp soaked through the unprotected plywood; and in the corners, long, wet drips developed. Inside, paper decorations wilted and streaks of blue, red, green, and yellow bled onto the white sheets. Although the old words of praise and thanks for daily dew and rain remained in the prayer service, they were mere reminders of a past life. Not since the Middle Ages, when Jews were still agriculturally employed, was rain appreciated.

In the synagogue, too, there was much to enjoy. Besides the extra readings and songs for the holiday, there were the honors to be doled out, hence the talk of who would be honored. Every year two men were selected, one to read the final chapter of the Torah, the second to read the first. Along with the others, Joel and Aaron enjoyed the speculations, guessing, and then the discovery of whether they were right. The second and higher honor was reserved for a scholar. The first one went to a man of means who could afford the kichel, herrings, wines, and liquors required to celebrate endings. If the man had a wealthy father-in-law, there might even be fish and noodle pudding. And people took such pleasure in eating. The young friends amused themselves by keeping track of how many slices of noodle pudding certain people ate. Seeing such enthusiasm for food, one wouldn't know this was a holiday in which most of the day was spent at the table eating, as if in compensation for the Yom Kippur fast. At lunch, a three-course meal of gefilte fish, egg salad, and an entrée of meat or chicken, after which you could only sleep. On waking, you had a choice of potato pudding and cakes with tea or coffee to carry you through to the next three-course meal of gefilte fish, chicken soup with matzoh balls, and the entrée of meat or chicken. By the end of the long week, after so much food and rest, most people looked forward to a return to everyday disciplined life.

The suspension of regular Talmudic classes provided Joel with an added benefit: the freedom to range wide in his readings and researches. In his notebook, he worked out a schedule for the week, which besides his daily morning sessions with Aaron included an hour of alphabetic meditations and time for reading.

There was one obstacle: No matter what he was doing, the image of the Ukrainian girl intruded. She occupied his dreams. On waking, Joel discovered that he'd sinned. After such involuntary transgression, abstaining from food and drink was the usual penance, but during the holidays, fasting was not an option.

After the third episode, Joel determined to speak with R. Yidel, but not wanting to hurt his father on the first joyous days of the holiday, he delayed. On the first weekday, after his morning study session with Aaron, he walked to the bookstore.

R. Yidel was just locking up. The store is on holiday schedule, he explained. It's open mornings only. But wait here, I set aside a book for you.

R. Yidel turned the lock to open the door, hurried in, and soon returned carrying the book.

Here it has been gathering dust and I think it will interest you, R. Yidel said. It's the doctoral thesis of a student at Hebrew University. As a Bratslaver, I recommend books written by one of us, and there are enough of those to fill a house. However, as a bookseller who must remain current, I know that the interesting recent writing on Reb Nachman has come from outside the community. To some extent this was also true in the early days. In 1932, when Hillel Zeitlin began publishing essays on the Rebbe in *Der Moment*, the Bratslav community didn't trust the work because it was written by a man they considered an outsider. Years later, his son Aaron Zeitlin collected and republished them as a biography, and since then the book has entered even the Bratslav canon. As a result of Zeitlin's work, other scholars became interested. In Germany, Martin Buber and Gershom Scholem. More recently, Joseph Weiss, Joseph Dan, Arthur Green, Arnold Band, a woman named Ada Rapoport-Alpert, and David Roskies.

R. Yidel talked as he walked, and Joel accompanied him to the back of the storefront, where he had parked his old station wagon.

I'm going to the Bratslaver *shtibel* for *minchah*, R. Yidel said. Perhaps you want to join me. We have a wealth of Bratslaver writings there, any of which you could pull from the shelf and read. The one stipulation is that they must be read and studied on the premises.

Though Joel knew his father wouldn't like it, the promise of seeing the entire collection of books, all of them in one place, was irresistible, and he accepted R. Yidel's invitation.

The town of New Square was a twenty-minute ride by car. Once en route, R. Yidel inquired after Joel's well-being and Joel confessed that something that had taken place in Uman had continued to trouble him. He retold the events of his late-night experience, complete with all the shameful facts.

R. Yidel nodded encouragingly during the telling. After, he remained silent for so long, Joel became anxious, wondering whether he'd offended him somehow.

R. Yidel didn't speak until he'd parked the car and turned off the engine.

I wondered if something like that might have taken place, he said. Several of us, myself included, have had the same experience with the girl, a veritable Lilith, it seems.

Joel stared. Could this be true?

As it turns out, R. Yidel continued, every one of us who reported the episode felt that it had been an important one, that one way or another it had brought with it some inner spiritual growth. In the end, we agreed that the experience was mostly beneficial. I'm of the opinion that the repetition of the incident indicates that it isn't mere happenstance, that the hand of Reb Nachman must be acknowledged.

Joel nodded. He too had benefited. The strange event had changed him. He wasn't certain how or why, but it had wrought something in him. He had yet to understand it better.

Sometimes, R. Yidel added cautiously, for those worthy of such experiences, descent, even into sin, is the first step toward greatness.

Joel nodded, and remembered what Nachman had written on the subject.

> When the *zaddiq* speaks with the wicked, and he uplifts his mind to bind himself to God, he also uplifts their minds along with his own, and he thus brings them close to God. The true *zaddiq* contracts his intellect, speaking to them with great cleverness and artfulness, binding all his words to God and thus bringing them [inadvertently] to repent. . . . The *zaddiq* therefore must go down and fall into this state of simplicity, and become a truly simple man for some time. In this way he brings life to all the simple ones, whoever they may be.

When they entered the *shtibel*, Joel expressed surprise that there were so many Bratslaver.

Holiday visitors from Brooklyn and Jerusalem, R. Yidel explained. Otherwise, on any given evening, there are hardly ten for prayers.

R. Yidel introduced Joel to several people, then walked him around the perimeter of the room and explained the shelving system.

On the north wall the books on the life, all the biographies in other words. On the south side, criticisms and interpretations of Nachman's work, which as you can see are as multitudinous as the seas. On the shelf in front of the room facing east, above the cantor's stand, and surrounding the ark, are the primary sources, Nachman's own writings: his *Liqqutim (Collections)*, *Sippurey Ma'asiyot (Book of Tales)*, the *Sefer ha-Middot (The Book of Moral Qualities)*, and the *Sihot ha-Ran (Conversations of Rabbi*

Nachman). Of course, R. Yidel said, it's difficult to make the case that the tales and even many of the *Liqqutim* are fully primary, since they were originally oral compositions. Among ourselves, since we know the scribe was the holy Reb Nathan, we accept them as primary.

R. Yidel put his hand on Joel's shoulder. Shall I leave you for a while?

Joel nodded. He walked the length of the shelves and back, paused to pull a book from the shelf, then moved on to the next shelf, next book. In the Bratslav synagogue in Jerusalem, Joel knew from his readings, Nachman's old carved chair stood, always vacant, its presence a constant reminder of the story of its survival and a source of hope and strength for present-day Bratslav followers. According to the storytellers, when Jewish communities in the Ukraine were forced to disperse, the disciples had taken the chair apart, distributed the pieces among themselves, and promised to do everything in their power to bring them to Jerusalem, where they would reassemble the chair. That every one of them survived the pogroms and wars to accomplish this mission was considered a miracle. Several reported that during the worst times they'd felt Nachman near them.

Though mystically colorful, such miracle tales brought Joel no closer to Nachman. They seemed designed to obscure rather than unveil, and yet it was possible that the knowledge he was seeking was to be found in this darkness. But how to enter it? He would have to begin the way he knew: in light.

In any research project, one begins with primary sources. In this case, there weren't many. All of Nachman's early writings, significantly the messianic material, had been destroyed at his own request.

In Lemberg, between Purim and Passover of 5568 (1808), he went into his private room and wept a great deal. With tears running down his cheeks, he called to R. Simeon, and, sighing, he said: "There is no one to consult." He then told him about a book which he had in his house, which had brought about the deaths of his wife and his children. He had also risked his own life for this book, and now he did not know what to do. He saw that he would have to die there in Lemberg, but if the book were burned he would live. He was in grave doubt, not knowing what was the proper course of action. It pained him to burn this holy and awesome book, for which he had already risked so much. Indeed, the true holiness of this book is beyond all description. Had it remained in the world, everyone would have seen the greatness of our master, face to face.

R. Simeon responded: "Surely if there is any reason to think that your life depends on this, it is better that the book be burned and that you remain alive." Our master explained that it would at least give him some more time; if the book were burned, his life would be lengthened at least a bit. But then he went on: "You don't understand how great is the sanctity of this book, over which I lost my first wife and my children! How much have I suffered for this!" He broke down and wept again.

It was finally agreed that the book should be burned, and Simeon set off for Bratslav to do as he was reluctantly bidden.

On the upper shelves were multiple copies of various editions of the tales in Hebrew, Yiddish, and bilingual editions. There were also several English translations. On the lower shelf, the collected anecdotes, sayings, conversations, and teachings. Below that, the *Moral Qualities* (*Middot*), a day journal Nachman had started in his childhood as a personal project and continued into early adulthood. And that was all. Not a large legacy. Still the books composed a kind of shrine. Reading them was the closest a Chasid could come to knowing his rebbe, just as in the study of Torah man comes closest to knowing God. This, it seemed to Joel, was true of all reading. Whenever he'd followed the mind of an author, the particulars and minutiae of his method and style, he felt he'd come as close as any human could to knowing another mind. Though

Bratslav Chasidim of this day didn't have a live rebbe to visit, Joel felt that their access to Nachman's mind might be greater than what was available to other Chasidim who might pray with their rebbes on a daily basis, participate in the communal table Friday and Saturday nights, and receive the rebbe's blessing in private chambers. Joel's own experience with the tales seemed proof of this. That the Bratslaver were called the "dead Chasidim" was simply perverse, an absurdity.

By the time the afternoon service began, Joel had accumulated a pile of books that would take some time to read. After prayers he told R. Yidel that he wanted to remain on the premises.

R. Yidel nodded. My wife's family is visiting; therefore, I may be held up. However, even if I don't arrive in time for the evening service, I'll return for you later.

Joel cleared a space for himself at a table. He wasn't in the room alone; others remained to talk or read, and Joel was comfortable, the hum of talk low enough that he could concentrate. Now and then he noticed someone's eyes on him, nodding knowingly. Joel didn't respond. He couldn't explain that this was not what it seemed, he had no intention of becoming a Bratslaver, at least not in the standard sense. What he wanted from Nachman was something less than honorable, the object of his scholarship, not transmittal and continuity. He was here to break the vessel that was Nachman's work to understand how it was made, and see whether he could reconfigure the shards his own way.

Two hours later, Joel was in the middle of the first book, and minyan for the evening service had gathered. Joel joined the men in prayer. He noted that R. Yidel hadn't arrived. He would have more time.

After the evening service, the *shtibel* emptied and Joel relaxed. If he'd known he would be here through the afternoon and evening, he would have brought an apple and perhaps some crackers. He was hungry, but not terribly. He had fifty pages left in the *Book of Moral Qualities*. A collection of sayings and proverbs, it revealed Nachman's preoccupations as a child and teenager.

How little a man changes, Joel thought. In the child, one could discern the adult and vice versa. Most impressive was the consistently heightened consciousness: Nachman had been a man who had lived every moment with urgency. In his thirty-eight years, he'd lived more than most men lived in sixty.

Oddly enough, according to the biographers, concentration was difficult for Nachman. Joel already knew from his readings that the BeShT (Ba'al Shem Tov) lineage had been a great burden as well as a motivating force, and that involuntary nocturnal sins had been a source of guilt and doubt. All this had led to an intense longing for a sign of approbation, a divine signal of endorsement that could expunge painful self-doubt.

In the silence of the room Joel was able to enter into Nachman's mind and feel his discomforts, because they weren't far from his own. If Nachman's temptations had been anything as powerful as Joel's recent experience, they would indeed have been terrible. Thinking about it, Joel felt himself immediately aroused. He squeezed his thighs together and hoped the sensation would go away. He tried concentrating on the page in front of him, but when he found himself on the same sentence minutes later, he pushed the book away in disgust. He considered R. Yidel's statement, that the hand of Nachman could be seen in this strange and shared experience. But what was Nachman's motivation? Joel wondered. Did he want every Chasid to suffer as he had? Was it simply a desire to bind others to the servitude of sexual desire as he had been? Since that moonlit night in Uman, Joel had felt himself no longer a free man. In the throes of arousal, he was shamefully, blissfully fettered. Under the table, beneath his clothes, in the skinny shadow of his thighs, he felt a growing discomfort, uncomfortable and glorious at once, pain and pleasure mingled. His thighs fell open, his hand moved toward what it shouldn't. He arrested it and pulled the book in front of his face, attempted concentration once more. In a house of prayer and study this was worse than shameful. But desire was stronger than the finest sensibility, body won out over mind, and Joel looked for a door that might lead to where he belonged now.

He stood with some difficulty. At the far end of the room, he found the brown door. He went down a narrow corridor of stairs, dark and humid, and groped for a light switch on the dingy walls, pawed the thick air, and there it was, the dirty dangling string. The bulb flashed on and then off. His luck. He would have to manage in the dark. He stood with his legs apart and tried to hold up his pants, but it was too much and they crumpled around his ankles on the damp floor. When relief came, it was slow and it burned. And what were the sounds from above? The sound of feet, several. R. Yidel had brought others? If he didn't hurry, R. Yidel would think that Joel had found another way home, but he couldn't move yet, he wasn't finished. Wood cracked and splintered in his head. Which hurt. And then he saw the girl again, dress lifted, legs apart, and the steady unashamed stream between them. Joel couldn't move. His legs were weak, rubber. He went down on his knees and stayed, eyes closed, until he was spent.

Long minutes passed and then Joel groped for the faucets of the small sink to wash his hands, and without pausing to dry them, ran up the stairs, wondering at the noise. Movement of benches and tables, but no voices. Perhaps an evening event had been scheduled, something R. Yidel didn't know of, though he would know such things. In any case, it was time to go. It must be past nine, he thought, and he had accomplished very little.

When Joel stepped into the light, he froze. What was this? Where was he? His sins below had created chaos above. Bookcases were overturned, benches askew, and at the podium in the center, fire—holy books on fire. How could he have done this? In what must have been moments. Ten minutes, fifteen, he couldn't say for sure. His legs were giving out again. He was out of breath. And who were these black figures, three men with the black gabardined bodies of yeshiva boys and terrorist faces shrouded in stockings. They were feeding books to the fire. This was a strange dream. Joel closed his eyes and waited before opening them. The table where he had been sitting, those books were still there. He ran toward them screaming: Fire, help, fire. Someone slapped him in the face.

Shvayg shtil, a voice said. The others came forward and looked at him.

Reb Moshele's son, one said. I heard he went to Uman.

Who are you? Joel asked. Demons?

He was shoved in the shoulder and, falling left, was shoved again on the other side. He fell forward. He felt a shoe on his back.

Keep him there, a voice said. We'll finish and go.

Let's go now. Let the fire do the rest.

What about him?

Leave him there.

Joel lifted his head. They spoke the Yiddish of the yeshiva, but they were hoodlums. What did this have to do with him? He pushed himself up and spoke. To date, to this moment, I believed only Nazis could think, speak, and do such things, that Jews weren't capable of such behavior. No matter what I heard about the Zionists in Palestine, I never believed it. Now I know better. And you call yourselves Chasidim?

He felt the heel of a shoe between his shoulders. Hold your tongue, he was told.

Joel lifted his head again, took a deep breath, and screamed as loud as he could. This was the town of New Square, there were plenty of houses nearby, Skvere Chasidim all around, with God's help, not all of them criminals.

What's going on here?

R. Yidel's voice. Joel felt the full weight of a man on his back, then it was off his back, but he couldn't move. Running feet. A long car horn, slamming doors, then nothing.

. . .

During the second half of Sukkot, Joel nursed two cracked ribs.

If only that were the worst of it, R. Moshele said.

Mrs. Jakob disagreed. It could have been worse. R. Yidel could have shown up too late, God forbid.

In the local synagogues and study houses, the story sprouted horns. Among the variations that developed was the notion that Joel Jakob was a collaborator. That he was taken to the hospital on a stretcher didn't convince otherwise; there were ways of explaining this, too.

After the holidays, before the new term began, R. Moshele was called in to meet with the faculty of the yeshiva, including his own brother and father.

It grieved R. Moshele to be going to such a meeting. This much talk about a seventeen-year-old boy was not good. And since the meeting was called without R. Moshele's knowledge, he had an idea that it wouldn't benefit his son. Of course they all meant well, Joel was their flesh and blood and a good scholar, but they were thinking also of the yeshiva's reputation, of its influence on incoming students, and of parental concerns.

The result of the meeting, the verdict, was that Joel could no longer consider himself a student of the yeshiva.

He's old enough and good enough to study on his own, the Berditchever advised his son. Let him sit in the *beis medrish* with the young newly marrieds. A month ago, I would have advised postponing marriage. Now I think a quick match with a good girl from a fine Bratslaver family is the answer. Such an engagement will squelch talk of collaboration. It will also provide Joel with the freedom to pursue his interests. At this late stage, the wisest approach is to let him exhaust the subject.

Joel's uncle, R. Moshele's younger brother and the first lecturer at the yeshiva, told his brother privately that Joel had been losing focus, and this could be for the best. He's not a boy who will squander his mind. If he doesn't become a great Talmudic scholar, he will achieve greatness in another area.

Alone, in the administrative offices, R. Moshele shed tears. This was his only son, for whom he'd had such hopes. And there was nothing he could do. Disciplinary action was out of the question. And accusations of blame would do no one any good. R. Yidel hadn't sought Joel out; he'd merely responded to the boy's requests. Allowing his children too much autonomy in their pursuit of knowledge might have been a mistake, but even that was ridiculous. If Joel wanted a Bratslaver book, he would have found ways to get hold of it, with or without the bookstore.

Perhaps the Berditchever was right: an engagement might be the answer. Married, Joel wouldn't stand out in the *beis medrish*. He could pursue his scholarship alongside his other interests. If necessary, a daily session with the Berditchever could be scheduled. But these were all second choices, and R. Moshele wasn't consoled.

That night, father and son had the long-expected talk, which deviated a great deal from earlier expectations. There were no reprimands, for which Joel was grateful. He didn't need them. He knew himself as guilty, he'd violated the purity of the Bratslav study house in the most shameful manner; however, he also understood now that his sins were necessary descents for the purpose of ascent. It was clear to Joel that not only had Nachman endorsed this descent, he was acting as a sort of guide, though it was an unearthly guidance and one that directed him into the netherworld. For himself, for the personal consequences he would have to endure as a result, Joel had no regrets, but the violence in the *shtibel* and his strange involvement was a shock to everyone, most regrettably, his own father. In an effort to ease R. Moshele's pain, Joel pointed out the positive in the event: that his presence in the study house that day had brought R. Yidel back, thereby preventing the complete destruction of the place itself, the books, and most significantly the Torah scrolls. If they had burned, a mourning period would have been declared, and the entire community would have suffered.

R. Moshele was both pleased and disturbed to find Joel in such a serene state of mind. The boy accepted the fact of his dismissal with a nod and agreed to arrange an alternate schedule of study. He seemed even to welcome the change, which was good in its way. The father didn't want his son's spirit broken. In the best-case scenario, Joel would apply himself with renewed rigor to his Talmudic studies and continue to grow as a scholar. And perhaps marriage was the right thing. Adult or not, recent events were shaping the boy's future, and there wasn't a thing R. Moshele could do to prevent it, which indicated that as a father he was no longer indispensable.

As requested, Joel submitted to his father a proposed schedule of study. Early morning, before prayers, an hour of meditation. Then, until three-thirty in the afternoon, the Talmud. Following the afternoon service, two hours of miscellaneous readings, including history, science, philosophy, Kabbalah, and Chasidism. In the early evening, Joel proposed to join his father's study session. After evening services, an hour's review session with Aaron, which would help gauge his own progress against the yeshiva's curriculum.

R. Moshele studied the handwritten schedule and nodded, satisfied that it was ambitious enough. He folded the paper in four and placed it in his pocket. He wanted to review it again in private. He wanted to think about the three hours a day Joel had reserved for his strange interests. Meditation in the morning. Not the newest thing on earth. It was common knowledge that Nachman's disciples were expected to spend time alone, engaged in soul-searching and meditation, but that was the eighteenth century. Today's Bratslaver weren't carrying out these teachings to the letter. It took an earnest seventeen-year-old to interpret such esoterica literally and put them into practice. R. Moshele also wondered whether these brain exercises could have an adverse effect on an individual prone to seizures. He would consult the neurologist.

The new circumstances suited Joel; he was released from the strictness of a yeshiva schedule and now everything was suddenly possible.

From his readings, Joel knew that the periods in history that produced the true greats—Abulafia, Saadia Gaon, Moses ben Maimon— were those in which Jews encouraged scholarship in such subjects as music, philosophy, and mathematics. Cultural eclecticism in Sephardic education gave rise to the early Spanish Kabbalists. Joel's goal, brought into sharp focus for him by recent events, was to become more than a narrow-minded, limited scholar. He would open his mind to what was new, to strange experience, even sin. He would encourage it, exhaust it, follow it to the end, until it took him somewhere higher. This, he understood, was the way to greatness: to embrace what was most fearsome. Joel was quite certain now that this was Nachman's great teaching, written one way or another into every one of his tales, most often in the motif of the hero's journey as a personal quest, an exhilarating adventure rather than the traditional joyless exile.

Joel felt the sharp stab of broken ribs every time he breathed, and along with it gratitude. He was grateful to the Skvere hoodlums for this pain that had granted him a vision of his purpose. He would reach for a deeper understanding of the world, for a knowledge that was difficult, divine. He would study and imitate the ways of the Kabbalists, of the rabbis who recited the alphabetic permutations. He too would know divine ecstasy, of which he felt he'd had some inklings, the too quickly passing moments in the presence of the girl, for example. He was beginning to understand coded references, connections, meaning behind meaning. According to a Talmudic passage, Raba, a disciple of Rav, the last of the Tannaites, was able to create a man with his knowledge of the alphabet; in Aramaic, *Raba bara gabra,* a variation on *Abracadabra,* I create as I speak. Joel was convinced that Nachman, during his oral, spontaneous compositions, had also experienced such heights.

The broken ribs limited Joel's activities. In his writings on alphabetic meditation, the Spanish Kabbalist Abulafia prescribed deep breathing at certain intervals, between certain letters, but breathing was still too painful for Joel. He determined to use his convalescence for preparation.

In bed, propped up on pillows, Joel studied the various systems for permutations, wrote them out in his notebook in large format to facilitate reading from a distance. Seated with his legs folded and his back straight, according to Abulafia's instructions, he would have to see these letters from several feet away.

He read and reread the texts, the various breakdowns and uses of the letters and vowels. The turning and nodding of the head.

Twenty-two Foundation Letters:
   Three Mothers
   Seven Doubles
   and Twelve Elementals.
   The three Mothers are Alef, Mem, Shin,
   Their foundation is
     a pan of merit
     a pan of liability
     and the tongue of decree deciding between them.
   Three Mothers, Alef Mem Shin
     Mem hums, Shin hisses
     and Alef is the breath of air
     deciding between them.

According to one source, man and woman were made with only three letters, *alef, mem,* and *shin—A-M-Sh* for male and *A-Sh-M* for female. Joel thought he might attempt permuting the letters that make a female, and as he considered the possibility, the girl floated into his mind's eye and he found himself staring straight ahead, at the far wall of his room, seeing and not seeing the letters. He took a slow, shallow breath and concentrated on the *shin*, the foundation of woman, her lower body, and *shinned* carefully, combining the letter with the Tetragrammaton, YHVH, attaching them to the vowels. Joel added the movements of the head, and engraved the letters, as described in *Sefer Yetzirah*, on the wall straight ahead, maintaining the torso of a woman.

He didn't blink, or breathe, but moved on to the *mem*, afraid she would disappear if he stopped, afraid not to see what happened. To continue, to form the lower body, the legs, he would have to complete the *mem* combinations, then the *alef* would have to follow. And through all this it was necessary to keep the middle intact, which meant keeping the *shin* combinations somewhere behind his eyes while also engraving and permuting with the *mem*, maintaining all of it in his head, and then onward to the *alef*, the vowels, the head movements, and breaths. Joel felt his mind stretching to accommodate the permutations, to hold on to them simultaneously, and he understood why only a truly omnipotent God could keep the world and all of humankind extant.

Thinking this, he lost his place, and the girl disappeared.

He started again, engraved the *shin*, then the *mem*, filling his entire consciousness. He took a slow breath, and understood that the secrets of heaven and earth are to be discovered in slowness. He paused, concentrated on what was already in his head, afraid to begin with the *alef*, afraid to lose the *shin* and *mem*. His brain simply wasn't large enough. He prayed for a larger brain, and for patience. One flicker of doubt, of chaos, and all would disappear. He pronounced the first vowel with the *alef* long and drawn out, stretching it to keep the rings of *mem* and *shin* complete and spinning. Then he heard steps, and someone at the door. Joel broke off and Ada came in bearing the chessboard already laid out for a game.

After midnight, when the others were in bed, Joel tried again. This time he began with the *alef*. *AoYo AoYa AoYe AoYi AoYu*, then five breaths, *AaYo AaYa AaYe AaYi AaYu*, five more breaths, *AeYo AeYa AeYe AeYi AeYu*, five breaths, and onward to the next vowel and letter, the next set of breaths, and again. He made room for the letters to expand in his head, to fill it. He permuted, weighed, and transformed with them, the ring turned and twisted, danced, and there was the head of the girl with the long silken hair, the strands wrapped around her neck. But this was grotesque. She needed a torso, a chest, and stomach to hold up the head. Joel moved on to the *mem*, her middle, carefully and patiently, beginning with the first vowel and letter, *MoYo MoYa MoYe MoYi MoYu*. He paused, inhaled, paused again, and *MaYo MaYa MaYe MaYi MaYu*, and on, careful to keep the ring of *alef* still engraved.

He imagined the outlines of a body, he carved it in the air, and there she writhed, a body without hips and legs. The girl floated and Joel was afraid to blink. He kept his eyes fixed on the writhing shape flickering in the air, a shadow on the wall, there and not there, solely dependent for her life on his concentration, on his maintaining the rings of letters and gates moving them, shifting, dancing. He took the twenty-five pre-scribed slow breaths, one at a time, counted, and prepared for the hissing *shin*. He was aware of a discomfort in his own foundation, but he didn't move or shift his weight for fear of losing the girl, her body incomplete. He entered *shin* hissing. *ShoYo ShoYa ShoYe* . . . five breaths *ShaYo ShaYa ShaYe ShaYi ShaYu*, five slow breaths. He felt his head expand again to hold this third ring, while keeping the other two engraved and dancing. *SheYo SheYa SheYe SheYi SheYu* and five more breaths, and then the fabric of his pajamas stretched tight and thin, and before he could take the next breath she was gone, the writhing shadow-shape along with the rings like tapestries on the wall. Only a scalding wetness remained, and Joel knew what Nachman meant—what it was to scream a scream so great it travels from one end of the earth to the other and no sound emerges.

It was four A.M. There was time to start again, but not here, not now. He would have to find a site for this work, a place at a distance from disruptive life.

He closed his eyes and mentally walked himself around the neighborhood, searching for a location appropriate for meditation, and came upon the culvert behind Ida Road. Installed in 1954 on the recommendation of civic engineers as part of Rockland County's extensive interconnected underground drainage system, it participated every spring in a minor reenactment of the Ice Age's great thaw, when snowmelt comes rushing down the hills and mountains of the Hudson Valley. But this was late September; the ground was dry. As children, he and Ada had used this culvert as a hideout and called it a cave. It would serve a similar purpose now, satisfying his need for privacy. On a rainy day, Joel mused, the sound of running water would be an added bonus: the Kabbalists were said to have stood in running water during their ablutions. Most appealingly, this man-made drainpipe would provide a meditative site as close to the atmosphere of the caves of Safed as anyone living in Rockland County could hope for.

The idea of conducting these exercises in an environment close to the real thing pleased Joel, though he realized that the Middle Eastern climate in which the ancient Kabbalists had lived was more suited for outdoor activities than the intemperance of North America. He would have to equip his cave with provisions against inclement weather. The pillows of the old green Naugahyde sofa could withstand the moisture, he thought. Several old mikvah towels would be useful; an old wool blanket, too. And he told himself that he had to be prepared to suffer; he wouldn't allow a bit of wet and cold to deter him.

A week later, impatient to try the permutations he'd copied out of Abulafia's meditative guide, Joel poked his ribs, declared himself able and sound, and announced that he'd be out of the house the next day.

Indeed, after so much time indoors, he was impatient for the day to begin and remained in bed only as long as it was moon dark. As soon as he could identify the alphabet on the walls in his room, he dressed hurriedly, walked in his socks to the front door, sat on the stoop outside to tie his shoelaces, and inhaled the moist morning, thrilling to the wonder of being the only conscious member of the household, of the street, of this town, his small world. He walked around the house to retrieve the Naugahyde pillows from the back porch. On the street, swinging them, one in each hand, he felt himself a newly sprung Adam, experiencing the freshness of the first dawn, with the still of night still in it.

He ducked to enter the drain and welcomed the smell of wet clay, a familiar clamminess, cousin to the dank of the mikvah, distant relative to the freshness of first raindrops, that mix of earth and water, the elements of life. He stood, shoulders hunched, in the center of the drainpipe. Even at this highest point of the curve, he couldn't stand upright. This would be a place of crawling and sitting. He set the pillows one on top of the other on a high, dry spot, bent his body, and folded his clumsy legs with some pain. Somewhere in his head, gray cells protested this position, alien to his bones. Joel's knees had resisted hard stretching and bending ever since he could remember. He'd learned not to attempt such things, when at the age of eight, he'd tried to perform a handstand, fractured a bone, and had to wear a splint for weeks. When Mrs. Jakob told the doctor how it had happened—that Joel had wanted to impress tiny double-jointed Lucy Lee, a natural gymnast whose family was the last of the non-Jewish ones to sell their house when the Chasidim moved into the area—Levine advised Joel to leave such mischief to the *goyim*. The only Yid ever known for physical agility, Levine told Joel, was a famous magician named Houdini, and even he died performing one of his stunts.

You, my boy, Levine said, as if he were pronouncing something of grave significance, are built like a skinny lummox—the word *lummox* comes, I believe, from the biblical Lemech, the blind giant who clapped his hands together and smashed his grandson's head. My dictionary, however, lists the origin of the word as unknown, then dates it circa 1820.

Levine ended by clapping a heavy hand on Joel's flimsy shoulder. The boy's surprised knees buckled, and the nurse had to lend Joel her arm to help him regain his balance.

The unconcentrated mind has the ability to track two or more events simultaneously, but the word is a linear thing. Sitting in the drainpipe with his legs crossed, Joel attended to his physical discomforts; he remembered the old pain of his fractured wrist, felt his newly healed ribs. He welcomed this kinship with the student initiates at Safed who sat on hard rocks and stood in cold running water.

Joel also opened his notebook to the page of alphabetic arrays and, with his mind still on his aches and pains, intoned his first set of permuted letters. He arrived at the second array, started it and stopped, disturbed by the strange sound of his voice tunneling into the pipe and echoing back to his ears. Since water is a carrier of sound, he realized, anyone who happened to be walking past any of the hundred culverts in town would hear him quite clearly. Even without the water, the shape of the water pipes themselves was working like the cardboard paper towel tubes of the game of telephone. And since these pipes, these fat fingers, crept into every neighborhood of Monsey, they had the unusual advantage of multiple channels, a publicist's dream. In no time—faster even than the human grapevine, whose efficacy had been boosted by the invention of the telephone, enhanced by its cordless and wireless variations—in no time at all, word would be out: *Abracadabra*, Joel Jakob is making a man.

Knowing that sound waves travel initially in the direction they're sent, then bounce off hard surfaces, Joel turned to face the exit of the pipe rather than into its depths. And if he kept his voice down to a low rumble and slowed the pronunciations, he calculated, the sound emerging at any given entrance or exit would be virtually unintelligible.

He adjusted his pillows, inhaled, and began again.

AuYu AaYa AiYi AeYe AoYo
AuHu AbHa AiHi AeHe AoHo
AuVu AaVa AiVi AeVe AoVo
AuHu AaHa AiHi AeHe AoHo

He paused for five slow breaths as prescribed and went on to the second letter.

BuYu BaYa BiYi BeYe BoYo
BuHu BaHa BiHi BeHe BoHo
BuVu BaVa BiVi BeVe BoVo
BuHu BaHa BiHi BeHe BoHo

He paused to breathe again, unfolded one leg, then the other. This was a strange, uncomfortable exercise in strange surroundings and his mind refused to remain focused. It would take getting used to. When the act of reciting became familiar and habitual, when he could forget all outer distractions, only then could he expect results. The dew on the grass had seeped into his shoes, and Joel's toes were stiff. He made a mental note to bring an extra pair of socks. Then he reminded himself that discomfort is an aspect of the ascetic life, and he would have to learn to befriend and welcome it. He tried again. But his mind, distracted as it was by physical discomfort, demanded alternative positions and he kept shifting his weight, his legs. In one Talmudic passage, Joel recalled, disciples were described as having walked in circles while reciting. When they found themselves stuck waist-deep in the earth, their master suggested reversing the order of the alphabetic permutations and walking backward. Joel thought he might do better walking or pacing, but in this pipe, walking in circles or even in straight lines was out of the question. He felt unusually agitated, impatient to move, an impulse that was strange, unlike him. Disciplined for so many years to spend most of his day swaying over books, he was a prime candidate for concentrated meditation. What then was the problem? He tried to still his mind. He closed his eyes, inhaled slowly, keeping his breath shallow, above his healing ribs, and recited the array of the third letter. Then he stood, leaned the pillows up against the curve of the pipe, and left quickly.

It wasn't until after the morning service, when he was seated on the narrow, un-ergonomic bench of Jewish study houses everywhere, that Joel realized that in all his years of bench pressing, he'd never truly sat still. He noted the continuous sway of his torso, forward-back, with the occasional switch to left-right, and the constant movement of his hands, his right thumb arcing into the Aramaic *Ade-raba*, on-the-contrary, the therefores, and the from-this-we-learn. A recent study by the University of Chicago found that adults and children presented with a series of math problems and memory tests remembered twenty percent more of the material when they were allowed to gesture with their hands rather than keeping them still on the table. The results of this study, according to the journal *Psychological Science*, suggest that the brain has to do less cognitive work when the hands are in motion. According to R. Nathan, Nachman created his oral fictions with the movements of his hands. Early disciples claimed that only in their live telling was the full power of the tales revealed. Joel determined to veer from Abulafia's recommendations and allow natural body movement into his meditative posture.

Rather than lose his study partner, Aaron informed Joel that he too would leave the yeshiva and they would continue studying together as always, with only a change of setting.

Joel shook his head. He wouldn't hear of it. He didn't want Aaron's future on his conscience, for one thing. More significantly, a study partner would restrict his freedom. They were walking on Maple Avenue, the last stretch of their twice-a-day walk to prayers at the study house.

Right now, Joel pointed out, it's not even in your best interest to be known as a friend of mine.

Aaron responded quietly and firmly. In such things as friendship, public opinion plays no role.

Your father won't allow you to do it, Joel argued. Have you talked to anyone at the yeshiva, my father, for example?

Your father is the last person to talk to right now, Aaron said. He'd say so himself. Unless there's some reason you want to study alone, I don't understand or accept your objections.

Joel finally admitted that he was overjoyed with his newfound freedom, that he wanted to remain unbound by a schedule that would require his appearance in a particular place at a designated time. Of course, I will abide by a personal-study schedule, Joel explained, which includes our regular evening session, which I hope you'll agree to continue. But during the day, I want the liberty to deviate without notice.

Aaron was troubled about his friend's health, his strange preoccupations, the recent violence that had resulted in his dismissal from the yeshiva, but they'd been friends long enough that having his offer turned down wasn't a personal rejection. Indeed, as schoolboys, their bond was compared to the celebrated friendship of David and Jonathan. But Joel's recent secrecy was unprecedented. In all their walks together, back and forth from prayer and study, he hadn't said a word about an impending trip to Uman. Not that Joel was obliged to tell. The two friends generally avoided unnecessary obligations. They were adults. Their lives were already so programmed, they didn't need added commitments. Going and coming to and from prayer and study, they didn't wait for each other. They relied on the similarity of their schedules to bring them together. Indeed, they both smiled over an absurd episode in their early friendship in the fourth grade, when rather than part for the evening at the corner of Suzanne and Frances, where, to proceed homeward, Joel was required to turn left onto Frances Place, Aaron to continue straight along Suzanne Drive, they had continued walking each other, back and forth and back and forth, until it was past their bedtime and their fathers were sent to look for them. In all these years of walking, they'd developed habits of talking. Now Joel seemed to be losing the habit, he was drawing inward. Of course, these were extenuating circumstances. He'd been ill, he'd traveled, broken his ribs, which made breathing and talking difficult. Still it was odd, too different from what they'd shared for twelve years. Until recently they'd been able to cover every topic under the sun more than once, and still there had always been more to say.

Of the conversations they'd had before Joel's illness, some examples:

The old pedagogic controversy, Chasidic versus *Litvak* styles of education, breadth versus depth, superficial skimming versus in-depth analysis, was in the news again and Aaron took the Chasidic side. Logically, he argued, before delving into a particular passage, a child—any scholar, really—should have some breadth, the overall picture. Without an awareness of the whole, the study of the particular is flawed.

Joel took the other side, not because he supported *Litvak* ways, but in every argument, in all fairness, both sides needed an advocate. He pointed out that brooding over one paragraph at a young age was a way of habituating the mind to profundity.

Aaron, who thought it might be nice once in a while if they didn't have to act out this charade of fairness, sighed and stated in the quiet authoritative way he had of making such pronouncements that everything we know these days about the development of the child's brain points to the obvious fact: at the age of eight, nine, even twelve, a child's mind isn't advanced or patient enough to remain on one paragraph for a whole month. To force the issue is an act of brutality. Not that mankind hasn't proven itself capable of such acts, he added.

Early September, when families returned from their Catskill summers, a joke about the Lubavitch sign on Route 17 circulated among Satmar Chasidim: The frequency of the traffic jams this year were due to motorists who read Moshiach Is Coming and stopped to wait.

Aaron said that if the Messiah had indeed arrived in Brooklyn in August, he would have found no Jews. The yeshivas are empty. Every Chasid is sitting under the cool pines of Pine Hill, New York, or bathing in the loch of Loch Sheldrake in Sullivan County.

Joel had this to add: Rumor has it that in the mausoleums of the old rebbes there are now fax machines that receive requests for prayers all day and night. Indeed the machines run out of paper so frequently, a gravekeeper suggested raising funds for machines with memory. His argument, a persuasive one, I think, is that the absence of a physical hard copy is in keeping with the metaphysical quality of the dead rebbe's spirit hovering in the ether.

Another recent conversation:

When Joel mentioned a recent outrageous performance by the local wedding *badkhn*, Yankel Yankevitch, Aaron came to Yankel's defense: There are so many weddings these days, the man often works two a night. I don't know how he does it. He must be desperate. Besides, it's the job of a *badkhn* to outrage his audience, to expose euphemisms and lies, destroy illusion, and still play the fool. The best of them, that is, the most original ones, suffer consequences. I read that Hershele Ostropolier, the court *badkhn* of Medzhibozh, where Nachman was born and raised, was always in trouble. In one story, he insulted the wealthiest man in town, a Solomon Rapoport—of course a wealthy man would be named Rapoport, Joel said before allowing Aaron to continue. This man, Aaron continued, financed the entire yeshiva and town synagogue single-handedly. To appease the mogul, the local rebbe placed a monthlong ban on hiring Hershele. The problem: The youngest Rapoport girl was getting married that month, and all the women, including the bride, were in tears over the ban. Solomon loved his daughter too much and couldn't bear the sight of her tears. The day before the wedding, he called a private meeting, attended by the rebbe, Hershele, and, of course, Solomon himself, at which Hershele agreed to arrive in town disguised as Laybele Furth, the renowned wedding jester from Vienna. He was to cleverly reveal his disguise to townspeople, generally let it be known that he was not Laybele Furth, and that the disguise was only intended for the father of the bride, Solomon Rapoport. This way the bride and her friends would know that Hershele Ostropolier had performed at her wedding, while the proud Solomon could continue to pretend that he had hired Laybele Furth.

According to the agreement, for this act Hershele was paid ten times his usual fee, a number that the rascal claimed barely compensated for personal financial damage, since the ban had prevented him from earning a living. Of course, it was known to all the parties involved that Hershele had been performing every evening under various disguises and aliases. After the meeting, the rebbe, who was no dupe, pulled Hershele aside and warned him that next time he wouldn't get off so easily.

If you think about it, Joel said, the very fact that Ostropolier survived as a *badkhn* indicates that he always worked within the tradition of the *badkhn*, delivering his common doggerel rhyme, which means he wasn't all that original. Perhaps a comedian can never be very original.

.   .   .

On the subject of Spinoza's monism, his apostasy, Joel said, Never mind the man's denial of God, which wasn't a pure denial, since he identified nature as God. Spinoza's overarching idea that humans are capable of overcoming their emotional and psychological vulnerability to the environment through understanding is worthwhile. Knowledge rewards. It is with the knowing mind that one can control the desirous body. Human salvation depends on knowledge, since if man knows and accepts that nature, therefore existence, is necessarily flawed, he can't be caught off guard. He has the ability to confront every ill that befalls him with a certain equanimity. Equanimity is salvation, blessedness, the Christian grace.

You place too much trust in knowledge, Aaron said. Hitler loved science; encouraged research in technology, medicine, and biology; even couched his sins in scientific language: the great experiment, the final solution.

Bypassing Aaron's point entirely, Joel went on: A simple example of how Spinoza's ideas can help mankind, he said. Mrs. X sees that Mrs. Y and Mrs. Z have large, beautiful homes. She asks herself why she doesn't have such a home, and the question seethes within her all day. That evening she tells her husband that she too wants—no, needs—a grander home. Now if the homes of Mrs. Y and Mrs. Z were as small or smaller than that of Mrs. X, she would have remained satisfied with her own. And if she had understood that the root of her desire was entirely external, that she was merely at the whim of an unnecessary wind, that there was no reason to care what Mrs. Y and Mrs. Z live in, then she could have controlled and overcome her dissatisfaction.

That's beautifully theoretical, but it's not how the human mind operates, Aaron replied. A question comes up: Does Mrs. X covet merely what Mrs. Y and Mrs. Z have, or does she want more than what they have? I would argue that if Mrs. X is someone who knows the uselessness of material objects in this world, then she would maintain her inner peace without Spinoza. If, however, Mrs. X is a person who places emphasis on the material, Spinoza's advice might give her at the most a moment's rest, and then the seething would resume. Her mind would find ways to rationalize her helplessness in the face of every whim. She might even concede that she's weak when it comes to such things. Remaining in the end, though, would be her desire, which has all along only been gathering momentum.

÷

It didn't take more than a day in the study house for the fact of Joel's dismissal to become widely known, and not a full week for Yankel Yankevitch, who dabbled in matchmaking—as he said, *shadkhones* (matchmaking) is good for *badkhones* (merrymaking)—to devise a way to benefit from the disaster. Desperate for a financial windfall that would alleviate accumulated domestic expenses, he put a call in to R. Moshele and proposed Aaron as a son-in-law.

R. Moshele, for whom the idea of Aaron as a son-in-law was not new, was prepared with a response: My daughter is the second-born, therefore Joel must go first. As you know, my wife and I have only these two precious children, therefore we are in no hurry to marry them off. Of course, if the girl is extremely fine, and the boy's family is ready and willing, in other words, if the fit is perfect all around, we wouldn't stand in the way of a double engagement.

The lucrative potential of a double engagement wasn't lost on Yankel, and he set to work in earnest. First he discussed the situation with his wife, who knew the Chasidic female population and was good at matching a girl to the boy at hand.

Joel, Yankel explained, has a complicated reputation. On the one hand, a penetrating scholar with a unique cast of mind. But as every father knows, such a mind comes with some danger of derailing. Joel's recent foray into Bratslav, his voyage to Uman, which may or may not have been taken with his father's blessing, and his presence at the New Square fire were providing plenty of fodder for gossip at the mikvah. And if the men were talking, Yankel concluded, the women were almost certainly crowding the phone lines.

Mrs. Yankevitch nodded. She'd heard some things, also rumors of a recent illness.

Yankel rubbed his head. It's a difficult one, he said, because despite all the negative talk, suggesting anyone less than worthy of the family would insult R. Moshele and compromise the fruition of either match.

The Yankevitches spent the next day thinking long and hard. There were so many girls of appropriate age, his wife knew many of them, but which one would be right for Joel? Before Yankel could approach R. Moshele, he would have to talk to the father of the girl, to be sure that there was interest on the other side. Having R. Moshele turned down by another family wouldn't do. These rabbinic cases had to be handled with kid gloves. In the afternoon Yankel found himself in the town of New Square, near the Bratslav *shtibel*, and on a sudden impulse stopped in for the afternoon service.

Inside, Yankel noted that Mendel Moshkovitz was present. Word on the street was that the man had a houseful of women, not one son. As was known to happen in such cases, the first son-in-law became the long-hoped-for son. R. Mendel was a renowned scholar, well respected in scholarly communities. Yankel wondered whether any of R. Mendel's daughters were of age and would R. Moshele consider a Bratslav family for Joel. A year ago, perhaps not, Yankel reasoned, but now, after all the recent events, such a match was more likely. An important question remained: What did the Bratslaver think of Joel, and his role in the fire? They couldn't possibly think the boy guilty. What would be his motive? Skvere Chasidim, on the other hand, were reputed for their lasting grudge against Bratslav, and for good reason. Everyone knew of Nachman's persecution of the Shpoler Zeide, the Skverer grandfather, whose folksy style of leadership was held in contempt in the elite Bratslav court. In 1800, when Nachman was only twenty-eight years old, he moved to Zlotopolye, a small town within the Shpola's territory, thus issuing a challenge to the old man's authority and making an enemy for life. But Joel was entirely unrelated to Skver or the Shpola. He was closer, if anything, to Nachman because on his grandmother's side there were indeed some Bratslaver.

Ambitious matchmakers don't allow themselves the luxury of tact, and even for a member of his species, Yankel was known as aggressive. When he needed information, he asked for it. Before the service started, he turned to the man nearest him at the table and asked, What's the word here on R. Moshele's son?

The man shrugged. A fine scholar whose misfortune it was to find himself here, normally as safe a place as any, at the wrong time. I'd seen him earlier that evening, reading studiously.

In the *shtibel*, Yankel discerned the faint smell of fire, but no other signs of the violence. As always, the shelves were crowded with Bratslaver *seforim*. Word on the street was that the Skvere rebbe had sent funds for the purchase of the new books, and that the sum was large enough to cover several months' rent on the *shtibel* itself, which was a miracle, since no one ever knew from where the necessary monies for rent and upkeep would come. The local Bratslaver were all men with families to support.

After the service, Yankel went up to greet R. Mendel. They shook hands.

What brings you here? R. Mendel asked.

Yankel drew him aside to avoid being overheard. I want to propose a match. R. Moshele's son for your first daughter. To you, I don't have to sing the boy's praises. You're well aware of them.

Mendel Moshkovitz nodded slightly and stroked his beard. Does R. Moshele know of the proposal? Would he consider a girl from a Bratslav family?

You're the first to hear of this. If you're interested, I'll take it further.

But since on that side the subject of Bratslav is a touchy one, I wanted to clear it with you beforehand. Do you have any objections?

R. Mendel shook his head. Of course I'll have to mention it at home, but at the outset, from my perspective, I'd say the match is of great interest.

The men shook hands and Yankel hurried home excitedly. This was just the thing for R. Moshele, the finest family, though a Bratslav one. It seemed so sure a thing that Yankel found himself already spinning the wedding rhymes. They would be brilliant, he thought; there was enough material here to go on for hours. But when things seemed too certain they more often than not fell through, and Yankel, who had some experience in these matters, forced himself to slow down and consider the possible obstacles carefully. It wasn't until he told his wife about his conversation with Mendel Moshkovitz that he learned of a definite one.

R. Mendel's daughters are good-looking girls, she said, one of them is even a good friend of Ada's, but they're all quite chubby, which is bound to put off Mrs. Jakob. And who could blame her? Think of the contrast, for one thing. Joel is a beanpole.

Chubby? Yankel said. How fat are they? Beyond acceptable standards?

He felt a pressure in his head. He had enough to think about without the problem of weight, which he decided with some resentment was an American disease possible only in this land of plenty. In the old shtetl world, he was quite certain, where Jews lived in poverty, matchmakers hadn't encountered such difficulties.

Perhaps a diet, Yankel's wife said. After a week or two of fasting, she'll look better. Of course, she'll never be thin. A person with the body and appetite of a fat person remains fat. A fat child becomes a fat adult. But perhaps until the wedding, as a bride, at least, something could be managed.

Dieting is women's talk, Yankel said, annoyed with this unexpected factor.

His wife smiled and let her eyes drop to her husband's belly, which reminded him that even he, a man, would benefit from such women's talk.

I know, I know, he said. He pulled his stomach in and adjusted the waistband of his pants. Although he had always been tall and wiry, he had developed a skinny man's paunch, as his wife had noted.

You know very well, he protested, that I can't suggest to a father that his daughter be put on a diet.

Maybe there's someone close to the girl who can say it, in the kindest way, his wife said. I'll look into it. But you'll have to give the girl a chance to drop five to ten pounds.

Joel sat at the foot of his bed in the evening and copied into his notebook variations on the arrays of letter combinations. He started with the twenty-two letters on the first line. On the second line, he wrote every other letter, on the third line, every third letter, and so on, until the end. There were twenty-one lines and twenty-two columns, which he paired off to form eleven columns that produced the 231 letter combinations. In bed, on his back, he pictured, in the style of the Kabbalist Isaac of Acco, a circle on the ceiling above his head, the twenty-two letters in a ring, and the 231 connecting lines between the letters, known as the gates of wisdom. They formed a spirographic shape, a round tapestry spread above his head, and Joel followed the instructions, to "engrave them like a garden, carve them like a wall, deck them like a ceiling." He started with the *alef*, followed its lines to the twenty-one others, then moved on to the *beis*, and so on. It wasn't long before his thighs opened. This time he didn't struggle against the change in his foundation, he welcomed it, fell silent, and allowed the letters or the girl or whatever it was that brought him to this state to have its way with him. It was good, it was holy. He fell asleep soiled and content, with the outer rim of the ring, the gates between the *kuf*, *resh*, *shin*, and *taf* incomplete.

In the morning, sitting cross-legged on an old cushion in the drain-pipe, he looked straight ahead into the round opening of the pipe and formed the tapestry there, carving each letter in air so it stood vertically, and then the lines between them as paths.

After two weeks of practice, Joel found that he could keep the tapestry in his mind's eye and follow the paths between the letters, all without notes on paper. He congratulated himself on his progress. Two months earlier, he hadn't been able to recite the alphabet backward. Now, on good days, he was able to retain the shimmering ring of letters in front of him as he walked back and forth from the study house to home and from home to the study house, which added an extra hour a day of meditation. One morning on his way to morning service, he found himself in the middle of Suzanne Drive, made aware of his endangerment by a furious blaring horn. After this he avoided the main roads—indeed, he went out of his way to walk through backyards and extended properties, grateful that on Jewish properties dogs were rare. When he arrived at the study house without having completed the combinations, he circled the building and continued meditating until he came to the final letter, followed it down its twenty-two paths, and arrived late to service.

Several people noticed Joel's strange circling and wondered. R. Moshele, who was keeping an eye on his son, noted that Joel was frequently late, that he prayed without a minyan. He didn't say anything. He knew the lateness wasn't due to oversleeping, it wasn't mere sloth, the boy was out of the house before he himself was awake. Still Joel's strange pursuits were occupying a good deal of his time, taking up too large a share of too good a mind. But even in a world in which sons generally obey their fathers, in this instance there was nothing R. Moshele could do. Joel had a single-mindedness that would pursue this terrible project to the end, and R. Moshele could only hope that this end was near. In an attempt to understand what was engaging his son, he looked into Nachman's *Common Book,* read the recommendations and arguments for a daily hour of solitude, and told himself that at Joel's age, he too might have found all this fascinating.

Three weeks later, when Yankel approached R. Moshele with the name of R. Mendel's daughter, the anxious father was more receptive to the idea of Bratslaver in-laws than he might otherwise have been. He promised to give it some thought, which Yankel understood to mean that he would discuss it with his wife. Yankel didn't mention the girl's weight; therefore, when R. Moshele told Mrs. Jakob about the proposed match, he was surprised by her angry response.

He walked away deep in thought. There were worse things in the world than excess weight, and it wasn't like his wife to protest so vehemently. He wondered about the quickness of her response, she hadn't taken a moment to think about it. After all, R. Mendel was a reputable scholar, an admirable man all around, and from every angle with the exception perhaps of the girl's weight, an excellent solution to the problem of Joel's reputation. Besides, R. Mendel could serve as a mentor to Joel in his strange pursuits, which was probably the best argument for the match.

R. Moshele decided not to say anything, at least not yet. A week later, when his wife said she'd been informed that the girl had lost weight and looked better than ever, he felt rewarded for his silence. Mrs. Jakob also reported that Ada knew the younger sister of the girl well and liked her. She said that the sisters are known for their excellent sense of humor and sharp minds. Ada even claims, Mrs. Jakob went on, that Joel has already promised to marry the eldest, for the very reason that she's fat, and that I was a witness to this promise, which I may well have been, but you know how our children talk, everything's a joke. Such promises cannot be taken seriously.

R. Moshele smiled. This son and daughter of theirs were an odd pair, and very attached to each other. You'd think they were twins, he said to his wife. He wondered aloud whether it would be best to bring the two of them to the table for a discussion, let them decide between themselves whether the proposed matches were of interest.

The world changes quickly, Mrs. Jakob said. When I was seventeen, I turned red in the face at the mention of a match. Even now, admitting this, my face feels warm.

R. Moshele caressed his wife's cheek, which still surprised him with its smoothness. She was forty-six years old. She would be a young and pretty mother of the bride and groom and, God willing, a young grandmother. Not that R. Moshele was much older. He was forty-eight, though he felt every moment of his age, now more than ever. Even as a child, he'd felt emotionally old. After raising his own children, and assisting in the education of young men, he understood that his premature adulthood had had everything to do with his own father's immaturity, the Berditchever's irresponsibility. Knowing what his household's response to a goat would be, his father had come home with a goat anyway because as a child in Romania he had milked goats. And because Gypsies had camped somewhere on the farm, he responded to Gypsy music. In the street, in a park, or at some civic event, where the presence of a scholar and man of his stature was noticed, he would stop, listen, even tap his foot. More strange, the pleasure on his face, the joy Moshele perceived in the Berditchever's face when he stood watching the hula dancers at Great Adventure, where they had taken the children one summer, was beyond explanation. For a scholar and head of a yeshiva, the man had odd and primitive tastes.

At the dining room table, used for Sabbath meals and other special occasions, both Joel and Ada were eager to talk about each other's potential match: Joel said that Ada had belonged to Aaron since age three, when in play they'd performed a wedding; Ada countered that Joel had promised to marry the fattest girl in Monsey, but now that the girl was losing weight, she might not qualify. They joked about each other, but when asked for a serious opinion on their own behalf, declined marriage altogether.

Joel said he couldn't possibly consider it right now, that he was too involved in research and study and didn't want distractions. Ada pointed out that she had a business to tend, and the busy season was approaching. Besides, she argued, if Joel postpones marriage, she certainly would, since she wouldn't marry before her older brother.

R. Moshele and his wife looked at each other. They'd raised a couple of independent thinkers. But they were parents and had to look out for their children. R. Moshele shook his head. How much time do you need? he asked his son. Two weeks? A month? Because indefinite postponement isn't an option. It isn't fair to your sister or to the families who are waiting for a response.

If I concentrate exclusively on this project, if I spend twenty-four hours a day with it, then perhaps a month will be enough.

R. Moshele hesitated. What Joel was proposing was what no father would want for his son: a whole month away from Talmudic scholarship. However, if four weeks of concentration could cure Joel of his obsession, perhaps it would be worthwhile.

When Joel walked away from the scene at the table, he wasn't entirely certain what exactly his father had sanctioned, but suddenly he had at least four weeks in which he would be expected nowhere at any particular time, unheard of for a yeshiva boy. This, he told himself, might be as close as he would ever come to experiencing the freedom of the Kabbalists of Safed, who renounced all worldly possessions, left their families behind, and traveled far to live in the hills and caves. This was a golden opportunity, and it behooved him to do everything in his power to use it fully and well. He would spend every waking hour in the drainpipe, practically live there. If in these weeks he failed to achieve a level of ecstatic concentration it would prove once and for all that he simply didn't have the capacity for it.

In his head, Joel calculated that to complete in one sitting the recitation of a full round of alphabetic permutations required thirty-five hours of continuous meditation, or one and a half days of sitting cross-legged in the pipe. And that was without interruption, with no pause even during ecstatic moments and no indulgent recess after. He'd have to experience the ecstasy on the move, without stopping, which would mean maintaining it, extending it to longer minutes, perhaps hours, days. Thinking this, he felt his body rise to it, desire it. But though he'd made good progress, he wasn't yet capable of meditating for eight continuous hours, let alone thirty-five. During the first days, half an hour had been too much. Now he was able to remain in position for two and a half hours. On a good morning, he'd gone for three. It's a muscle, he told himself, and like any other muscle, it requires training. Since this was a difficult goal, the only chance for success was strict strategy.

Mathematically, Joel figured, if he increased the length of time of every session by an hour a day, he would get to the twenty-four-hour mark by the end of a month. The problem: There would have to be days in which he would sleep only an hour, and then finally not at all. But this was too methodical, too plodding. It didn't allow for magical leaps and bounds. He knew that even marathoners don't train that way. He had to figure that after a given number of hours of meditation, the body could keep going forever. It was said that after twenty-four hours of fasting, the sensation of hunger was no longer experienced. After a certain point, he would have to rely on advancing by way of the other-worldly.

Practice means repetition. Therefore multiply the following scene, allowing for slight variations, to understand what took place during the following two weeks. Joel spent entire mornings in the drainpipe, five to six continuous hours. There were days of frustration; there was also progress. He learned to subdue his physical needs. He allowed the unused parts of his body to go to sleep, and welcomed the deadening of these limbs, the peculiar pin-pricking. Asleep, they didn't interrupt, didn't demand unbending, stretching. When he did finally let go, he allowed himself to rise and stand, stomp his feet and rub his hands to restore circulation.

He was fortunate weather-wise. Although the days dawned crisp, with the feel of fall in the air, by late morning, when the sun moved high in the sky, golden light bathed the fertile grass at the entrance of the pipe. Now and then Joel stepped outside to feel the sun on his face, while attempting to keep the tapestry of letters extant. The more he practiced, the better he became at keeping the ring in place, still turning and shifting, even through a pause to eat from the box of whole-wheat crackers he brought with him. First thing in the morning, he folded a dry towel over the damp Naugahyde pillow, sat, and breathed deeply to quiet his mind. Without serenity, concentration was impossible. He closed his eyes and formed the spirographic circle on the wall of the drainpipe or on the ground in front of him and carved the connecting lines. He inhaled and found a voice to work with, low enough to avoid strain, the hum of the letter *mem*. He *memmed*, mmmmmmm, like the Sanskrit *om*, and felt his heart and mind slow. He started with the first letter, *alef with them all and all of them with alef*, using each of the five primary vowels in combination with the four letters of the tetragrammaton, the *yud, heh, vav, heh* (YHVH) that make up the name of God.

He took a single breath as directed and recited.

AuYu AaYa AiYi AeYe AoYo
AuHu AbHa AiHi AeHe AoHo
AuVu AaVa AiVi AeVe AoVo
AuHu AaHa AiHi AeHe AoHo

He started again, this time in combination with the head movement recommended for each vowel, beginning with his head in straight-ahead position, lifting upward for the *cholam* (˙), moving from right to left for the *kametz* (ַ), left to right for the *tzereh* (..), lowering the head down for the *chirik* (.), and forward for the *shirik* (...). He worked slowly, backed up for corrections, and repeated from the top. He was determined to be patient. He prayed for patience, without which nothing can be achieved.

He took five slow breaths and proceeded to the second letter, *beis.*

BuYu BaYa BiYi BeYe BoYo
BuHu BaHa BiHi BeHe BoHo
BuVu BaVa BiVi BeVe BoVo
BuHu BaHa BiHi BeHe BoHo

Five more breaths, and on to the third letter, *gimmel.*

GuYu GaYa GiYi GeYe GoYo
GuHu GaHa GiHi GeHe GoHo
GuVu GaVa GiVi GeVe GoVo
GuHu GaHa GiHi GeHe GoHo

And on to the fourth, fifth, sixth, seventh . . . all the way to the twenty-second letter. From there he went on to the harder task of articulating all twenty-two letters with one another, keeping the image of the ring shifting and moving, dancing in the air, on the clay wall, sometimes on the ground in front of him.

He moved from the *mem,* mmmmm, to the *samach,* ssss, from the *ayin* to the *peh,* and on to the hissing *shin* and final *taf.*

Variations on the Above

After a long morning of imperfect concentration, he was too hungry to continue and stepped outside to eat. He sat on a stump in the sun, chewed slowly, and noted the attention with which his body received the food. Hunger had the ability to obliterate from the mind everything but this basic need for sustenance, an example of the body's mastery over mind. Achieving the reverse, mastery of mind over body, was the great challenge. Of course the body has the advantage of hundreds of involuntary muscles conditioned to ensure its survival. If Spinoza was right and the mind, as *sub specie eternitatis*, is immortal, then it may be the only organism in the world that ought to exist without the anxiety of self-preservation. To make such immortality worthwhile, however, is not easy. Even the trained and disciplined mind, Joel discovered, is an unruly thing.

The difficulty? The alphabetic exercises were completely abstract, the permutations and combinations meaningless. But the stillness of mind that such concentration on the abstract produced was powerful. Joel was a person whose mind was habitually in high-speed motion. Aaron had once dubbed it a constant rush from the *Rahn* and run to the *Rosh*, two Talmudic commentaries. When Joel was a schoolboy, a teacher had asked him to slow down, to finish a word before moving on to the next one. One teacher told R. Moshele that when Joel was excited about a passage, he became almost incomprehensible. His mind ran so fast, his sharpest colleagues were left behind.

With age and recent experience came change. The meditative mind, Joel discovered, was like a dark room without walls or doors, deep as the heavens, with infinite time and space, therefore without time and space, unlimited. Like the heavens, the mind was a place in which a tempest could storm for years, or lie dormant in a black hole. It was grand, grander than he'd ever imagined, and silent. He remembered that an awareness of this grandeur had first come to him in the fish store when he had fallen unconscious; on awakening, his head had ached with the shortcomings of his own paltry, hop-about mind and with knowledge of the quiet depth of the mind of God. Joel understood as he hadn't before that quick thinking was his limitation, that for a chance at wisdom he would have to develop the habits of the slow, deep mind.

Hearing one day that a cold spell was expected, Joel purchased at the hardware store chemical foot warmers, which were to be placed underneath the ball of the foot inside his shoes. He'd read about them in the new-products column of a monthly science magazine and thought they might be useful.

To activate the chemicals he shook the packets, and they kept his toes toasted for hours. After that he tried additional foot warmers on various parts of his body. He placed one underneath his bottom, which warmed the pillow and made his seat more comfortable. He inserted a pair into his gloves, and the palms of his hands became warm and malleable. The comfort this technology provided was amazing, miraculous, even—but would a true ascetic, Joel wondered, resort to such tricks?

Rodents in the field were attracted to the meditative *memmm*. On his second day Joel noticed a squirrel at the entrance, standing on its hind legs, listening, as if transfixed. Curious, envious of the squirrel's stillness, Joel paused, at which the squirrel moved away. Joel picked up where he left off, took the necessary breaths, moved to the next letter, and the squirrel returned. A second squirrel arrived. It was joined by a rat. Remarkable, Joel told himself. God's creatures, too. He wondered what the sounds meant to them, whether they triggered memories of previous lives. Was it possible that animals, who retained greater intuitive knowledge than man, recognized these sounds from as far back as the event of Creation, or if in previous lives, they lived as humans, the creation of the story of Creation, its promethean authorship?

Joel resumed his recitation and another rat joined the group. He was becoming a regular pied piper. He threw a pebble, hissed, and the rodents ran off. He resumed humming, *memming*, but now his stomach hummed louder, a growl. He was on empty. He recalled that it took Raba and his disciples a week to make a calf, which they ate, and then had to begin at the beginning; they had to learn how to do it all over again. Creating one calf didn't help them create the next one. Each one was separate and different. Of course Talmudic stories weren't intended literally; the achievement might have been a figurative or mental one. If Raba and his disciples had the ability to create a calf, they would be capable of satisfying their hunger mentally. With enough power of mind, one could overcome almost anything. But the persistent gnaw in

Joel's stomach displaced every other ambition and proved him a shameful neophyte. He stepped out of the drainpipe into the sun, found a seat on a tree stump, said the blessing, and chewed meditatively on his dry crackers, welcoming the warmth of food in his body, even this brittle warmth. A squirrel stopped to look, or beg, and Joel offered a piece of cracker; then there were more squirrels showing their white bellies, demanding their share.

At the end of his first week in the pipe, Joel conducted a review of what he had accomplished. He could sit in one place, recite and permute the alphabet for six, sometimes seven hours at a time. Using the letters, A-M-Sh, he was able to conjure up one part of the girl, her legs, or her torso, keep that part writhing in the air or on the wall of the clay pipe for a brief period. With one part on the wall, it was always a struggle to control his body and mind and attempt the next part. After an hour, he was exhausted and he allowed himself sexual relief. Then he had to rest for an hour. And still, in his dreams, when he wasn't conscious, she returned and had her way with him. In his dreams, with his mind at rest, he wasn't in control of his body. He considered the use of indulgence rather than delay and denial: Would allowing his body release after release provide a different strength and concentration? With desire expended, his mind would be freed of lust, out of bondage. If not for this, if not for the strength one acquired via experience, to what purpose the temptation?

Joel knew that sexual desire had been Nachman's life struggle. The other Bratslaver who had experienced the girl were also aware of Nachman's difficulty, and this knowledge lent perhaps too much significance to their own experience, not especially singular in the lives of most men. Indeed the more mature Chasidim soon relegated the incident to the category of the inexplicable; some spoke of the temptation as a test, an opportunity to overcome it. But Joel's mind had taken a baroque turn, and he remained intent on analyzing every aspect of his life, seeking out meaning, getting to the bottom of every potential teaching. To this end, he determined to try everything and anything, and in the days that followed, he engaged in an orgy of arousal and release.

In the second week of Joel's emancipation, on the seventeenth day of the second month, the heavens opened wide and rain fell upon the earth for three days and three nights.

On the first day, in the basement of the Jakob home, suitcases and boxes floated. Ada tied her skirt in a knot, slipped off her stockings, and went down to fetch them. She lined them up and stacked them in a row at the top of the basement stairs, where it was dry. By late afternoon, the suitcases were again afloat, and she had to move them a second time.

Outside, Rita Avenue was fast becoming Rita River. Water gushed down Jill and Ida Road, ferrying in its wake Big Wheels, twisted aluminum chairs, tree branches. Ada and R. Moshele ran out to gather whatever loose objects might present some danger to motorists—What motorists? Ada wondered aloud, seeing no cars on the road—and stored them in the flooded garage. The rain pelted their heads, shoulders, faces, streamed past their brows into their eyes, which made it difficult to see. Through the watery blur, R. Moshele noted that the rain drains on the corner were overflowing, therefore it was no wonder that normally dry basements were flooding. It was a strange and awesome sight, water roaring down every incline as if a dam had broken, and it was loud, a raging sea.

The flood redux despite the promise, Ada shouted. Which was what they were all thinking.

Mrs. Jakob hoped that Joel wouldn't attempt to walk home in this deluge. He has food and water with him, I packed it myself last night.

Walking from room to room, window to window, she discovered various roof leaks and put her saucepans to work catching water.

When Joel didn't show up for dinner, no one thought it strange; he was often late these days. I always beg him to carry some change with him, Mrs. Jakob complained, enough at least for a phone call.

In the morning, it was still raining. Roads were flooded and cars were stranded everywhere. Taking the old station wagon was out of the question, but R. Moshele said he would walk to the study house. He took with him a freshly packed brown lunch bag for Joel, who had probably slept on a bench.

When in the afternoon, he returned with the lunch bag, Mrs. Jakob worried. R. Moshele said nothing. He had an idea that Joel had perversely returned to the Bratslav study house in New Square, and had been forced to remain there overnight.

In the news, there were stories of houses and cars that had washed away. Also the rain had eroded away enough dirt to wash up coffins at the Mount Bailey cemetery, which raised concerns about the drinking water. As a result, there was a run on bottled water and the A&P posted Sold Out signs. Mrs. Jakob thought it foolish that with a surfeit of water there should be a run on water. She filled her largest pot with the rainwater pouring out of the house rain gutters, brought it to a boil, then allowed it to cool on the stove. Sieved through the Brita filter system, she said, the water should be as drinkable as anything bottled.

When Joel didn't arrive home for dinner the second night, R. Moshele telephoned R. Yidel. The bookseller didn't know what to say, he hadn't seen Joel. He himself hadn't been to the *shtibel* in New Square, but he would do what he could. Phone lines are down in places. He would try to get through to someone within walking distance of the *shtibel*.

An hour later, when the phone rang, the Jakobs held their breath. It was indeed R. Yidel, but with news that there was no sign of Joel in the

Bratslav study house. And as far as anyone knew, he hadn't been there before the rain had started.

When Aaron also had no information of Joel's whereabouts, R. Moshele turned to Ada, the one person who knew Joel better than anyone else. Where could he be? he asked.

Method

Ada awoke in Joel's bed, surrounded by Joel's smell, though she hadn't thought of him as having any in particular, since he didn't use fragrance. After a shower he always smelled of Ivory soap, the squeaky-clean smell of their childhood, of their joint bubble baths until the age of three. But this was a smell of slept-in sheets and something else she couldn't identify. She adjusted the pillow, her own firm pillow brought in from her own bed because Joel's was too thin, inadequately stuffed. He was a back sleeper, she slept on her sides, alternating between them, but she rolled onto her back to see what Joel saw on waking. Getting into character, Joel had once called it. He'd read about the Stanislavsky method: seeing, feeling, and thinking what another human had seen, felt, thought was one way to get to know another. But whom had Joel wanted to know and why, Ada wondered now. Nachman? She hadn't thought to ask him at the time. He picked up odd bits of information from his readings, thought about them, told her sometimes. Not knowing what else to do, Ada determined to try this actor's method to learn what she could about Joel.

From the center of the room, where his bed stood, an island surrounded by books, Ada saw what anyone stepping into the room would see, the alphabet, a kind of alphabet primer whose pages were out of order, whose lines and pairings were deliberately confused to thwart meaning. She'd seen it before and liked it, but this morning, the letters gave her a feeling of nausea, or vertigo. She covered her eyes, massaged the space between them to clear her head. When she looked again, she was able to see only form and shape, pure hieroglyphic beauty, an abstract pattern. She knew what Joel would say: that the impulse toward meaning is a human limitation, that an abstract universe had been good enough for God, but before He could make a man, He had to create a concrete, representational world, complete with narrative laws of cause and effect, and language with which to describe it. Therefore concentrating on individual letters so exclusively, avoiding meaning, was an attempt to step beyond the human toward the Godly. Was this what Joel was up to? But where was he now? She hoped he wasn't ill; though it would hurt their father, she hoped Joel had gone renegade again. For all she knew, he was on a plane somewhere and soon the phone would ring.

It was too early in the day for Ada, though already later than Joel's daily start. Like all Chasidic men, R. Moshele and Joel took their daily shower at the baths in the study house, after the ritual dip in the mikvah. Since she was a woman, she couldn't wear Joel's clothes, couldn't go to the men's mikvah, couldn't attend services at the study house. Her execution of the actor's exercise was necessarily incomplete, the differences between male and female a source of imperfection. But Ada had never resented her difference as a woman; she relished it, stretched the freedoms Chasidic womanhood provided, greater than what the men allowed themselves. And she was no purist, no slave to the tyranny of rules. The exercise would serve her purpose and not the other way around.

The sounds and smells of the automatic coffeemaker, attending to its daily task even though the members of the household were off their regular schedules. Unusually, Ada would have the morning's first cup, Joel's cup on any other day. She found her slippers at the foot of the bed, and padded silently into the kitchen, poured the coffee. She took her cup to the back door and stood looking out. A murky day with drizzle, not weather for outdoor activity, still an improvement over yesterday's downpours. Even through the closed glass door she could hear the sound of water, water everywhere. The dark bark of the black oaks glistened. Two of the green Naugahyde pillows were missing from the sofa, which should have been brought in. Though intended for outdoor use, the Naugahyde was only water resistant, not waterproof. She would have to step out to retrieve the pillows. She considered which of her many shoes and boots would serve in this waterlogged world, and came up short. None of her own were a hundred percent waterproof, but the tall fireman rain boots R. Moshele had used would be.

Minutes later, Ada went out through the back door, wearing her father's tall boots and long, dark raincoat over her flannel nightgown. She walked to the side yard, didn't find the pillows, and on a sudden impulse, seeing no cars coming, splashed across Rita Stream, which flowed into River Ida, and emptied into Frances Ocean. She didn't swim with the current, but waded out to the blind banks of Ida, what they used to call no-man's-land because it belonged to all men, the townships of Orange and Rockland. The site was familiar and not. But then she hadn't been here in, she calculated, eight years, when suddenly secret hideouts ceased fascinating, along with secret languages in which the first two letters became the last two, or, in another variation, two arbitrary consonants, say *t* and *l*, were added as a prefix to every odd word and *u* and *q* to every even one, hence the name, "tlon, uqbar." When the enemy, another schoolgirl clique, complete with its own secret language, came close to deciphering this tongue, complications had to be added and the rules of two or more languages were combined to make the language of "tlon, uqbar, orbis, tertius." In all those years of intrigue and treason she had never seen so much water here, the drainpipe so thoroughly at work, swallowing gallons, unlike the usual trickle and sip. Following the flow of water, she soon stood in the opening of the pipe and waited as her eyes adjusted from dim to dimmer. From the water marks in the clay, she knew that the water level had dropped. R. Moshele's knee-high boots would keep her dry; the long wool socks would keep her warm. She stepped into the round pipe, careful to negotiate the unevenness, and immediately remembered how: A foot on either side of the curve, arms akimbo for balance. It was easier now, her legs and arms were longer. Automatically, as if she'd been here only the day before, her fingers found and gripped the occasional handle conveniently set into the cement, making it possible to take a longer, steady stride forward. She inhaled the dank, humid air along with another familiar smell. Was it an illusion? There was something here with the essence of Joel's bed. She bent her head to her shoulder, brought the ruffled collar of her nightgown to her nose, recognized the tuberose in her own perfume, and underneath the damp metallic earthiness she was now identifying as Joel's smell.

She moved farther into the pipe, deeper than she'd ventured as a child because she'd feared the water rats. And she was still apprehensive, hoped not to see them, tried not to think about the slippery slime her fingers scraped against. Gloves would have been welcome. Slowly, slowed down by the water and dark, she arrived at a bend in the pipe, a turn, and deduced that she was just under Jill Lane. Knowing her approximate location aboveground was comforting. A hundred yards farther, there was another bend to the right; this time the pipes forked, and she encountered the proverbial diverging of two roads and only one to be taken. She looked both ways, wished she'd thought to bring a flashlight, took a few steps straight ahead, turned back, vacillated, convinced that there was one right way. She took some steps to the right, sniffed; for want of more definite signs, she made instinct her guide and found her reward at the next fork, where she turned right again, thereby imposing an organizing system on the unknown, and came upon one of the missing green cushions caught on a protrusion in the juncture between two pipes.

Seeing the familiar object, her heart jumped. Was this what she'd come for? She unhooked the waterlogged cushion. Water streamed from every seam. A summer of suns would dry it out. In the meantime, the airless stuffing inside would grow mold. She hesitated, saw the answer above her head like a cartoon balloon, and hooked the cushion onto it. It could remain here to drain. She would retrieve it on her return. But how far and deep would these pipes take her, and for how long would she follow? She was no longer certain of where she was. She didn't know whether she was under Suzanne Drive, or to its right, somewhere near Leon or even as far as Phyllis Terrace. Underground, she had lost her bearings. If the pipes continued providing right turns, she ought to come full circle, find herself at some nearby starting point. But how wide a circle and how nearby? Her feet were heavy, weighed down by the wet ruffle hem of her nightgown, which dragged, and she regretted not taking the time to shower and dress. She squeezed the water out and tied a knot. She moved forward determinedly, in a hurry to arrive, though arrival was hardly the purpose of this journey. To learn anything, an unhurried, fearless embrace of the unknown was necessary. But though Ada was courageous enough aboveground, in the dank cave she didn't feel very meditative or fearless. She kept a lookout for rats, shuddered at the slime and the smells, hesitated at the bends, unable to see what was ahead. But she was determined, bold, and if will is character, as Schopenhauer proposed, it was in her character to see this challenge through to the end, though gropingly, uncertain of what the end should be, of what she was seeking, or what she might find. In the dim humidity, in this concave circularity with its bends, forks, and junctures, she saw as if driving with parking lights in a thick dark fog. Joel, she knew, was not afraid of rats; they had never stopped him.

At the next turn, she came upon watery detritus, the flotsam and jetsam of that particular neighborhood, made up of copious families in which one child follows on the heels of the other, a crowded kite of siblings, near enough in age to take up not yet retired push toys, Big Wheels, bicycles, dolls, with the result that very little survived intact. Since the Jakobs, with only two children, were the exception—Mrs. Jakob had suffered a difficult miscarriage and the doctor had warned against another pregnancy—Joel's and Ada's toys had been passed on to the neighborhood children to endure their usual fate.

Here was the afterlife setting for the man-made. Still recognizable: a pair of twisted training wheels, a spent stroller, a broken Big Wheel, parts of a ruined canopy from a large old-fashioned perambulator, several severed, once flaxen-haired heads of Beth-Anns and Barbies, their armless and legless torsos, also the missing parts, arms, legs, and then what Ada recognized as old Mrs. Beasley in her original gingham dress and white apron, a gaping hole where her white head of hair and thick brown glasses ought to have been. Youth and beauty had never been Mrs. Beasley's qualities; sociability was. And no matter how old she got, Mrs. Beasley retained her memory, unlike some grandmothers Ada knew. Old Beasley knew who she was and had the ability to say so. Even before Ada picked her up, she was prepared for the particular timbre of the gravelly, Hello, I am Mrs. Beasley. What's your name?

She turned and straightened the doll to engage the talking mechanism and the feeble voice emerged watery, Hello, I am, and broke down.

She turned the doll again and Mrs. Beasley said, I am, Hello, I, and stopped. Ada did what as a child she had done out of curiosity. She lifted Mrs. Beasley's dress to extract and examine the mechanism stitched into the lower back and found stuck to it an imperfect square of lined paper, edges ragged. She peeled the paper from the wet back and made out a smudged *taf*, the final letter of the alphabet, in black marker.

Joel, Ada said, and the name traveled into the pipe and back. Mrs. Beasley responded. Hello, Joel, I am your name.

Excuse me, Ada said. She was hearing things.

She shook the mechanism vigorously, squeezed the cloth parts of the doll to drain the water, and Mrs. Beasley talked nonstop. Hello, Mrs. Beasley. What's your name? Hello. What's your name? Hello, I am, what's your? Hello. Hello. Hello. Mrs. Beasley. Mrs. Beasley. Hello.

Ada stared at the beheaded, chattering doll in her hand, then slipped her through one of the handles in the curvature of the pipe, where the babble continued.

Ada moved forward, onward, to the next bend, right again and right once more, and emerged at the culvert on Hopal Lane. She was a mile from home, wearing a nightgown and boots two sizes too large. Schoolchildren were at their bus stop, doing what children at bus stops do. One child saw Ada and waved. Ada waved back. Did he think she was a fireman? She stepped back into the pipe. She couldn't walk the streets like this. She would remain in the pipe. But first some fresh, open air.

She stood in the opening of the pipe, breathing, and in the mound of soft mud at the entrance, her eyes discerned another white square. She picked it up and found the *shin*. These squares of alphabet were signs of Joel. He'd been here. And there had to be more. She hadn't been looking hard enough. She hadn't known what to look for. She walked back into the pipe, searching, her eyes focused now on the ground in front of her, on the walls, in the water at her feet. Would the next one be a *resh*? Echoing in the pipe was Mrs. Beasley's voice, which seemed to have grown louder, dispersing the geriatric wisdom of someone who has lived long enough to know, a Virgil to the afterlife of the inanimate.

The next squares of paper that revealed themselves bore the watery lines of the *resh* and *kuf*. She was gathering the alphabet in reverse order. Why the reverse order? she wondered. What did it mean, if anything?

When she unstuck the two squares, she found another between them, and it was either the *vav* or the *yud*, it wasn't clear which, the differential being the length of the vertical line, which was smudged. Either way, *yud* or *vav*, it was out of order, which though a reverse one, had provided something to work with. Which means what? Ada asked aloud. That she was looking for coherence where there wasn't any? But she couldn't help herself. She was desperate. Joel was missing, and no one seemed to know where he was. If only he would call. But she couldn't just sit and wait. She didn't want to sit around imagining the worst. She had to do something.

The squares that followed arrived in the following order, or lack of order: After the debatable *vav* or *yud*, came the seventh letter, *zayin*, which suggested to Ada that the previous one might be the sixth one, or *vav*. But when the *zayin* was followed by the fourth letter, *dalet*, and the pattern of minus three emerged, she reread the *vav* as a *yud*. The next letter turned out not to be the *alef*, which repudiated any pattern, and Ada paused to reconsider the events.

In the beginning was the *taf*. Which is to say, in the beginning was the end.

But before the *taf*, Ada reminded herself, came Mrs. Beasley. And before Mrs. Beasley, a pair of twisted training wheels, a spent stroller, a broken Big Wheel, parts of a ruined canopy from a large old-fashioned perambulator, several severed, once flaxen-haired heads of Beth-Anns and Barbies, their armless and legless torsos, also the missing arms and legs. Then Ada remembered the green cushion, which came first. And before the cushion, the rain, water. Would it be possible to arrive at the beginning of this story?

In the beginning was the flood. A return to the primordial state, with water over the firmament, heedless of separation and bounds. Water. It brought forth life, swarms of biblical creatures. But too much water also threatens life, sets man and ark afloat, with no ground to walk on, no earth to till, no harvest.

In the way of any story maker, Ada paused to question the various parts, to begin with the drainpipe system as setting, which suggested mystery, or at least adventure. She wondered whether Joel had selected this setting for a specific reason, with expectations of cause and effect, of crisis, complication, and resolution.

She considered the disparate details and tried to separate the circumstantial—mere foils that served as distraction—from the truly revealing. She reasoned. The pillow could have washed down into this drain along with the Big Wheels, stroller, dolls, even the alphabet. It was possible that Joel hadn't set foot in this cave since childhood. Her instincts could be misleading her. So far, she'd proven nothing. She walked back to the first fork and hesitated. Which strand of possibilities would she follow this time? Within every strand, substrands branched off. Instinct directed her leftward; system suggested remaining with the right. Ada had been in business long enough to value efficient strategy. If she continued to proceed systematically, she'd know which ground had already been covered and could avoid unnecessary repetition.

She took the road not taken, then returned to the rigorous strategy of hard rights and found herself once again beneath Hopal Lane.

She retraced her steps slowly, thoughtfully. Would all paths lead to the same place? It was too soon to tell. There were at least four left turns that might have led elsewhere. This time, at the first substrand, Ada abandoned strategy and switched into the left path. When she came to another fork, she went left, calculated that she might be under Frances Pl., came upon a confirmation in the form of a miniature street sign in abbreviated form, Fr. Pl., which gave her confidence. Now she knew where she was. It made sense to her that this underground network should mirror an aspect of the world above, since its purpose was to serve the world above. Just as man is made in the image of God, and every garden features aspects of the Edenic one. Since rain drains were at the edges of the road, drainpipes ought systematically to run underneath them. She was so involved in her planning and deducing, so determined not to think the worst, that she forgot about the inhabitants of the netherworld until she heard their all too distinctive sounds. She came around an elbow in the pipe and found a busy nest of rats, massive adults surrounding and nourishing their young. And what were those bits of white? Ada's first impulse was to run. She hated rats and had one foot already headed the other way, but she stopped herself, looked back, the example of Lot's wife notwithstanding, and froze: Joel's squares of alphabet were papering the rat nest. And something else. Amid the mix of grasses, twigs, and paper, were the pale blue covers of a notebook. Joel's?

Determination and character dissolved. Faced with a pack of yammering rats, Ada ran.

She ran until she stepped out into daylight, onto the banks of Ida, waded across Rita, and home.

Or, in an alternative hell that allows the story to adhere to a basic rule of the storyteller's craft—if there is a gun it must go off: She ran, took a wrong turn, turned back, but she must have taken another wrong turn, because nothing was familiar. She turned back again, and came upon a miniature one-way sign. It was so small, she might have missed it the first time. To convince herself that it was real, she reached up to touch it, and it came off the wall. In her hand, it became a key. The key to what? It was familiar and not, a regular Medeco, but rusty. She pushed onward, wondering how a one-way drainpipe would differ from the others. So far it was equally wide; two people could pass each other easily enough. She calculated that she was somewhere under Suzanne Drive. Then she came upon a metal circular stairwell, with stairs that led down. Below was a metal door. Leading to what? She would take a look. She stepped down the narrow flight, positioning each large-booted foot sideways, turned the knob on the door, and found it locked. She inserted the key in her hand and the door swung open, onto another set of stairs. She took the next flight down, then stopped to peer below. It seemed there was a round chamber with shrubs and trees growing within. She looked straight up. Light for the trees and shrubs came through the holes of a drain above. This was interesting. She'd look around, she told herself, then leave. No, the damp and dark were getting to her and she didn't want to continue this strange descent; she'd leave now. She turned and lifted her foot to place it on the stair above her, and discovered she couldn't. She tried stepping up with her other foot, and again the stair repelled her as if she were an opposing magnet. She remembered the one-way sign and opened her palm to look at the sign that had become a key, and recognized it as the key to her family's front door. Was this the key that Joel had dropped? And into this rain drain? She closed her fingers around the key, then opened them, and once again they held a one-way sign.

In the logic of dream, Ada assumed that this one-way staircase had now reversed itself. Tentatively, she took the first step up, then sprinted the rest.

Non-Explanations

R. Moshele and his wife were anxiously waiting at the door. When Mrs. Jakob saw Ada wading across the street in her father's large boots and coat she felt relief and rage at once, and reexperienced a moment she remained ashamed of, when Ada, as a three-year-old, had chased a ball into the street and come close to being hit by a passing car; with one arm, her mother had scooped her up into a hug, while with the other hand, she smacked the child's bottom, expressing two emotions at once. But Ada was grown up, too old to smack, and Mrs. Jakob had to satisfy herself verbally.

Ada apologized. Then explained. I woke up with a feeling about the drainpipes.

And? Mrs. Jakob asked.

It's possible he was there. It's possible he wasn't. I don't know.

R. Moshele shook his head. I don't want you to go there alone again. I called the police and filed a missing-person claim, which means the fact of Joel's absence will soon be widely known. I had no choice.

Get dressed, Mrs. Jakob advised. Aaron will be here in minutes.

Ada nodded. I'm going to take a hot shower.

In the shower with hot water running down her back, Ada considered the accumulated facts and what they might reveal. She thought about Joel's trip to Uman. The fire at the Bratslav *shtibel*. How did all that fit together? And the letters? The lost key. It was confusing enough to make her head hurt. The details were dots, and though she considered herself good at such games, she was having difficulty connecting them. Perhaps if she were a detective, a Sherlock Holmes, or a skilled story-teller who found pattern and consequence everywhere, she could connect the disparate details and find Joel. If she gathered all the squares of alphabet and threw them into the air, would they line themselves up into words and sentences and reveal what had happened to him? She dressed, stepped across the hall, and opened the door to his room, half anticipating that the letters on the walls had organized themselves into coherent paragraphs.

She remained standing at the door. Her eyes lighted on the letters of Joel's name and she wanted to accept this as a good sign. He was alive, he would be all right. But in crisis she was allowing herself to grow superstitious. She reminded herself of the insignificance of names, of the mundane names of the streets around them, Rita, Ida, Jill, Suzanne, Frances, harmless street names, and meaningless to the inhabitants of the area. There was no Rita or Ida or Jill or Frances living on any of these particular streets; quite probably, there never had been. Nor were there any Ralphs, Ronalds, or Carletons, male names reserved for the larger streets that led to the more significant routes and byways, as if hero-ically leading the way to grand adventures. They were all indifferent names selected from a book by a land developer.

In the kitchen, R. Moshele and his wife sat with Aaron, asking the occasional question, brooding silently. On the table in front of Aaron was a glass of water, the only one of Mrs. Jakob's multiple offerings he'd assented to. All three looked up hopefully when she entered, as if she had answers. She disappointed quickly.

Here's what I know, Ada said, forming a zero with her forefinger and thumb.

What did you find underground? Aaron asked.

Ada went to the coatrack, took out of the pocket of her father's raincoat the squares of paper she'd picked up, and spread them out on the table.

Nothing we didn't already know, she said. Joel was obsessed by the alphabet. They're all over the walls of his room.

The alphabet? Aaron repeated. Why the last four letters? Aaron asked.

The rats are using the others to paper their nest, Ada explained.

Despite the cups of coffee, Ada found herself unable to think at her desk, and decided to lie down. She was good at closing her eyes for twenty minutes, after which she was always more productive, came up with quick answers. She closed the door to her room and listened with eyes closed to the sound of water dripping, to the variant tones of irregular off-rhythm drops splashing into one of six saucepans distributed through the house. They needed emptying. They would wait another twenty minutes. For now, she remained in bed.

And with her eyes closed, she slipped out of the house and returned to the underground complex, convinced that she was doing so in order to accomplish two things: to retrieve Joel's notebook and traverse the byways that remained unexplored. Both required that she brave the rats. This time, Ada came equipped with a flashlight.

When Ada stepped into the opening of the drainpipe, she felt that Aaron was there, and this gave her courage; more than that, it attracted her. She didn't know where he was, in which fork or subfork, the first right or first left, second right or left, or a confusing mix of both. She didn't know him well enough to know what he was likely to do. Though they'd played together as children, there'd been little personal contact in recent years, in which time they'd grown, changed, and yet remained the same. He was still Joel's best friend, she was still Joel's sister, destined to become man and wife.

She lifted her foot to take her first step and felt herself carried through the familiar space all the way to the first fork, into and past the first left, and onward. Not having to make the decisions, she lost track of the turns, of the paths taken. She floated toward Aaron's open arms. Afloat, their clothes blew away, their legs intertwined, arms fell into place, her body became his, his became hers, and underneath them a soft carpet of alphabet, above them a blanket of warm water. Cradled in the soft and warm, they knew each other, and with this knowledge made a man, though they didn't yet know it. His name would be JakobJoel. Eight years later, a home video would show JakobJoel at the age of seven, front teeth missing. The camera would zoom in and an off-camera voice would ask: What do you want to be when you grow up?

I am going to be a *badkhn*, JakobJoel would declare.

P A R T

÷

Two

When the waters receded, Joel's body turned up on the muddy shore of Frances Lake. Since Jewish law prohibits autopsy, the cause of death remained undetermined. This didn't prevent interested parties from pursuing the full story. Indeed, the absence of information seemed to stimulate the desire for detail, and local police and hospitals reported an unprecedented increase in Yinglish speakers calling with questions. Certain details emerged, sequence was guessed at, coherences cobbled together, and a story of what might have happened began taking shape, or rather a series of stories, since there were numerous versions. In Leibniz's theory of the monads (or souls), the perception of an individual monad is necessarily subjective, because it is dependent on its point of reference; the subjective perceptions of multiple monads become an assemblage of points of view, therefore more objective and closer to truth. But is absolute truth ever knowable?

THE MONADS

÷

Readers of Newspapers

Local papers reported that the police recovered a body on the shores of Frances Lake, that it had been identified by family members as that of Joel Jakob, and that the cause of death remained undetermined, though drowning was considered likely. They reported also that all suspicions of foul play had been dismissed, and that the deceased was scheduled for interment at the Mount Zion Cemetery on Route 306. And finally, they noted that weather conditions were ascribed as cause of death in three additional fatalities in the Orange and Rockland area.

Readers from the community understood that the family wanted to avoid publicity. At stake was not only family reputation but also the yeshiva's well-being. It was also in the interest of the religious community to keep Joel's involvement in the recent violence at New Square out of the press. If the suspicion of foul play became credible, an investigation would follow, and the story along with names of the culprits made public.

Only the hard-core gossips and a small group of Bratslav Chasidim emphasized the possibility of foul play. They made the point that if the Skvere hoodlums could strike once, why not twice? It wasn't as if they were off the streets, in jail. After a personal appeal from the Skvere rebbe, the Bratslav community and the Jakobs had agreed not to prosecute, and the perpetrators had suffered at most a harsh reprimand. Was it so far-fetched to consider this second strike a form of revenge?

Dr. Levine

At breakfast, when Shirley Levine brought the article in the *Journal News* to her husband's attention, he said, The boy must've had another seizure. Alone, with no one to urge him back to consciousness, he could have been without oxygen for too long, in other words, there could have been brain damage. And if during the seizure, he inhaled water, he would have drowned.

Will you say anything? Shirley asked.

If I'm asked, Levine said. Where there's no patient, there's usually no doctor. He shrugged, reached for the two-day-old *Science Times*, and immersed himself in an interview with a theologian/scientist on the ethics of artificial intelligence. It was the professor's double specialty that interested Levine. Was it possible for one person to believe in both religion and science?

Nugel & Nugel

At the local hardware store Nugel & Nugel, husband and wife debated whether or not to release the information that two weeks earlier Joel Jakob had purchased at their store a new product, a chemical that reacted with one's body heat to produce more heat. It wasn't as if they'd advocated for the product. He'd known about it beforehand, because when he came in he had asked for it by name. The packets, sold in pairs, were kept behind the counter.

Mrs. Nugel remembered other odd purchases. About a month or two earlier, Joel had stopped in for a magnet and roll of twine. And the following day, he'd returned for watch batteries, if she remembered the timing of this correctly.

Mr. Nugel thought that nothing ought to be said. A new product, untested on the market, is vulnerable to blame and it would be too easy for people to create fictions around it. For the business of Nugel & Nugel, it wouldn't do any good to be associated with this scandal.

Besides, a foot warmer isn't exactly a dangerous product. As for the magnet, twine, and batteries, they were innocuous enough. Anyone could
have a need for these things. Indeed, he could have been running an
errand for his father or mother. Mr. Nugel argued that it would be insulting to the family to release such information.

During her weekly update of the store's accounts, it occurred to Mrs.
Nugel that since Joel had purchased some of the items on credit, sooner
or later Mrs. Jakob, who surely reviewed the bills before she paid them,
would discover these charges and could do with the knowledge as she
saw fit. In this, as in most things, she told herself, Mr. Nugel had proven
himself wise. Still, as she entered the debits and credits in her neat
accountant's handwriting, the particularity of the items remained sug-
gestive and she pondered their use. The foot warmers were easy. If you
were planning to spend several hours in the cold, warm feet would help.
It was also possible, that with his toes toasting, Joel could have fallen
deeply asleep. Could it be that on falling into the lake, the cold water
wouldn't have awakened him?

The magnet and twine were an obvious pairing. Joel could have
dropped something metal into the water and was attempting to retrieve
it. It was possible that it was his watch that he had dropped and
retrieved, and the batteries had been affected by their immersion in
water. One question remained: Why would a yeshiva boy spend so
much of his time beside the lake?

If Mrs. Nugel had spoken of the Jakob tragedy to the local locksmith,
she might have learned that on the day Joel purchased watch batteries,
he'd also had keys made, which would have clarified some things,
obscured others. If it had been keys that were dropped, then how did
watch batteries enter the story? Mere coincidence didn't occur to her as
an answer. Though she was as religious as the next Jew and took the
daily leap of faith that belief requires, she would have remained uncomfortable with coincidence as an explanation because it wouldn't have
explained anything at all.

R. Yidel

After a long conversation with two of his colleagues, R. Yidel came to several conclusions. If the story of Joel's encounter with the woman in Uman became public knowledge, it would create a scandal, give the enemies of Bratslav more fire. For R. Moshele, the knowledge of such an event in his son's life would bring only more pain, confirmation of the dangers of Bratslav pursuits, and a lifelong resentment against the community. Besides, there was no way of knowing whether Joel's misfortune was in any way related to his experience in Uman. The boy had developed his initial interest in Nachman without anyone's help, which indicated that even before his trip he'd been walking off the beaten track. The bookseller recalled the many not quite kosher books that Joel had been reading, and he determined that this too would remain unreported. Readers trusted him; he would continue to deserve that trust.

In the privacy of his own room, R. Yidel ripped the collar of his own shirt and sat on a low stool for an hour, the abbreviated mourning ritual a disciple performs to honor the death of his teacher. He had come to love and admire Joel. The boy had a determined curiosity and bright humor that had made conversation with him an unusual pleasure. And he had barely begun his studies of Nachman. With his particular cast of mind, he could have gone on to accomplish great things. And who knows what he might have done for the community of Bratslav with new scholarship or otherwise? Losing Joel at such a young and promising age was terrible and wasteful, not only for family and friends, R. Yidel felt, but also for the Chasidic community at large.

When he tried to speculate about what might have happened, he turned to the question of Joel's seclusion. It was unusual for a yeshiva boy to spend so much time alone. It cast suspicion on his activities. Furtiveness was an indicator of aberrant behavior, which suggested sexual sin. R. Yidel conceded in his heart that Joel's youth in the face of his experience at Uman could have intensified the sexual temptation. Unlike himself and the other men to whom that Lilith had exposed herself, Joel was at an age when such desires are at their peak. Unmarried, he would have had no acceptable outlet, therefore control would have been difficult. It was quite probable that Nachman's early marriage to Sosia had prevented much evil. In the end, R. Yidel recommended to his colleagues that the experience of Uman be limited to married men.

Aaron

Aaron couldn't sit still. When he found the atmosphere of mourning in the Jakob household most unbearable and was certain that R. Moshele wouldn't be alone, he walked. He covered Joel's daily walk, including their shared stretch, and he raged. He walked and raged from Ida Road toward Frances Place, then left on Suzanne, which ran alongside the perimeter of the lake. He recalled various conversations with Joel, strange moments. He remembered looking out the window of the study house during prayers one morning and noticing that Joel was circling the building. Joel's behavior, the strangeness these last months, his illness, his interest in Bratslav, the concentration on the *alef-beis*, pointed to one explanation. For such misfortune there could be only one explanation. Tosefot tells the story of four men who attempted entry into the heights of the universe. Only Rabbi Akiva, the greatest scholar in the history of the Jews, returned successfully. The others came to terrible ends. Ben Azai died, Ben Zoma lost his mind, and Elisha ben Avira, known also as Acher, lost his faith. Aaron believed that with his illicit pursuits, Joel had brought upon himself a variation or combination of these deaths. And for no good reason. He had been doing well without them. Together they'd been tackling the most difficult passages of *Sanhedrin* with ease. Which had been gloriously gratifying. But Joel had demanded more, and in the process had destroyed himself and others. Aaron grieved for himself and for Ada, for R. Moshele and Mrs. Jakob, those who had loved Joel and would have difficulty going on without him. For long hours at a time Aaron trembled with anger. He kicked at the pebbles in his path, at a stone on the side of the road. He walked deep into the drainpipe on Ida and screamed, Joooeeel, Joooooeeeel, Joooooooeeeeeeeeeel, Jooooooooooooooooooooooeeeeeeeeeeeeeeeeeeeeeeeeeeeeel. The name echoed back empty.

R. Moshele

Sitting on the low mourner's stool, the ripped fabric of his caftan flapping, R. Moshele swayed in pain and spoke as if to himself, his voice low, his sentences short.

Why the setting of the drainpipes? It's a mystery to me. He and Ada were fond of them as children, I remember. They're cavelike. Children like hiding places. Unfortunately, unlike desert caves, these pipes carry water. If Joel had another seizure, and in his unconscious state he was submerged, well . . . R. Moshele paused, swayed, unable for the moment to go on.

He wasn't the kind of boy you kept in bed. He wanted to continue living, studying, and he was always thorough. When something took his fancy, he pursued it exhaustively. Pursued it, R. Moshele repeated, swayed, repeated finally without sound, body swaying, lips moving. Pursued, pursued it exhaustively, pursued, exhaustively, it, pursued it exhaustively, exhaustively, pursued exhaustively, pursued it exhaustively, pursued, pursued, it, exhaustive pursuit, pursued it, exhaustively, pursued it exhaustively, pursued, exhaustive pursuit, pursued exhaustively, pursued it exhaustively, pursued, pursued, it, exhaustive pursuit, pursued exhaustively, pursued it exhaustively, pursued, pursued, it, exhaustive pursuit, pursued exhaustively, pursued it exhaustively, pursued, pursued, it, exhaustive pursuit, pursued exhaustively, pursued it exhaustively, pursued, pursued, it, exhaustive pursuit, pursued exhaustively, pursued it exhaustively, pursued, pursued, it, exhaustive pursuit, pursued exhaustively, pursued it exhaustively, pursued, pursued, it, exhaustive pursuit, pursued exhaustively, pursued it exhaustively, pursued, pursued, it, exhaustive pursuit, pursued exhaustively, pursued it exhaustively, pursued, pursued, it, exhaustive pursuit, pursued exhaustively, pursued it exhaustively, pursued, pursued, it, exhaustive pursuit, pursued exhaustively, pursued it exhaustively, pursued, pursued, it, exhaustive pursuit, pursued exhaustively, pursued it exhaustively, pursued, pursued, it, exhaustive pursuit, pursued exhaustively, pursued it exhaustively, pursued, pursued, it, exhaustive pursuit, pursued exhaustively, pursued it exhaustively, pursued, pursued, it, exhaustive pursuit, pursued exhaustively, pursued it exhaustively, pursued, pursued, it, exhaustive pursuit, pursued exhaustively, pursued it exhaustively, pursued, pursued, it, exhaustive pursuit, pursued exhaustively, pursued it exhaustively, pursued, pursued, it, exhaustive pursuit, pursued exhaustively, pursued it exhaustively, pursued, pursued, it, exhaustive pursuit, pursued exhaustively, pursued it exhaustively, pursued, pursued, it, exhaustive pursuit, pursued . . .

Ada

In the kitchen, where the women received condolence calls from friends and family, Ada listened to her mother's attempt to retell the story, complete with regrets, sighs, pauses, and breakdowns when she was unable to go on.

Joel fasted too often. He was an extremist. I had to beg him to take some food with him, to drink enough water. The doctor told us that in athletes seizures were often a result of dehydration, a deficiency in electrolytes.

It wasn't until the nth recounting, when Mrs. Jakob had begun to recite the phrases as if they composed a mantra and Ada felt she couldn't stand hearing any more, that she suddenly wondered at the frequency of Joel's fasts. There must have been a reason. Why hadn't she thought of this before, why had it not occurred to their father? Joel had been doing penance for something. Recent personal desires informed her that the sin was likely sexual. The particular stink of his sheets came back to her, she smelled it suddenly on herself, in her hair, it was everywhere, as if she were again in his bed. She stood up abruptly, excused herself, and went to his room. She sat on his bed and cried.

This explained some things. His sudden interest in the alphabet. He had been struggling for control, for concentration, as a way to prevent the sin of spilling seed. In men, the sin is indeed great, but that something as natural as a bodily function could be the source of such pain was repulsive.

Nachman's *Book of Tales* was on the chair beside Joel's bed and Ada picked it up. She turned it this way and that, allowed her tears to wet the pages. To understand more about her own brother, she would have to read Nachman.

A week earlier Ada might have said with confidence that she knew and understood her brother inside out; now she wasn't so certain. Was it possible to know anyone, even those closest to you? She had come up against one of the mysteries of life, that it was unknowable.

What separates real life from fiction? E. M. Forster asks, and answers: Fiction is knowable.

Ada understood that though she had lived as Joel's sister for almost seventeen years, she hadn't known him. And now she never would.

Yankel Yankevitch

I was preparing the most skillful rhymes. More than once in those weeks of waiting, waiting for the girl to become a little less of herself, my wife caught me with that ear-to-ear grin that only a good turn of phrase begets. But what happens when the words that create a character suddenly disperse? What action can there be when the protagonist is no longer able to act? He arrives in this world by way of the alphabet, and exits the same way, with such words as The End; but what if it is not yet the end, what if he hasn't yet answered the questions raised, hasn't fulfilled his potential? The story has to continue, though in unexpected ways.

All my great Berditchev-Bratslav barbs and re-barbs, whole paragraphs that would and should have made history in a book on the artistry of the *badkhn*, had to go back into the world-bin of unusable lines. Financially, I admit, I came out ahead, since the mere possibility of a match between Joel and R. Mendel's eldest daughter, though unrealized, wrought a miracle. It didn't take a month for R. Mendel to find his palms lined with gold. Suddenly the wealthiest fathers were prepared to pay good money for any one of his daughters, even when he inserted into the contracts, as he did for his two youngest, three- and four-year delays as conditions.

It would be too hard, he said, to go so quickly from a houseful of lively girls to the quiet of an empty nest. My rebbetzin, he explained, would be devastated.

Fortunately for me, these postponements didn't affect my earnings because a *shadkhn*'s fee is due at the signing of the contract, that is, on the night the plate is broken. Possibly the most honest man alive, R. Mendel showed his gratitude to me generously. Even when other matchmakers were involved, he insisted on compensation for me, albeit not always the agreed-upon full amount of $700 per girl. But though I became for a short time successful as a *shadkhn*, I lost out as a *badkhn*. When all my rhymes on Joel's behalf became worthless—and I had spent more than seven days creating them—I salvaged what I could for the occasion of Ada's marriage. And it was this performance that turned out to be my last one for several years to come. Losing Joel was a terrible blow for everyone. We all descended into an abyss for a while.

Nachman

On Saturday evening, the second day of Sukkot, he asked that we lay him down on his bed. He was terribly tired then, and said that he had gotten tired out by sitting so long on the chair. Then he turned to us and said, "Do you remember the story . . . I told you when we first came to this place?" A shudder passed through me. I remembered that story very well. The Ba'al Shem Tov had come to a certain place, and had seen many great souls there which turned to him for redemption. And he had known that the only way he could redeem them was by his own death.

I stood there trembling as he added, "They've had their eye on me for so long already, beckoning me to this place. What can I tell you? Thousands of them, tens of thousands . . ." He turned his face toward the wall and spread out his hands, as though to say, "I give my life; I am ready to accept all for Him, bless His name. . . ."

On that Monday evening, the eve of the last day of his life, his disciples Reb Naftali and Reb Simeon stood before him (for we were

sleeping in shifts, so that he was never left alone) . . . and he again spoke
of the souls that longed to be redeemed, and how many there were in this
place. Naftali answered him, saying, "But didn't you tell us in the teaching
'Boaz said to Ruth,' that the truly great *zaddiq* could do it all within his lifetime?" He replied, "But then I only revealed a part of the thing to you;
really one has to die to do this."

THE SEVEN FAT BRIDES

singing Steve Reich's *Tehillim* (Psalms)

for Voices and Ensemble (30:27), two to a part, except one

(Excerpt follows)

Score in C

TEHILLIM

Part I

Steve Reich
(1981)

Ha - sha - my-im meh-sa-peh - reem Ka - vohd Kail_____ u - ma-ah - say ya-dive mah -

JakobJoel:
The Last of the Monads

JakobJoel hurried across Harvard Bridge, head tucked down and into his Michelin Man jacket to avoid the raw wind slicing at his face and chapped lips. He passed the halfway mark, if the painted "Halfway to Hell" could be trusted as an accurate measure, and steadied himself. He was no lightweight, as Dr. Levine, the old family doctor, had liked to inform him when at fourteen he grew a half-foot, another half at fifteen, and reached five feet nine at sixteen; but today, with no breakfast in his stomach, he felt as if he might be lifted off his feet and blown into traffic, or worse, into the icy Charles. His first class, intermediate Japanese, was scheduled to begin in ten minutes and he was still fifteen minutes away. He might have just enough time to pick up something to eat on his way to signals and systems, his second class. In the meantime he would eat one of the Luna bars he kept in his backpack for emergencies, though he didn't look forward to the grainy lemony texture first thing in the morning. And so much sugar on an empty stomach wasn't good, the voice of his mother may as well have spoken, because he heard her just as clearly. She followed him everywhere, riding on his left shoulder, advising. Hovering and leaning on his right shoulder, intruding whenever he became interested, was his uncle Joel, whom JakobJoel had never met. It seemed to JakobJoel that his dead uncle was taking unfair advantage of his nephew's life on campus; he was living the MIT life vicariously and with none of the pressures of exams and papers, no need to prove himself. Right now his uncle was preoccupied with citing the midrash on the giants that men once were:

In comparison, today's man is said to be a puny thing, though declarations about the good old days are generally hyberbolic.

JakobJoel understood that the midrashic statement wasn't intended literally, that the gigantism referred to the genius of ancient man, but he didn't believe that, either. Why should man have been smarter then? Science has proof that at least physically man was smaller, since nutrition was poorer; archaeological finds support the theory of diminutive rather than immense proportions. And if we've evolved physically, why not intellectually? Man's brain evolves along with everything else, therefore intelligence must have progressed. Even if in the course of such growth we've stood on the shoulders of giants—Einstein's, for example—it's also true that as a result we are able to see farther than they did.

You're too young to understand the value of mythic hyperbole, his uncle pointed out—dismissively, JakobJoel thought—then moved on to another subject, the very much beside-the-point length of his nephew's sideburns. In a hurry, JakobJoel, who had only recently begun to shave at all, had cut too high on one side, and they were uneven. What did his uncle expect, *peyos*? If Joel took a look around campus, if he achieved any understanding of what went on in this institute of science, he would understand that such things as curls, beards, fringes, caftans, *gartlech*, and *shtreimlech* were unnecessary frills, the decorative accessories of Chasidic life that could only get in the way.

Frills! their grandfather, the pious Berditchever, would lament. In the Old World, Jews died for what this grandson was calling frills. Nowadays such things were dispensed with for the sake of convenience. It was no longer a matter of life and death.

Right now—JakobJoel interrupted and shook his head to clear it— even this conversation on this subject was in the way.

He had three hours of classes this morning, and the second one was always difficult because the professor's delivery was particularly plodding. The material itself was stimulating, the presentation was not. And throughout his stomach would distract him with its rumble, insist on being heard until someone would turn to acknowledge it, smile or frown, depending on the particular individual's state of mind and stomach, sated or hankering. And he, JakobJoel, would apologize for something out of his control, the inner workings of his body. But that wasn't entirely true. He could control it. He could feed it.

After classes, JakobJoel ate lunch and went directly to a carrel at the library, where he worked for two hours, juggling differential equations, solving initial-value problems for wave functions, radioactive decay, population models of fish in a stream, compounded interest for bank balances, until he could no longer concentrate. Going at it right after classes, while the equations were still in his head, helped him make quick progress. And the allotment of two hours a day seemed right, about all he could take of it in one stretch. He was always glad when he was done.

He walked from the library to his computer systems group meeting. Their current project was to design a peer-to-peer file-sharing system like Napster's, but without a central control that had the ability to shut down, unlike Napster. The various tasks were quickly divided, the next week's meeting scheduled, and after some talk about this and that— the upcoming on-campus preview of Spielberg's *A.I.*, the debate over the university's role in loco parentis, which had become a hot topic since *The New York Times'* cover article about a recent student suicide at Harvard—the group dispersed.

At three, JakobJoel walked across campus to meet with his team from management psychology to finalize plans for the survey they were conducting for the Humanoid Robotics Group, which was planning to redesign Cog's facial features. Even though Cog was a machine, the Robotics group wanted her to appeal to humans on an emotional level. She would be the first robot with a head that approached the physical attributes of a human. To this end they wanted to learn what types of features elicit a caregiver response.

Three of the five members were already there when JakobJoel arrived, sitting on top of the desks instead of at them. Although he'd grown up knowing not to sit on study tables, where holy books are kept, he hesitated for a second only—these aren't holy books, he told himself—then took another desk top, feeling that he'd earned the right after a whole morning in a seat.

The goal for this meeting was to identify and distribute the various parts of the survey. They began with some of the assumptions already in the works. First, that children, because they're small, inspire sympathy, therefore Cog was considered a toddler. Furthermore, if Cog were blond, blue-eyed, and cherubic, like the Ivory Snow baby, she would be more lovable. Someone suggested that Cog should have Asian features, since Asians made up the majority of the population at MIT, but fair representation wasn't the goal. Their assignment was to learn whether it was true that a particular age, shape, or color would benefit Cog. The survey would have to confirm or refute these ideas. Each member took the responsibility for a different facial feature. JakobJoel volunteered to write the survey questions for the eyes. He thought there was some truth to the idea that Aryan-blue eyes were more sympathetic, but he was interested in why humans considered the color blue more attractive and what such information might reveal. His own eyes were brown;

brown-eyed children had been dominant in the Jakob family ever since
he could remember, though there was the occasional green-eyed newborn. He'd heard or read stories about the Nazis experimenting with
turning brown eyes blue with dye injections. Was there any truth to
them? He would do some Google searches on the subject.

They spent the next half hour discussing the statistical methods to
use in their analysis of the gathered data, scheduled the next meeting,
and adjourned.

JakobJoel walked to the Microsystems Technology Lab on campus, where he was designing a wireless-network simulator on which
various protocols for use in larger projects could be tested. He was also
one of two interns who'd been assigned two hours a week of interaction
with Cog, the robot whose outer appearance was still in question. For
internal change she depended on human interaction. This was how she
learned.

When JakobJoel was first introduced to Cog, he was disappointed.
Given the attention the robotics group received both on and off campus, he'd expected something much more advanced, a machine with
signs of real intelligence. He'd imagined conversations with Cog, wondered whether the equipment was advanced enough to recognize
speech or whether he'd be typing on a keyboard, at which he was slow.
He'd imagined the stories he'd tell Cog, educational ones, the way one
would begin with a child. When he considered which stories to begin
with, he thought of beginning at the beginning, with Genesis.

After such expectations, the actual tasks assigned him were a let-
down. Though computers had admirable capacities for storing information, they were not good at using that information as knowledge.
Imagination was still way ahead of technology. Thousands of years
before artificial intelligence had become a subject of study, there were
medieval legends of golems, man-made beings, all of which originated
in the Talmudic tractate *Sanhedrin* 65b: Rava created a man and sent
him to R. Zera. When R. Zera realized that the man couldn't speak, he

told him to return to dust. In another passage, the *Sefer Yetzirah* (*Book of Creation*) is identified as the source of knowledge for the *amoraim*, the third-century Talmudic scholars from Israel and Babylon who created a calf and ate it. During the Middle Ages, the *Sefer Yetzirah* became more widely known as an instruction manual for magical creation, though for the Kabbalists who studied the various transformations and combinations of the letters, the purpose of the power to create was symbolic and contemplative. Mystics of the twelfth and thirteenth centuries considered the creation of a golem an ecstatic experience that served as a celebration to mark a level of achievement. They gathered virgin soil, shaped a human form known as a golem, meaning an imperfect being, a body without soul, then danced around it, while combining the secret name of God with the alphabet in an attempt to give their golem life. Various popular legends took shape around this ritual; the Golem of Prague is the most recent and most renowned, though it has no grounding in the historical life of Rabbi Loew, who is credited as its maker, or in the history of the Altneuschul synagogue. In mainstream fairy tale and fiction, Pinocchio and Frankenstein are two noteworthy golems. In film, Stanley Kubrick's HAL. But even in the year 2001, HAL was still way ahead of what was possible at the most advanced laboratories. True intelligence is just too complicated. Even simulated intelligence is still out of reach. The three basic approaches to AI—case-based, rule-based, and connectionist reasoning—remain unsatisfactory, each with its own shortcomings. To solve a problem, the case-based approach requires the computer to search a database of hundreds of problems and find the closest matching case. But cases don't always match one another perfectly and the computer can be stumped. The rule-based system begins with a large database of rules, but no matter how many rules it stores, there's also always the possibility of a breakdown, because there will always be a situation in which none of the given rules applies. Connectionist systems, based on the way the nerves in a brain work, use networks of simpler components to form one large neural network. This system also has limitations. It operates well when presented with a single type of problem but fails when attempting something more complicated, something that requires moving between subjects, say intertextually. Because of these limitations, the most powerful chess-playing machine, Deep Blue, remains a classic brute-force-based AI machine, capable of searching up to 200 million chess positions per second. Deep Blue is also capable of what's called "selective extensions," which enables the computer to search critical positions more deeply to discover difficult, even profound moves. But still, a search is a poor substitute for real reasoning. Although Deep Blue can play grand master–level chess, it is only machine-style chess; it finds solutions via the search, which means it doesn't have general intelligence. Despite huge leaps in microchip technology, which helped advance chess-playing machines, 2001's fictional HAL, who plays a human-style game, is more intelligent than IBM's Deep Blue. For one thing, HAL has emotional capacity, which means he can appreciate his own chess moves.

JakobJoel felt his uncle Joel hovering, wanting to say something, and turned his back on this shadow. He had no time for ghosts. He was here to study science.

Another reality at this most advanced of AI labs: Simulation of deductive reasoning, as limited a substitute for true intelligence as it was, was far ahead of simulated physical intelligence. Robotic movement remained in the most primitive technical stages. Automated arms used in factories all over the world were still jerky mechanized contraptions with none of the fluidity of the real thing. When JakobJoel heard the graduate students refer to Cog as a toddler, he thought the word was used to justify everything that she was still unable to do. She had yet to learn the most basic tasks. This week JakobJoel's assignment was to touch something on his face, his nose or eyes or lips, and ask Cog to imitate him. The reasoning behind this exercise, according to his assignment sheet, was that the human intellectual experience is bound up in its physical one, that without knowing how to move in space, there can't be true intelligence, artificial or otherwise.

But was this entirely true? JakobJoel wondered.

In any case, Cog was in the process of learning how to move her arm through space and find her own nose. First she had to be programmed to register the gesture with her camera eyes, match the human hand to her own extremity, move it in a controlled manner to her face, and so on. The smallest physical movement, when broken down for analysis, revealed multitudinous faculties required to perform it. It was impossible not to pause and admire the high intelligence that might have made man.

Of course his uncle had something to say on this subject.

High intelligence, Creator, God, call Him/It/She what you will, his uncle said, it's His felt presence that matters.

If He's a real presence, JakobJoel replied, why doesn't He reveal himself? Why does He allow everything, nature, for example, to seem so natural?

But you could also say He reveals himself daily, his uncle argued. Your perception and admiration of creation, even if momentary and passing, is a kind of revelation.

It's too hidden and mysterious, JakobJoel said. Besides, how or whom does the acknowledgment of a higher being benefit? What good really is admiration?

On the MIT campus, populated as it was with some of the most brilliant minds—brilliant enough to humble a Talmudic mind considered one of the geniuses of Berditchev—JakobJoel found himself compelled to gawk and admire. And what did gawking do for him? It left him dissatisfied with his own mental powers, doubtful of achievement, disabled, in bondage to what he admired. Therefore he wondered: Was the purpose of revelation simply a way of keeping humans in bondage to God?

For once his uncle didn't have an answer.

Working with Cog was slow. She understood that she was being asked to match or imitate the gesture, the way children do; she registered the gesture with her camera eyes, but these eyes, set to look outward, were of no use to her in the map of her own face. The scale between a human face and Cog's was approximately one to three, Jakob-Joel calculated, but approximation wouldn't help her. She needed an accurate mathematical equation with which to figure the location of her own nose.

When JakobJoel suggested this to the grad student who happened to be there that day, engaged in building Kismet, the next-generation robot, Rex became irritable. You weren't hired for your mathematical genius, he said. If you must know, we thought you might be useful to us in dealing with Professor Droer.

Sarah Droer was a theologian and computer scientist brought in by someone outside the robotics group, a wealthy alumnus from the divinity school, who had an idea that a theologian would raise questions about artificial intelligence that scientists would not. Ever since she'd come on board, she was getting all the media attention and for work she hadn't done. When JakobJoel's application arrived along with hundreds of others, his Talmudic background was noted, and on someone's foolish suggestion a decision was made to counter Droer with their own in-house rabbi. Of course, this had nothing to do with the real work at hand.

JakobJoel spent half an hour processing this new bit of information: He'd been hired not for his grades, or for his keen interest in science, or even for his award-winning Westinghouse Science project. This wasn't the first time his religious education had helped him in this institution. In his essay application he'd suggested that his interest in science was a result of having grown up with so much that wasn't based in fact, with a way of life that was based on faith in God, whose existence despite thousands of years of intense Talmudic scholarship remained impossible to prove. And it was this religious background that had separated him from the pack. Ironic, perhaps, but understandable, he now realized. On paper MIT freshmen all seem alike, clones really. Trekkies, fans of Isaac Asimov, avid readers of *Wired* and Stephen Hawking, with excellent SAT scores.

He'd had enough for one day.

Outside it was dark and he debated whether to walk home for dinner or go directly to the computer lab at the Athena Cluster, where he could begin working on the sharing system. If he arrived too late for dinner with his housemates, he would eat cold leftovers. Also he would miss the half hour before dinner, when they were all in the kitchen, a kind of family. Living with these people for an extended period, he'd become part of something larger and liked it. On the other hand, if he went home now, he wouldn't relish crossing the river again later, when the wind was stronger and colder. On a bicycle the trip was fast if not pain-less, but his bicycle had been stolen the previous semester. JakobJoel stood with his backpack on his back, debating, then turned toward the warmth of home. He needed a break. He would try borrowing Rick's bicycle. If that didn't work, he would catch up on textbook reading, and work at Athena the next day.

Decision made, JakobJoel set out to follow through. One thing he'd learned: Too much debate about minor things costs too much time, and the rewards were too small. He saved indecision for larger issues.

He put on his headphones and listened to Air, which he'd down-loaded the night before, on Julia's recommendation. And the synthe-sized sounds and sound effects were cool. That was the way to describe Julia, JakobJoel mused: Cool. With that breezy quality he'd encountered in all the Californians he'd known, admittedly not many. If not for Julia's partial Asian background, JakobJoel thought, she might have appeared too standard for his taste. He was drawn to students with mixed back-grounds probably because he himself wasn't so all-American. MIT, unlike Harvard, for example, populated as it was with people from dif-

ferent places, had turned out to be a good fit for him. Everyone on campus was slightly odd. Oddity was the norm. Rockland High had also
been a mixed group, and he'd liked that. It was where he'd met Ludmilla,
whose family had emigrated from Russia. When he visited one night for
dinner, Ludmilla and her siblings gave a mini-concert, with Ludmilla at
the piano, her younger sister on the violin, and her brother on bass.
JakobJoel had been impressed. After he heard her play with the school
orchestra, he decided to learn an instrument, and she had helped him
select the trumpet. In the end, though, Ludmilla had decided to major in
science rather than music, JakobJoel still wasn't sure why; she applied
and was accepted at MIT.

The wind was at his back now and he felt himself buoyant, feather-
like—a strange, even pleasant sensation. He was flying home. His size
was another thing he was comfortable with at MIT. At yeshiva, where
most of the boys were shorter, he'd catch himself stooping, a giant
amongst Lilliputians. At Rockland, there were students and faculty
members taller than he. He'd noticed that shorter people responded to
height with what seemed a touch of awe; the physical adjustment they
had to make to look up took on the meaning of being looked up to. He
thought of short Ludmilla, and acknowledged that the principle that
governed those looking up also worked in reverse: having to look down
at Ludmilla, he'd expected something childlike. He'd loved her cute-
ness. This year she was a freshman at MIT, and though they were no
longer going out, he saw her now and then, and always stopped to say
hi. And he thought of her quite often. More than a year after he'd held
her the last time, he could still feel her diminutive body tucking into his
and remember the pleasure it had provided. She would hold the place of
first girlfriend forever. He'd loved the way she'd stood in front of him on
tiptoe and arched her back and neck to look into his eyes. She'd had no
choice, she was five feet one, but it wasn't just a matter of height. Her

body seemed to know to give him pleasure, without doing much at all. Somehow women knew what men liked without being told. He was quite certain this was a subconscious knowledge, instinctive. If Ludmilla had faked it, JakobJoel felt certain he would have known. Such responses came naturally to her only when she felt a certain way. And still he'd grown bored. He'd loved their first days, the process of getting to know her, and then the possibility of variations on this experience began to appeal. Each one would be different, yet similar also. He knew Ludmilla well enough to know she wouldn't like his desire for variety and it had taken him a while to gather the courage to tell her. During one of their late-night telephone conversations, he suggested that it would be better for them to begin the next year uncommitted. We'll be living in different cities, going to different schools, he said. Meeting new people. I think we should both be open to new things. Next year, when you leave for college, you'll want that, too.

But if I get into MIT, Ludmilla argued, we'll be separated for only a year. And we'll see each other when you come home and I can visit you.

He didn't tell her that he wished she would apply elsewhere. He thought her determination to apply to MIT, even to major in science rather than music, had begun with her desire to be near him, but if Ludmilla said she wanted to study science at MIT, who was he to tell her not to. She had been a good, encouraging friend; she'd believed in him, celebrated with him. When in her senior year she was working on her own Westinghouse Science project and he was already at MIT, he'd wanted to support her.

Ludmilla cried. Hung up. Called back. And cried more. This was how it felt to be heartbroken. It was true that men always broke your heart.

She was experiencing her first pain in love, and JakobJoel was the boy who'd provided it. He didn't like being the one, but finally he merely shrugged. It had to be someone. And even in this, the breakup, there was much to learn. Her sobbing elicited the guilt he was meant to feel. On the subject of guilt, he felt himself experienced. It would have been

impossible to grow up as he did, to leave tradition for a modern education in science, to go from Berditchev to public school and then to MIT,
without knowing that his choices had caused suffering.

After two days of crying, Ludmilla had turned angry and refused to
talk. When he called, she wouldn't come to the telephone. He'd read
that there were preset and named stages for everything, and without
having endured a breakup before, without having any previous experience in the stages, Ludmilla suffered through every one. She was a natural in suffering, too.

Cog, if and when fully realized, would be different, JakobJoel mused.
As a machine, she could give equal attention to every act, which meant
that even suffering would be a contemplated emotion. She would calcu-
late that it was now appropriate to suffer, look up the algorithm on suffering, and find that there were twelve stages of mourning, each one
requiring a decent interval of time. She would adjust her eyes and mouth
to give herself the facial expression suitable for each stage. And she
would know in advance the human reaction to the expression. And so
on. Since all of this was programmed, therefore non-instinctive, since
every manifestation of mood and response was artificial, Cog would
always seem a touch manipulative, a bit evil. There were ways around it.
Programmers had given her variations on every mood's manifestation,
but these variations were finite, and the camouflage worked only for
those who were new to Cog and didn't know better.

One inhuman aspect of Cog was enviable: She would never experience a day, an hour, not even a moment of pain or self-doubt.

It occurred to JakobJoel that in the next meeting he ought to point
out that they all referred to Cog as female, and that although the decision regarding her gender had never been discussed, if the goal was to
make her seem just helpless enough to elicit sympathy, it had to be
admitted that making her a girl was the right choice. Five minutes later,
JakobJoel reconsidered his ideas about the female from the point of view
of the two females in the group, and understood that such a comment

would be insulting. Then he asked himself whether this wasn't a perfect example of how intuitive thinking is compromised by overthinking, an ostensible human advantage turned to disadvantage. Sometimes unsympathetic inhuman decision-making could be useful.

At home, he found a message on his machine from his mother. They spoke once a week. Ada always asked for details. She wanted to know what he was learning, what ideas he was forming. JakobJoel understood that his mother's interest in the details of his life was at least in part the way she kept track of his state of mind, religious and otherwise. Often, she'd have a response to something they'd discussed the previous week, as if she'd been processing the information. In this she resembled Cog, who sometimes took several long seconds to respond to his prompt. He would tell her that she shared a behavioral characteristic with a robot. Of course, JakobJoel knew that her delayed responses were a result of a conversation she'd had with his father, who didn't talk on the telephone. It was always his mother who provided him with family news. The health of the Berditchever. The pace of his father's work, the book he was working on, an encyclopedic gathering of commentaries on a particular subject or idea or law that interested him, and the conclusions drawn from the varied sources.

JakobJoel welcomed news of Aaron. His gentle father's pained silence in the face of his son's pursuit of an education in science saddened him. But the silence had also made it possible. Aaron didn't argue against it. He presented a resigned demeanor, a kind of admission up front that nothing he could say or do would change anything. Regrettably, Jakob-Joel's choice of a life in science stood as a critique of his father's exegetical work and, though unintended, would remain forever as a wall between them.

His father, JakobJoel knew, received from Ada a full replay of what was said, with the details that might disturb elided. In turn, he received an edited version of his father's responses. His mother performed this role as mediator and go-between with seeming ease, taking everything in stride. She was amazing. All women, JakobJoel thought, were amazing. Like men, they fulfilled their tasks and jobs; unlike men, they also made the world go around, tending to everyone's feelings, providing words of comfort as needed, talking, scolding, encouraging, all while getting their own work done, and also putting dinner on the table. But apparent ease didn't mean that the tasks themselves were always easy. His mother, JakobJoel knew, had experienced a terrible year. A month after his birth, they had moved back into his grandparents' home because Ada was unable to get out of bed and someone had to take care of the newborn. The pattern-making business was put on hold, the apartment newly furnished for the young couple was sublet.

Ada's condition was identified as deep postpartum depression, but it was understood by those closest to her that she was mourning her brother. They lived in the Jakob household for almost a year. Ada and Aaron slept in Ada's old room. His uncle Joel's room, which might have remained an untouched shrine otherwise, was quickly transformed into a baby room, with appropriately enough, the alphabet on the walls. JakobJoel lived his first year in the care of four adults, every one of whom was in mourning. In the end it was his grandmother who pulled through as primary caregiver. And R. Moshele became the one who brought in a daily draft of fresh air, and for whom JakobJoel performed. For his twinkling, hazel-eyed grandfather, JakobJoel took his first steps, spoke his first words. In the meantime Ada and Aaron missed Joel terribly and struggled with their own and each other's grief. Then, suddenly, days before the anniversary of Joel's death, Ada arose one morning with renewed strength and determination. A week later the young family was readjusting to life in a small apartment, and Ada and her friend Malke were back at work as designer and pattern maker; Mrs. Jakob agreed to serve as sales and office manager. Within two years, Ada and Aaron purchased a house on a corner lot in the neighborhood and threw themselves into its redesign and renovation. One thing didn't change: No one wanted Ada to risk another bout with postpartum depression, and JakobJoel remained an only child.

Smells from the kitchen wafted up to his room. JakobJoel looked at his watch. He would call Ada after dinner. Downstairs, Kimee was cooking with Fred's help. Elena was also there, setting the table. Kimee and Fred often chose kitchen duty as a way to fulfill their house hours. They said they enjoyed it. Elena pitched in when she had time, as he did. Jakob-Joel knew too little about cooking to attempt it for the group; his position as house treasurer qualified as a household chore, and he put in an additional two hours in cleanup duty twice a week to satisfy the hours required of every resident. This year there were twelve residents, and though the new ones understood the concept of a cooperative house, they weren't as committed to the community as the previous year's group had been. JakobJoel missed the companionship of last year's housemates, in particular those who had graduated. The older residents had always done more than their share. On or off duty, they pitched in if only to get dinner on the table sooner. In time, the new residents might become more generous, but right now they didn't even always arrive at the dinner hour. When they did show up, they didn't stick around. If it wasn't their night for cleanup, they didn't do much more than remove their own plates.

As soon as Kimee saw him, she said, You're just in time. Could you rinse the lettuce and tear the leaves into medium-size pieces, smaller than the last time and larger than the previous one?

JakobJoel laughed. Anyone tell you you're a taskmaster? What are we having for dinner?

Wednesday is spaghetti day, Fred chanted.

I know, but what kind? JakobJoel wanted to know.

Red meat sauce, Kimee said. I'd planned on meatballs, but didn't have enough time.

As long as there's meat, JakobJoel said. I could eat a cow. I've been hungry all day. Actually since yesterday.

We had fish yesterday. Oh, right. You don't like fish.

JakobJoel took the spinner into the pantry to the extra sink, ran cold water on the lettuce, drained it, and spun. He liked the contraption. His mother didn't use one because it bruised the lettuce, she said. Her lettuce leaves air-dried on a towel.

In the dining room, some of the others had gathered. Greg was pouring water into glasses. One of the new people hovered, not knowing where he belonged, and JakobJoel said, How's it going?

He made a point of being nice to new house members. It was only a year ago that he himself had been new, and it wasn't easy to live surrounded by new people twenty-four hours a day, with no one you'd known longer than a month. What had helped him was to concentrate on the work, and there was always enough of that. Social life eventually took care of itself.

Julia arrived and thanked JakobJoel for his help with her math problem. For the first time, she said, I understood what was going on in class today.

She wore blue jeans as usual, everyone wore blue jeans, but her tops were never plain T-shirts. They had drawings or ruffles or fringe. And they were always tiny. When she moved, JakobJoel could see slices of smooth belly or back. Sometimes her belly ring was exposed. Ludmilla had always worn baggy pants and baggy shirts, her hip-hop Brooklyn look, and he'd liked that, too. Whenever he'd hugged her, her diminutive body beneath all that fabric had been a pleasant surprise.

JakobJoel was relieved that Ludmilla didn't attempt to move into his house. She was living in the famous and infamously dilapidated Mies van der Rohe house that Ada had recommended when he was trying to decide where to live. It was a groundbreaking design in its time, Ada had said.

But when JakobJoel toured it during his campus visit, and noted the dingy hallways and rooms, the decrepit windows, he decided against it.

Design, he called home to say, can be admired from outside. I don't have to live in it.

Even over the telephone he could feel his mother shaking her head, thinking: Youth has no respect for greatness, but maybe that's what makes them fearless in their own pursuits. Besides, Ada thought, irreverence in the face of genius was probably a sign of psychological health. She was glad her son hadn't inherited Joel's intensities, his extremism. He was a being who tended to swim with rather than against the current of life. And he had accepted her advice on the wall art in his room. The university offered on loan to incoming students a work of art, and after consulting with his mother, JakobJoel requested a black-and-white Cartier-Bresson photograph.

The humanity of these loans impressed Ada. The university didn't just cram their students full of science, they nurtured them also with art. MIT students might go to sleep with overworked minds but they also awoke to the product of excellence.

At dinner Julia sat beside him, and JakobJoel ate less than usual. She replaced his appetite with something else. He couldn't help himself. With Julia, you sort of knew without really knowing how she would look underneath. She dressed like a woman, though not a grown-up one. She wore colors, pinks and reds and yellows and greens. And always jeans. Always sitting low on her hips, which was how he knew her skin was smooth and tan. And she seemed to like him. JakobJoel liked her, too, but told himself sternly that it wasn't fair to start anything with a freshman. Besides, he didn't want a girlfriend. They were both too busy for dating anyway. And she lived in his house. It would be much too complicated. They ought to just be friends. And yet, minutes later, he found himself asking her whether she wanted to go with him to the *A.I.* preview and promo party. Announcements had been posted all over campus.

Elena and Rick said they were going.

I love Kubrick, Julia said. I've seen *2001* about two thousand times. And I know that Kubrick started the project, but Spielberg finished it, and I detest Spielberg. When is it? she asked.

This Friday night, JakobJoel said. It's sponsored by the lab, but paid for by the film studio, so the food might be decent.

In his room, JakobJoel asked himself what he'd done. If he started taking Julia out, Ludmilla was certain to hear about it or see them, and she'd feel hurt. Even if that weren't an issue, and it shouldn't be, he ought to know better than to start something. But whenever his critical brain questioned his behavior, another part of him rejoiced. He wasted fifteen minutes thinking about Julia, about how she knew and wasn't shy about saying what she liked, which he liked about her. Then he looked at his watch, and calculated. *The Simpsons* was on in five minutes. He had done no work all evening, and he hadn't yet called home. It would be a late night. But first *The Simpsons*.

The regulars were already gathered. *The Nanny* was just finishing and no one was listening. JakobJoel took his seat on the rug in front of the television. If you sat on the sofa or chairs, beside the others, there was a good chance you would miss the best lines because someone would be talking or laughing, and Simpson lines lost their humor exponentially in retelling. If it was a rerun he would skip it and use the time to call his mother, unless it was a rerun of one of the better episodes.

Rick and Elena were bickering for legroom on the sofa, and JakobJoel interrupted—stop, you two. Hey, Rick, are you using your bicycle tonight?

Nope, I'm stuck for the night with statistics.

I need to work at Athena.

You can use it until eight A.M. tomorrow. I have an eight-thirty class.

Elena poked Rick affectionately with her toe. Genius, she said, he'll be home before eight A.M.

At this rate, definitely A.M., hopefully before two, JakobJoel said.

Erica, Pam, then Julia entered and JakobJoel found himself hoping that Julia would sit beside him on the floor and was disappointed when she didn't, even though she was near enough that he could reach out and touch her toes. A year ago, almost everyone in the house gathered every Monday, Tuesday, and Thursday to watch *The Simpsons*. Even those who didn't make it in time for dinner were usually in the parlor by eight. This year, several of the residents had small televisions in their own rooms and stayed there.

In his room alone again, JakobJoel warned himself not to start anything with Julia if he wanted to avoid the inevitable breakup. And it was inevitable, he told himself. They couldn't be expected to stay together at their age, and as exciting as the beginning would be, the end would be devastating, especially for her. He didn't want that kind of responsibility. He exhaled. He had to admit that ending the relationship with Ludmilla had been stressful. He was glad they were friends again, if distant ones.

He called home. Rather than work his way around to Julia, like the mature person he was becoming, he simply blurted it out.

I think I just made a mistake. I invited Julia to go with me to a screening.

Why is it a mistake? Ada asked, quickly coming to her son's defense. If you deny yourself female friendship you'll miss out on half the population, she pointed out sensibly. Besides, self-denial usually results in something worse. There's nothing wrong with taking a friend to the party, as long as you leave it at that. Have a good time without complicating the situation. She might think she's in love with you, and you also will feel pleasure in the sensation, but you don't have to fall in love in return.

That's good advice, Mother, JakobJoel said, and smiled. He'd started to call her Mother when Mama seemed too infantile and Ma too abbreviated. She was cool. He'd once overheard her telling another mother that she wanted to be a mother whose son was comfortable telling her everything. And it was true. He wasn't afraid to tell her things. His first semester, when for the first time in his life he realized there were minds more brilliant than his, he called home in despair.

How smart? an incredulous Ada asked. It wasn't only as a mother that Ada thought her son as brilliant as any mother could want. Her brother, Joel, had been considered a genius, but he'd had an impractical edge; though she'd loved Joel for his singularity, it had led to death. Unlike Joel, JakobJoel combined the brains that made him a remarkable student with a healthy intolerance for nonsense. He was a born skeptic, and though characteristic disbelief doesn't lend itself to religious faith and even stirred up some trouble at Berditchev, she had taken care to encourage the tendency. Even after one of JakobJoel's teachers had called a meeting to discuss the boy's freethinking inclination, Ada had continued to support it.

So smart, JakobJoel answered, they can't walk straight.

That's your strength then, his mother said. I, for one, would rather have a son who doesn't walk into trees, who relates to others, who knows how to live. Social skills are important for survival. You work well with others, which makes you more employable.

About your job as treasurer, Ada said, your father and I have been thinking about it, and it seems to us not the ideal position to be in as a Jew among non-Jews. I know that this is a different era, that we're not living in anti-Semitic Europe, but human nature hasn't changed. People are strangely touchy when it comes to money, and to be in the position of handling others' finances is never a good thing. It would take only one student to say one thing, and that would be enough to cast aspersions. If it's too late to turn down the position this semester, certainly reconsider for next.

It is too late, JakobJoel said. I told you about this treasurer position two weeks ago. I meant to tell you, Mother. You and Cog have something in common. Delayed reactions.

Ada laughed.

JakobJoel asked about business. She'd recently expanded to include children's styles and also patterns for the larger woman, and she'd hired two office assistants to help Mrs. Jakob, who continued to work as office manager.

It's busy, Ada said, too busy, but that's good, because otherwise I couldn't justify the additional salaries.

How is Zeide? JakobJoel asked, referring to his grandfather, R. Moshele.

Well, but growing older, slower, Ada said. Call him. He always enjoys talking with you.

For the *A.I.* preview and panel discussion, Julia wore what she usually wore, jeans, but paired with high heels and a sparkly red top. With three inches added, she came up to JakobJoel's upper chest, and he wondered how it would feel to kiss her. He wouldn't have to bend down far and she wouldn't have to stand on tiptoe. She would be grounded and balanced on her own feet, if anyone can be balanced on heels. Given her shoes, she walked relatively well. When he said this aloud, she laughed.

I can run quite fast in heels, she said. It just takes getting used to.

They took the bus across the Charles to campus and then walked to the conference center, where the event would be held. They got in what they thought was the end of a long line, but then it grew longer, and only minutes later they were approximately at the halfway point. The doors aren't open to students yet, they were informed, but JakobJoel noted that for the press, the doors were very open.

When it was almost seven—according to the posters, the film was scheduled to begin at seven—and there was no sign of anything changing, the students started banging on the door. Someone came out to see what was wanted, and after whispered consultations, and much entering and exiting through the barred entrance, returned to inform them that the film wouldn't begin until seven-thirty.

More reporters arrived with cameras and recorders and were rushed through a side door. Outside there was much grumbling. When seven-thirty came and went and the doors remained shut, students started threatening. In response, the gatekeeper indicated that it wasn't at all definite that students would be allowed to enter. If there's room, perhaps some of you will get in, he said.

Your attitude is insulting, someone shouted. This happens to be our campus and our home, someone else said. You are merely visitors.

This behavior is disrespectful, someone with an enviably loud voice roared. You advertised and we came, stood in line. You have absolutely no right to be wasting our time. We have work to do. Important work.

It's too disgusting, Julia said. They're obviously using MIT merely as a way to promote their film. Spielberg has no interest in MIT's population, the people who actually work in AI.

JakobJoel agreed. He'd heard a rumor that Spielberg wasn't even showing up.

Suddenly, though, the doors did open and the students were directed to the upper half of the auditorium. They found seats in the dark and then the trailer for the movie came up. After that they were shown a video in which Steven Spielberg spoke of MIT's significance. Finally it seemed the movie would start, and JakobJoel settled into his seat, and felt Julia relax in hers. A scene in which a scientist discusses what he calls his idea to create an android capable of emoting was shown; then the reel was stopped.

Students booed, and were hushed as a panel of experts took their seats onstage to discuss ethical questions raised by artificial intelligence—one scientist referred to it, surprisingly, Joel thought, as machine religion— issues such as machine rights, the ethics of enslavement, whether programming is a variation of brainwashing, none of which covered anything MIT students hadn't heard before. The screening was resumed and continued to the end, uninterrupted. Then the producer and the actor Haley Joel Osment, young David Swinton in the movie, went onstage to take questions from the audience, most of them from the press. One student persisted and was finally passed the microphone.

I want to know, he asked, why Hollywood reverts to the same pattern, makes the same stupid movie over and over, all with robots who grow touchy-feely and fucking human, who desire nothing so much as to find their place in society. He listed so many titles, the audience laughed. Even, he went on, when a sci-fi movie does have some ideas in it, as in *The Matrix*, it quickly descends into an action film filled with cool special effects—not that I mind action and pyrotechnics, but still, it's a cop-out.

An MIT professor pulled the microphone away from the student and said: Welcome to MIT.

Along with a group of others, JakobJoel and Julia stopped for pizza, and continued deriding Steven Spielberg late into the night. Then someone suggested going home to watch 2001, but by the time they arrived home, they were too tired. They said good night, Julia with her shoes in one hand and a blown kiss for JakobJoel in the other, and parted.

JakobJoel dropped onto his bed in his clothes. Despite the disappointment of the event itself, the evening had been worthwhile. Sometimes a flop was more of an experience than a success. He'd enjoyed standing and sitting beside Julia, grumbling in line. And the question-and-answer period. Osment's answers, which suffered—JakobJoel smiled at this idea—from Cog's problem: they were thoughtful and succinct, and not spontaneous. Of course, he was about ten or so, a kid; still it was obvious that he'd been coached. He'd memorized a set of answers, and during interviews his brain simply searched to find which one fit the context of any given question. This was a good example of case-based reasoning, the human mind working like a machine, and it was quite common. At any party or social situation, there was always one person who hardly listens to what's said before he responds with a this-reminds-me-of and launches into a story. If you meet that person at more than one party, you soon realize that he has a given set of stories to tell and that's what he does, that he is merely a storytelling machine. The problem: Such a person isn't using his intelligence, merely his storage facility, which machines can also do, and which is the way AI works. Which was interesting. Would Osment realize that he was behaving machinelike in life, not just on screen? That might have been a good question. But already JakobJoel could think of the possible pre-stored answers. Osment could say that this was a successful example of how actors enter into and become their characters. Of course, he was only a ten-year-old and the question might have been lost on him.

On the sameness of Hollywood plots, JakobJoel wasn't certain he entirely agreed with the criticism but it was something to think about. For one thing, there was always the contrast between the emotional machine and the rational scientists who create them. In 2001, only HAL allows his emotions to run rampant. But why would super-rational scientists build an emotional computer? For JakobJoel, as for all sci-fi fans, Star Trek's Mr. Spock and Data were the unemotional patron saints of computer scientists. Though Spock and Data both recognize their emotional incapacity as a shortcoming, JakobJoel thought, they also know that they're valuable to the Enterprise precisely because of it. It should be possible to develop a plot without engaging emotions and needs. Cog could be coldly ambitious, for example. Without self-doubt or self-questioning, since a machine doesn't suffer these emotions, without the usual human-style indecision and delay, she'd march straight toward her goals. She'd know that her memory and computational abilities exceed human capacities, that in this she resembles God. To give herself the full stature of a god she'd go on a mission to acquire all knowledge. And the motive? Omniscience and omnipresence. To remain, like a god, forever extant. But did this desire to be a god already make her too human? Besides, coldly ambitious celluloid androids were plentiful. *The Matrix* and *The Terminator, Terminator* 2 and 3, and so on.

There is nothing new under the sun, his uncle Joel intoned, using the traditional chant of Ecclesiastes.

JakobJoel shut his uncle out and continued. Cog would observe that although she was God-like, she was not yet God. In order to be God, a good number of humans would have to be convinced of her divinity. Thinking like a machine, Cog would follow the logical step-by-step process to achieve her goal. She would study various Creation myths, *The Epic of Gilgamesh,* the *Mahabharata,* the Hawaiian *Kumulipo,* the *Lord Song* of the Bhils of Central India, and the Judaic Genesis.

It would occur to Cog that if to be a god, one depends on human faith, then perhaps humans, not gods, are the highest beings in the world. She would wonder why the highest beings would have the need to create someone above themselves. It indicated an inferiority, some deep insecurity. To better understand human psychology, Cog would assign herself a course in the human psyche. She would read books on psychology, process the information, and confirm her initial diagnosis: the presence in humans of an insecurity that manifests itself in various ways, therefore not simple to recognize or categorize. She would learn that there are only a handful of superhumans—Nietzsche, for example—who made a great point of not believing in God, but that such unbelievers were in the minority.

JakobJoel became aware that he was composing a heretical being, but Cog was a machine, not an emotional human. This shortcoming, Jakob-

Joel mused, her inability to be weakly human, could somehow lead to the end. But how?

He paused to consider the originality of this plot. Despite good intentions, he'd fallen into the Hollywood trap. He'd eliminated the robot's desire to be a man among men, or person among persons, he corrected himself, only to fall back into it. In the end, Cog came around to the same old thing.

Originality. Of course his uncle Joel had something to say on the subject:

After Creation, he pointed out, no creator is original. To attempt originality is to enter into competition with God. Merely to create the not-new, the Lurianic breaking of the vessel is required; in other words, a breakdown of the perfection that has been, so that one may put the shards back together. Since the shards are reused, everything new is based on what came before.

And he quoted Nachman saying about himself that "never has there been such a novelty as I."

Originality, JakobJoel understood, is every creator's first anxiety. Nachman's statement was the best indication that it had been a concern. And that Joel quoted Nachman was also revealing. His uncle must have been anxious about his own ingenuity. Like many young hopefuls, he'd hoped to absorb something through proximity, as if creative capacity could rub off. Always a mistake, JakobJoel told himself. Meeting famous men could lead only to nothing. It was never the creator himself who was great, but rather the creation, therefore learning could only happen through study. And of course in the process of creating. JakobJoel paused. Would his uncle have anything to say about this?

For once there was no response. Or, rather, silence was the response. But silence was difficult to interpret. It could mean one of many things. His uncle could be regretting his early naiveté. He could be considering the possibility that it was the created world that was great, not God, the

Creator. Or he could be attempting his own version of the Kabbalistic withdrawal to see what it would produce, attempting to prove the usefulness of his presence via absence, a way to inspire his nephew's appreciation. And it worked. JakobJoel missed Joel's close attendance.

Before dinner the next evening, JakobJoel told Julia about his attempt at a non-Hollywood plot.

I can see why filmmakers fall into the trap every time, he explained. No robot story can completely avoid it. It has something to do with the nature of a plot, which is a story complete with a crisis that leads to success or failure, which is a rise or fall, a happy or tragic ending, which means it's entirely unmachinelike, since machines don't emote.

If you write the plot, Julia said, we can analyze it to see where Cog goes Hollywood. Maybe originality in a story isn't in what happens so much as how it gets there. At least your Cog wants to become a god, which is better than wanting to be a sappy human, like Osment. What I don't get is why Cog decides that man is greater than God and how this leads to what you're calling her fall. And why does every story have to have one?

You didn't understand it because I was summarizing too much, JakobJoel said. He took a deep breath. Cog knows she's man-made; she also knows that to be a god she must somehow rise above her makers, achieve something greater. She understands that to be greater than another being requires knowing that being better than it knows itself. One way or another, she would have to become the greatest human, a superhuman.

Cog quickly wades through courses in psychology and biology, history and biography. She reads about the lives of generals and kings, of saviors and messiahs, and has difficulty choosing the world's greatest man. She considers Alexander the Great, Augustus, Napoleon, Jesus

Christ and Shabbatai Zevi. She might consider the Ba'al Shem Tov and his messianic grandson, Nachman of Bratslav. She changes direction and looks at philosophers and scientists: Aristotle, Galileo, and Newton. Albert Einstein and Marie Curie. She thinks Leonardo da Vinci might have been the world's greatest genius. She reads up on Nietzsche and Freud, rates Mary Shelley, the creator of Frankenstein, as one of the greats. She changes direction again and considers Bach, Mozart, Beethoven. She finds she likes music, but not emotionally, not the way Frankenstein enjoyed it. When Cog listens to music, she bases her judgment of a piece on the complexity of the physics in the work, not the melody it forms. The melody to her is insignificant. Her brain doesn't respond to it. She decides finally that there were many great humans, but however admirable they were, each was great in only a limited area of knowledge. Humans have the capacity for greatness in one or two particular areas; they can be only local experts. Often enough genius in humans originates in a physical or emotional deficiency elsewhere. Short life spans and a regular need for rest also limit the human ability to receive data. Cog understands that an unlimited capacity for information is her strength. And since she is free of time, she can acquire all knowledge. She has already covered much ground and plans to continue.

JakobJoel paused to see whether Julia was still with him. She was looking at his face, nodding, as if transfixed. He was impressing himself, too, composing as he went, and delighting in it. He didn't want to stop. He was creating as he talked. He rushed on, elaborating.

Since Cog is a machine, she doesn't ever give up. There's always more to know. Just reading all the newspapers every day is consuming. And then there are texts and journals and so on. All her functions are subsumed by this task of knowing.

Julia nodded excitedly. The challenge will be to make the end unlike anything else. No chase scenes and deaths, no tremendous conflagration. You'll have to come up with something quiet and disappointing.

It may be too quiet and disappointing, JakobJoel said. For the audience anyway. Cog will be working on this project of knowing forevermore. The story ends with Cog's circuits continuously in operation, and as we know, there's nothing dramatic about accumulating knowledge. On film you'd simply see the light on the machine blinking, but it would keep going and going until the audience, bored and tired, would walk out on the story, realizing that Cog will continue into infinity. Someone might suggest that unplugging Cog would be a merciful act, but then one of her off-site backups would take over and continue her work. It's potentially a story without an end.

Interesting, Julia said. The nonending makes it profound. And humans can relate to Cog thematically. For example, when we become too obsessed with one thing, we lose ourselves as humans. I know when I get like that, it's as if I'm wearing blinders. But also, seeing the use Cog makes of her immortality, humans might wonder whether mortality might be preferable despite the tragedy of death. The story could make us rethink our attempts to escape temporality. You could try to sell this as a screenplay, Julia said, but not to Spielberg. He would turn Cog into a sobbing nincompoop. And the ending would be some overheated form of a giant meltdown. Here is the headline I, for one, would like to see: MIT robotics student writes non-Hollywood script and sells it for a six-figure advance.

And gets himself thrown out of school for falling behind in his work, JakobJoel said. Since I'm not Cog, I'm behind in my reading. And besides, I didn't come to MIT to write stories. You could say I came here to avoid storytelling.

Oh, everyone at MIT is behind, Julia said. It's our existential state, scrambling to catch up, and always falling farther behind. The MIT experience is the ultimate paradigm of the post-Edenic human condition, because we're on limited time. Unlike Cog. Did I just say that? Julia asked, and spun on her toes, a 360-degree pirouette. I'm impressing myself. That's what I love about you. You make me feel smarter somehow.

She came off her toes and became serious again.

You know, from Cog's point of view there's no such thing as a fall because she isn't human; she exists outside human limitations. Only mortals think in terms of rise and fall.

JakobJoel laughed. She was on a roll. At this moment, he loved Julia for her mind. She was not only pretty, but wonderfully, articulately smart. An unbeatable combination, he thought.

They sat across from each other at dinner and Julia told the others about Cog.

There's your future, Rick said with his mouth full. MIT robotics major shows Hollywood how it ought to done.

Elena looked at JakobJoel and shrugged. Sorry to be a downer, but I'm willing to bet that half the MIT student body has a robot script in their files. Besides, have you read *Galatea 2.2*? Your Cog sounds more than a little like her. Maybe also a little like Neo in *The Matrix*.

I read *Galatea*, Julia said. I can see why you'd think her similar, especially since they're both female. But Helen the cyber-student knows only one subject: English literature. And she's not self-propelled like Cog. The driving force behind her is an unhappy former professor/writer. He's programming Helen to somehow compete in the GRE exam against this student he loved. I don't recall all the details, but the story is about this professor, and the relationship he forms with Helen, who becomes a substitute for the other woman. Now that I think about it, I might add that because his relationship with a flesh-and-blood woman was too difficult, he made himself a cyber woman whom he could more easily control.

You know, JakobJoel said, if it's true that half of MIT's students have scripts in their drawers, then there's a strange contradiction going on. Because if we're all here to learn the facts of science but what we really want to do is write fiction, well, I don't know what that says about us or about MIT.

Says nothing, Rick said. Contradiction is perfectly normal.

You know, this isn't even about a script. Anyone can do that, Julia said, but not everyone is capable of something unusual enough to succeed.

Not true again, Rick said. Based on the work that succeeds in the world, it's clear that the best doesn't make it. It's persistence, the big P, that achieves success.

There won't be a script. It was an amusing mind exercise, JakobJoel said. I happen to hate writing. And now I'm gone. I've got work to do.

You'll miss *The Simpsons*, Elena said. That'll be a first.

You could record it for me, JakobJoel said with a winning smile.

Wait a minute, Rick said. My mom works as an agent, not in film, but she knows people who do. Let's send her your script for the fun of it. Just to see what happens.

But first JakobJoel has to write it, Julia said. It's all still in his head.

Here's some advice from a self-help book, Rick offered. You have to get it down before you lose the urgency. And you need the big P—persistence.

I can't write, JakobJoel said.

We'll help, Julia said. It can be a kind of house project. We'll act as your editors.

JakobJoel pushed his chair back. I'm leaving now, before I don't want to.

At Athena, it was some time before he settled in to work. He greeted and was greeted. He answered questions. No matter what time he arrived at the lab, it was crowded and buzzing. And there were always freshmen with programming questions. Occasionally there was a programming problem, some fatal error that had stumped everyone, and when you walked through the door, you were considered a fresh mind with a better chance of solving it. Presented with such a challenge, JakobJoel couldn't help himself. He blew an hour or more sometimes, but it was always worthwhile, especially when he found the solution and became hero of the week. When he felt himself a hero capable of anything, his own work seemed to write itself.

Three hours later, he was deep into his project, with no thought of anything else. This was his mind at its best, completely focused, refusing to be distracted. At such times, he felt that if he could maintain this optimal state for seventy-five percent of any given day, he would succeed at anything. At midnight, he ran the program, it returned the correct values with only two syntax errors, which he corrected and tested. Then he packed his bag and left for the night. The cold air and the bicycle ride revived him, and though it was past midnight when he arrived home, he wasn't ready for bed. He did what he always did on such occasions, he dialed into the Internet and checked his e-mail. He had a group e-mail from his management psychology professor with guidelines on how to write a survey. An invitation for the summer from Lazar, a yeshiva friend who was now living in Israel. If he could get the money together it would be fun to go to Israel for a few weeks, Jakob-Joel thought. There was a note from his friend Nick who was at Stanford, and one from his first physics teacher at Rockland High. A shipment confirmation from Amazon: his I-pod would soon arrive. And a good-night from Julia, to which he replied with a sleep tight. Then he went to brush his teeth.

Half an hour later, JakobJoel was still awake, and awake, he thought about his parents and grandparents. He considered his ambitious great-grandfather, the Berditchever, who started the yeshiva with only three disciples, two of them his own sons.

The story went thus: For the second term three additional students enrolled and the Berditchever rejoiced in lecturing to what amounted to a small class. The following semester, when his eldest son, Moshele, JakobJoel's grandfather, decided to study elsewhere and took his study partner with him, the Berditchever was down to four students, and if it were up to his wife, he would have closed shop and taken a lectureship elsewhere. But the Berditchever reconsidered. It was too late in the year to find another position; besides, he had no interest in elsewhere. He would make the best of things on his own. He would make of these four boys under his tutelage examples of what Berditchev was capable.

The desperate strategy turned out to be a good one. Within two years, the word was out: Berditchev turned out genius scholars, prodigies. As with all such stories, there were variations on this tale of making good of which as a grandson JakobJoel had heard a good number, but heroism was the essence in all of them. Depending on who was narrating, whether friend or foe, the Berditchever emerged as persistent genius or ambitious tyrant. As R. Moshele informed his grandson, things are never that simple, an either-or.

JakobJoel took great interest in what R. Moshele had to say, after all it was he who had delivered the blow. Indeed, when JakobJoel expressed a desire to leave Berditchev for another yeshiva he had his grandfather's full support. It is perfectly understandable, R. Moshele said, that Jakob-Joel would want to leave the safety of the family compound for a while. Leaving yeshiva for Rockland High's tenth grade, however, he was on his own. No one would help a Berditchev grandson leave his Talmudic studies, especially one with a mind as sharp as JakobJoel's. Only after he had taken the initial steps alone—convinced the physics teacher at Rockland that he could keep up, proved it in an intensive summer course of intermediate physics, and was then accepted as a full-time student at the school—did Ada begin to lend a hand.

He thought about his uncle Joel, who died before he was born and for whom he was named. The tragedy, shrouded as it was in mystery, had provoked JakobJoel's curiosity. It was expected that everyone would be sad, his grandmother especially, but in a family that told and retold just about every event, the reticence on this exceptional subject excited the boy, and he had made it a practice to conduct systematic searches whenever he was alone in anyone's house, his parents' or his grandparents'. One day, in his mother's most private drawer, something turned up. He had been surprised to feel a hard object in this drawer of slippery slips and silky cotton, where unlike his own underwear the garments refused to remain folded. The impassive presence of a stiff cover amid such softness insisted on his fingers' reaching and finding the thing. He brought up an old notebook with pale blue covers, what in grade school they'd called a *hefte*. Without pausing to consider the ethics of such an intrusion, he'd taken the notebook to his room and read it. Reading about alphabetic combinations, JakobJoel understood why no one wanted to talk about what had happened. Yeshiva boys who engaged in such activities were considered disturbed. He knew his uncle had suffered seizures, but that was a physical ailment. This notebook suggested spiritual derangement also. After reading it, JakobJoel returned the notebook to its place under the silks, and if he hadn't sworn his grandmother to secrecy and told her, no one would have known about it. She was trustworthy, he knew. Indeed, she kept her promise and the episode passed without Ada's ever finding out.

But there were other consequences. It seemed to JakobJoel that once he'd opened the notebook, and read the story of alphabetic permutations and the attempts at figure-making, his uncle Joel refused to return to the closed pages. He started talking to JakobJoel. He became a shadow riding on the young boy's shoulder, commenting on everything, talking, advising, cautioning, always talking. At first JakobJoel wasn't bothered, he even welcomed the constant companionship of this strange unknown uncle who'd gone from being only a received idea in his mind to a real presence. Later, his uncle became an irritant, but when JakobJoel was new on campus, he once again welcomed the company.

About the tragic aspect of his parents' wedding, JakobJoel had also learned through methodical pursuit of information. He knew from his grandmother that it had taken place before the first year of mourning had passed, which was unusual. It was decided by the Berditchever that the wedding ought to be expedited because it would be good for every-one involved. R. Moshele gained a son, and Ada found companionship with a husband who had been a close friend of her beloved brother.

And then you, dear boy, his grandmother crooned, came along and brought comfort to everyone. You were and still are the apple of your grandfather's eye. He sees in you the fulfillment of all the lost promise. You are his great hope and dream. I often have to warn him—don't worry, dear, I do it without revealing our secret. I tell him it's too much to expect of a young child to live his own life and also stand in for his uncle's interrupted one. But your grandfather has such faith in you, dar-ling. My JakobJoel, he says, is strong. He's blessed with Ada's clarity of mind and the Berditchever's physical vigor.

It occurred to the twelve-year-old JakobJoel that his grandmother thought these conversations were useful to him somehow. He'd sworn her to secrecy about the notebook, but that was when he was still a child. He no longer minded anyone knowing—by the time he was twelve he knew Ada wouldn't punish him for something he'd done when he was eight—but since his grandmother enjoyed having this secret to share with him, he left it alone.

JakobJoel understood that his parents' wedding had been a sad event, but what he learned by keeping his eyes and ears open, by maintaining an eager curiosity, was that something else had happened and the community had dubbed the wedding "the Trail of Tears." He learned why through the fortuitous purchase of a CD entitled *The Best of Yankel Yankevitch*.

The story of Yankel's penalty was widely known. For years he had performed at the best weddings, until one particular event, when his choice of entertainment was so inappropriate, he couldn't get himself hired again for several years. A family man whose wife demanded what every wife demands—a roof over her head, food for herself and her children, clothing, shoes—he was desperate for a living, and began appearing in the lineup of the poor at the entrances to wedding halls to receive donations along with the other poor. Members of the community suggested partial forgiveness. For the annual fund-raiser, the position of master of ceremonies was created and Yankel was hired to fill it. The following day murmurs about a miracle circulated because the annual event had never earned as much, but it wasn't clear who had started this talk of miracles. Then a wealthy father hired Yankel as entertainer for his son's bar mitzvah and started a trend. For the next ten years Yankel was performing in front of thirteen-year-olds one night, senior citizens the next. These gigs were of lesser stature than that of wedding *badkhn*, but Yankel accepted what he was offered and his repertoire expanded. It was said that the months without work had benefited everyone because Yankel was more lighthearted than he'd previously been. When he was in demand again, to prove perhaps that he'd been entertaining all along, or simply to earn a few extra dollars, he released a CD of his best work. JakobJoel, almost a bar mitzvah boy and a fan of Yankel's work—he'd heard him at a classmate's ceremony—bought the CD and listened to it on his Discman on his way to and from classes. On the final track Jakob-Joel was surprised to hear his parents' names, their gematrias, and then his grandfather's name. He restarted the track and heard a strangely dark performance, insane and desperate, JakobJoel thought.

It began traditionally enough, with what Yankel introduced as a historical nod to his forebear, the *badkhn*, as he developed in seventeenth-century Poland. Unlike the wedding jesters of Germany, those mere clowns, Yankel said, the Eastern European entertainer was an erudite scholar. As it says, Yankel quoted, "Be not a fool in rhyme." The following story, Yankel continued, about the great *badkhn* Laybele Furth is told. Lamenting the use of learning for mock discourse, the local rabbi quoted from the tractate of Taanith: A pity that such excellent wine is contained in such a poor vessel.

Proving himself excellent indeed, Laybele responded with a line from the same passage: Better a good wine in a poor vessel than bad wine in a good one.

Yankel proposed to continue his tribute to the *badkhn* by beginning with the traditional beginning, the gematria. He calculated that the numeric values of the letters in the names of the bride and groom, Adel and Aaron, added up to 301, and that the difference between the two was 11, and subtracting the 1 from the 1 left 0. Doing the math for the name of the father of the bride, Moshe, Yankel arrived at 345. And since the difference between 345 and 301 was 44, and 4 subtracted from 4 was also 0, Yankel concluded, the first dance should go to R. Moshele, father of the bride.

The audience booed. And they were right to, JakobJoel thought. Even for solipsistic gematria, this was a terrible example. It didn't have an ounce of cleverness. But already his grandfather must have come forward, taken Ada's hands into his own, and spun her around the room until she was dizzy and begged for reprieve. From the starts and stops in the singing, JakobJoel knew that R. Moshele must have escorted Ada back to her seat, pulled Aaron out of his, uncles, cousins, and friends joined, and the dancing continued.

When Aaron was brought back to his seat beside Ada, Yankel would have stepped forward, raised his arms. The audience would have grown silent, waiting. What nonsense would this man think of next?

As master of ceremonies, Yankel explained, the *badkhn* was expected to announce the names of donors and the gifts they'd pledged. To this end, he encouraged the well-to-do to begin pledging, promising them excellent value in publicity for every dollar spent.

Someone in the audience shouted that the old wedding jesters, the renowned Hershele Ostropolier and Laybele Furth, knew how to entertain, not just collect.

Yankel responded that only idiots were intent on laughing before the punch line. The task of the wedding jester, he said, was to make the bride and groom cry and the wedding guests laugh. Using my own not so paltry skills, I will show you how such miracles are wrought, providing of course that I am well paid for it. After a pause—he must have gotten a nod from R. Moshele, JakobJoel guessed—Yankel proceeded.

As was customary in the opening of a *badkhn's* act, JakobJoel could picture Yankel untying and retying the sash on his caftan, smoothing his *peyos*, finger-combing his beard, a performer's pre-performance ritual. Then he must have lifted his arms, to beseech the muses, hummed the first notes of the chant, and as expected, the audience joined him, completing the song's line.

> This is a story about a bride and groom
> yaididaididaidaidai
> whose future the Nazis nipped in the womb

The audience hesitated, unwilling to participate in such a story, and the line of the lament remained unfinished.

What? JakobJoel asked aloud and restarted the track to make certain he'd heard right.

> This is a story about a bride and groom
> yaididaididaidaidai
> whose future the Nazis nipped in the womb

Where could Yankel possibly go with this? JakobJoel wondered. Who would find anything about the Nazis amusing?

With no encouragement issuing from the audience, Yankel resumed without chant or rhyme. This wedding of this unlucky bride and groom, Yankel said, was interrupted. In the town synagogue, the plate was barely broken when the Polish peasants stormed in and stole what they could, what food and wine had been scraped together by the local families. In this town, as in too many cities and towns in too much of Europe, the Jews were quickly rounded up and crowded onto trains with the barest if any necessities. As it happened, the *badkhn* was in the car with the bride and groom and he took it upon himself to entertain, since, circumstances notwithstanding, for these two newly marrieds, it was still a wedding day. After ascertaining a few facts and details, the man began, as was customary, listing the wedding gifts received and the names of the contributors. Then he went on to consider the usefulness of each gift in the next world, where they were all going sooner or later, whether at the hands of the Polish, the Nazis, or the godly angel of death.

There was a pause. JakobJoel turned up the volume and heard what sounded like Yankel's large, bony hands rubbing together. Nervously? JakobJoel wondered. He ought to be. The man was nuts.

What the town *badkhn* couldn't have known then, Yankel pointed out, was the future of one gift, the story of a small feather pillow. As you all know, the dowry of every European bride consisted of a measure of goose feathers, enough, every village groom had come to expect, for a warm featherbed, perhaps even a pillow or two. Often the bride herself was employed in plucking the geese, then washing and drying the feathers. A capable girl might sew and stuff her own bed, thereby taking into her own hands both her comfort and her own worth. Well, rumor has it that among the village women, this bride's featherbed had been discussed for months. They frowned on and admired the girl's willingness to beg, borrow, and steal. In time of war, when there wasn't enough bread to go around, and the Germans and Russians were both approaching, Fraydl had produced a six-inch-thick bed. It was widely known that she couldn't have accomplished this feat without her youngest brother, the twelve-year-old Tuvye, whom she called Krepel, because he was short and stout, a small plump dumpling. Krepel learned to take advantage of every synagogue service and every gathering, approaching merchants and farmers for a few *groshen* to help out in Fraydl's wedding. And he didn't take no for an answer. After a while, the men reached into their pockets with a sigh as soon as they saw the boy. With his wit and persistence, Krepel would go on to survive the war and become one of the largest property holders in London. These days, Yankel digressed, the sons of Krepel, who acquired from their father the survivor's habit of living everywhere at once, fly the Concorde shuttle London to New York, New York to London regularly.

In the present of the story, in the last desperate hour, Krepel and Fraydl considered the featherbed. Clearly a six-inch-thick blanket wouldn't travel well; even if allowed on board, it would end by serving as a communal bed for crowds. The brother and sister decided that the bed should remain in the hiding place where they'd successfully kept it hidden through the year, while the feathers had accumulated. Seeing his sister's disappointment, Krepel suggested that the tiny flat pillow which she'd sewn thinking of a future infant could serve as a travel pillow, and this soothed Fraydl. In the final moments, in the bitter panic of forced packing and moving, Fraydl folded the little pillow in half and tucked it into the inner pocket of Krepel's coat, where it remained when he and another boy slipped out of line, and into the nearby woods. During the night, when he awoke with the discomfort of his head on a hard, cold stone, he remembered the little pillow in his pocket. Krepel and the little pillow survived, and no matter how many twenty-seven-inch European squares he found on his various grand hotel beds in various parts of the world, his sister's little pillow, her final gift to him, traveled with him everywhere.

As Yankel had predicted, by the time he came to the end of this story, the bride and groom were crying. Yankel had made Ada and Aaron cry at their own wedding! JakobJoel listened further. Members of the audience were shouting.

You've succeeded in making the bride and groom cry, but we the wedding guests are not laughing, someone said. Another voice accused Yankel of trafficking in the Holocaust business, which as he himself had put it, had become a good subject for writers. Everyone has a relative to write about. And if there isn't a relative, the writer makes one up. Even writers who aren't Jewish have taken up the subject. What critic would dare to write negatively about a book on the Holocaust?

But Yankel wasn't apologizing. The bride's tears weren't yet dry, and already he was asking for his entertainer's fee, calling it a profitable night.

The track ended and JakobJoel wondered why Yankel had included this punishing performance at all: for posterity's sake, or was this his way of marking Joel's death?

First JakobJoel interviewed his grandmother.

Liebling, Mrs. Jakob protested, I thought we went over all this already. I've told you everything I know.

You didn't tell me about Yankel's performance, JakobJoel pointed out.

That was a sad end to a sad day. Your mother had been crying all day, and she ended the day with more tears. What is there to say? We were all terribly sad. It was difficult for your father, too, the dear Aaron. Joel and he had been inseparable.

JakobJoel waited for the right moment to question his mother, and finally his patience was rewarded. He came upon Ada and her friend and business partner, Malke, sitting at the kitchen table with a pot of tea between them, sipping and reminiscing. He took a seat and said, Tell me about your wedding.

Ada and Malke smiled. Since when do twelve-year-old boys have an interest in weddings? Malke asked.

It's a personal project. I'm researching family history, JakobJoel said. Collecting stories. I want to know everything.

Ada leaned back and began. When she omitted something, Malke filled in, until the story of the engagement and wedding took shape in JakobJoel's mind.

The Engagement

Tongues were still wagging when, three months later, renewed impetus for gossip arrived with the announcement of Ada's engagement to Aaron. People said it was too soon, too close on the heels of what still remained a mystery. In other words, the Jakob name was still fresh on people's minds.

Within the circle of friends and family, there was full support for the engagement, not least because they knew that this union between Ada and Aaron had long been one of Joel's great hopes. Besides, a joyous occasion was much needed to counter the evil that had befallen the family, and everyone wanted to see a smile on R. Moshele's face. Indeed, the gathered guests were so certain of the rightness of this match, when the porcelain plate was broken, every family member, including the grandparents on both sides, the uncles, aunts, and cousins, as if enacting an old ritual, contributed his or her personal stomp, leaving the plate shattered and the fact of the engagement unquestionable.

Fortunately the porcelain had been carefully wrapped in a dish towel, as was practical in busy households. Mrs. Jakob shed tears, both bitter and joyous, as she guided the shards through the funnel neck of a small glass vase. Someone pointed out that there was no shard large enough for the usual bridal pin or charm, but Ada merely shrugged. She detested those pins and charms anyway and took the opportunity to inform her future mother-in-law that she had no interest in standard bridal gifts. I much prefer what's different, Ada said.

Thinking that the girl was bravely making the best of things, Aaron's mother kissed her new Adichke for the nth time, and promised that for her Aronke's bride there would be only the best. The woman hung embellishments on every name, and for Ada she had more than one version. Adele, Adichke, Adyeke. Perhaps, Ada thought, it wasn't clear yet which would stick, but they all made her feel one year old. She would wait for the right moment, after the wedding was probably best, to suggest that simply Ada was most comfortable.

She glanced at Aaron and saw him watching her out of the corners of his eyes. He blushed at being caught. Ada smiled. She was glad he hadn't turned argumentative when she'd denied him his request that she tell him what she knew about Joel, in other words, what Joel had been up to. The engagement had been agreed upon by both parties, and someone suggested that the children be given some time to get acquainted. To that end, they were sitting at the Jakob dining room table, doors closed to provide privacy. Ada responded to Aaron's request with her own request. She reminded him that in the way of the world the king grants the queen a request—up to half the kingdom—and not the other way around.

Aaron nodded. I'm listening, he said.

Her request: To be allowed to keep this secret. She explained that she had good reason not to say anything just yet, that in time, she hoped she could reveal more.

And that was that. Aaron had bowed his head in agreement.

Ada couldn't explain that she didn't want Joel to look bad, not even in the forgiving eyes of his best friend, her own future husband. She didn't want to mention the possibility of idol worship or the transgressions that seemed its result. Right now, even the most fleeting look of derision from Aaron would be too much, and Ada wasn't prepared to risk it. This fear was new to her. She'd never cared about the opinion of others and she wondered at this change. At its root was recent personal experience, an acquaintance with inner desires. That she could be moved to the prohibitive in dream made the potential for transgression great, the inconstancy within deep. For the first time in her life, Ada felt herself a sinner, and she didn't like the feeling. It was as if at bottom she knew herself to be dishonest. This changed everything. She'd fallen from a height. She was no longer Ada Jakob, the fortunate girl whose sense of freedom had come from the knowledge that she was much loved and admired by friends, parents, grandparents, brother, and ever since she could remember, Aaron. She had now this heavy feeling that if only they knew, their love would diminish, and with it everything that made her who she was. Up to this day, anything she had undertaken, no matter how far-fetched, couldn't go wrong; now, she felt, nothing would be right. For the first time in seventeen years, Ada felt herself vulnerable. Knowing there were sins she couldn't prevent, that in sleep she was without armor to deflect temptation, she felt naked and understood for the first time why Adam and Eve suddenly desired clothing.

With this realization of her own fallibility came a slow understanding that something similar also was to blame for Joel's recent strangeness, and this knowledge was a blow. Living with both her own and Joel's bad consciences, she became more aware of whisperings behind her back, the jabbering about the Jakob family's hubris and its fall.

And she was aware that her mother's nerves were overwrought and her father was in bad shape. He had aged seemingly overnight, grew thinner every day. A man who had veered toward rotundity, he was beginning to look more like his beanpole son.

At the Friday-night table, without Joel's voice to give weight to his own, R. Moshele sang listlessly. When Aaron joined them for a meal, he helped make of the melodies what they ought to be and the mood lightened. For the first time in her life, Ada wished herself a member of a larger family, with more siblings. If they'd had the Chasidic standard of eight to ten children, the house wouldn't be so silent now, her parents would be more distracted. It would be up to her and Aaron to fill the house with the sounds of infants. Ada felt herself already preparing for their first, their JakobJoel. She had inner stirrings, desires. From her friend Malke, who was due to give birth any day, Ada had learned about such things as intuitions and interpreted her own agitations.

The Berditchever grandfather had suggested that the wedding take place in three months, before even the year of mourning was at an end, which meant preparations would have to proceed at a fast, hard pace. Though Ada understood that the urgency was intended to help her parents, she regretted the need for it. There's a time for everything, and it was Aaron's time to be pampered as a groom. About her own abbreviated experience she was less concerned. She'd lived bridehood vicariously more than once, every time a friend got engaged.

Before the evening was over, the Berditchever requested a moment of privacy with the bride, his eldest granddaughter. Alone with him in the room, sitting again at the dining room table, Ada waited for him to take his seat and begin. He didn't take a seat. With his hands clasped behind his back, he paced the length of the room and back. Watching him, Ada noted that unlike her father, the Berditchever had a developed aesthetic sensibility. She had an idea that even when he turned ninety, his shoulders wouldn't stoop and round. He would remain unbowed by life. He was a man with an awareness of his long back, and a certain vanity attached to it.

At my engagement to your grandmother, the Berditchever said, speaking slowly, as if selecting each word, my grandfather, the holy Shimlauer, presented me with a task. It is this same task that today I want to bestow on you.

He paused to let this information sink in, and Ada understood that in the normal course of events Joel would have been the one honored with this task.

As you know, he said, a wedding day is the ultimate Yom Kippur, second only to the day of one's return to the next world. In preparation for this important day, I challenge you with the lifetime task of knowing yourself, the first step toward recognizing the presence of God within. Before one can hope to transcend the human limits of personality and ego, one must overcome them, and discover the place in which God represents himself as an individual, an I. Of course, for most people, this first step requires a lifetime.

Ada exhaled and waited. What did that mean, knowing herself? How was she to go about it? And if it was a lifetime task, how could she accomplish it before her wedding day? Besides, it seemed to her that she experienced some change every day, which would mean she was never the same.

The Berditchever nodded, acknowledging the unspoken questions, and suggested that she begin by reacquainting herself with the one great personal disappointment or challenge of her life, though he granted that until the recent tragedy, she'd had little experience in this area.

Given the happy, beloved girl that you are, he finished, eyes sad, Ada noted, but trying to smile.

Ada stood and looked the Berditchever in the eye. I accept the challenge on one condition.

The Berditchever interrupted his pacing. This granddaughter of his had an impudent streak, which had always interested him. He pulled out a chair, lifted his caftan, and sat. Seeing him seated, Ada started walking, and the Berditchever noted how quickly this girl had turned the tables on him. Though he'd called the meeting, she was doing the walking and talking. He sat and listened.

I accept the challenge, she repeated, if you will tell me what you learned about yourself and how this knowledge has made a difference in your life.

The Berditchever raised an eyebrow. In his time, the idea of not accepting the challenge had never occurred to him. Moreover he had never considered the practical usefulness of the task. He wasn't even certain he had an answer to this idea of utility. The challenge was intended to kindle an awareness of the significance of every living moment, of the presence of God in the thinnest blade of grass. It was a call to reach for heights, and as such, its effect on every individual was entirely personal. He wondered whether it was Ada's gender that gave her this oddly practical streak, then he remembered his own ethereal mother who couldn't be counted on to bring a pot of soup to boil. It was false to say that practicality was always a woman's domain. This was probably the first time this challenge was passed on to a daughter in the family, and the Berditchever had spent several hours debating the wisdom of this novelty. Having decided that Ada was as worthy a candidate as any son, he was determined not to leap to quick conclusions. Greater than the difference of gender, the Berditchever told himself, was the intergenerational disparity, largely enhanced by the influence of life in freethinking America. He was of an era that believed that grandfathers knew something about the making of better people. Ada had grown up in a country where youth knows best. Of course such a response would get him nowhere. Once asked, the answer to such a question couldn't be denied. He nodded his assent, but not without his own condition.

It is important, he said, that you learn about my own experience only after you have made some progress in yours, in other words, in a year or more, perhaps when, according to tradition, your bridal state will come to an end.

Fair enough, Ada said. She nodded and the meeting came to an end, but not before the Berditchever put his hands on her head and blessed her. May the four matriarchs, Sarah, Rebecca, Rachel, and Leah, assist you in your task.

For this particular task, Ada pointed out, the assistance of the patriarchs might have been more useful, since they were likely to have had more experience with it.

The Berditchever smiled. It won't do to denigrate your own kind, of which you are an exemplar.

Ada's initial response to the Berditchever's challenge was that the loss of her brother was her great disappointment, which was true, but to stop at that seemed too facile. What did it teach her? There had to be more to this question of disappointment than the act of merely naming it. She would have to learn something about it, force it to enlighten rather than obscure. Two and three weeks passed, she was making progress in everything else, but on the challenge to know herself she was stalled. Other than Joel's sudden and unnecessary death, nothing she could think of qualified as an answer to the question of disappointment. It seemed to her that until recently she'd suffered no great discomforts. Her childhood had been a happy one. She recalled the joy of learning to read, even overtaking Joel as a reader. When they were older—they were only a year and a day apart—there were the rounds of chess and the games won. How proud her mother had been. In a world in which girls and boys received equal educations, Mrs. Jakob had said, her daughter would have been a fine scholar. At home, they'd always been equal rivals. Ada brooded on the question of equality, on the moment she'd understood that because she was a girl, she wouldn't have the same opportunities as Joel, that she wouldn't be trained as a Talmudist. She wondered whether this could have been a great disappointment to her, then cast the idea aside. There was simply no truth in it. If the search and find were to have any value to her, she would have to be entirely honest. Fact was, she'd absorbed the notion of difference between herself and Joel with equanimity, and she'd never felt less significant because she was a woman. Just as they were different individuals, so too they operated in different spheres. Ada even believed that of the two, life as a Chasidic female was the more privileged one. That men were required to give thanks for their manhood every morning was for her a sign that the better life belonged to the female.

She became frustrated. How could she have lived close to eighteen years without experiencing some meaningful moments? If nothing in her early life had registered as an injury, she could hardly think of herself as a growing human being. The general wisdom that the passage from childhood to adulthood was painful wasn't true for her. If she'd had passing moments of pain, they'd been twinges, mere immature aches of hypersensitivity. She asked herself what Joel would have come up with. His unfinished project might have been an answer, but this same strange project was also indirectly the cause of his death. She was appalled by how little she or anyone knew, both about themselves and about another. She had thought of herself as knowing Joel, but if she'd known him she would surely have intuited more of what had been going on. A talk with him on the subject of not knowing might have made all the difference. Even when their conversations weren't about a particular subject, when they simply went at each other in their particular teasing banter, somehow talking had always helped. After such an exchange, Ada returned to her work in a lighter, better mood, and lighthearted, less desperate solutions followed. From this, Ada had extrapolated a certain set of rules for herself: She would never be so serious about designing that the work became drudgery. She understood that particular circumstances were necessary for her best work: a light heart, a good time, and a full schedule. As soon as she didn't have enough to do, the designs became heavy-handed, flat-footed. When she tried too hard, the quality of the work sank.

Taking her own advice, she decided to leave the Berditchever task alone.

The Wedding Day

No Jewish wedding is complete without an opulence of tears, but in the marriage of Ada and Aaron all averages were exceeded.

Ada awoke tearful that morning. She could hardly speak when Malke called to tell her of the day's schedule. Asked why, she was unable to answer. She wasn't certain why, a hundred whys. For one thing, she wasn't ready after all. She hadn't fulfilled the Berditchever's challenge.

Malke advised water. Even though you're fasting, make it an eight-glass day, she said. You'll feel and look better.

Ada agreed to drink water, then laughed.

You're crying one minute, laughing the next, Malke said. I'll pick you up at eleven. We should at least begin on time.

Before leaving her room, Ada stuck her head out the window and inhaled. It was a clear, blue day, and cold. The chill dried her eyes and cleared her head, but though she tried her best to spare her mother, Mrs.

Jakob looked at Ada and her own eyes filled. R. Moshele was beside himself. At the breakfast table, at which no one was able to eat, he told the most amusing story he could think of, and was rewarded with a half smile from Ada and more tears from his wife. Then all three broke down again.

They were interrupted by the doorbell. When Ada opened the door, a huge bouquet of white roses was placed in her arms. Grateful for the perfect timing, R. Moshele overtipped the delivery boy, and all three followed the flowers into the living room, where they were set down on a low table, and the envelope detached. Ada unfolded a letter addressed to "My beloved queen, rare as pearls," and sat down to read. To give her daughter privacy, Mrs. Jakob took R. Moshele's arm and led him back to the kitchen table, where she poured more coffee and reminded him of the letter he had sent her, of which she recalled every word. R. Moshele confessed that he didn't remember writing it, that on their wedding day he had been overwhelmed with fear and trembling.

Ada was almost dressed and ready when Malke arrived. While she waited, Mrs. Jakob slipped a $100 bill into Malke's hand.

Keep her busy all day, she said. If necessary, get yourself massages. I don't want her to spend the day in tears. And I don't want her father to see her.

Malke kissed Mrs. Jakob's cheek. It was perfectly obvious to Malke that Mrs. Jakob also had been crying. On this day, every one of the Jakobs could use a full schedule of appointments.

What time are you due at the facialist's? Malke asked. Should I send the car back for you?

I have until two. In the meantime, I have to drop off a check at the caterers' hall, then stop at the cleaners'. Reb Moshele will drive. It will keep him occupied.

Malke nodded. They both turned to see Ada emerge from her bedroom looking beautifully bridal, in a pearl gray knee-length dress and white overcoat, her hair pulled back in a neat chignon. When she turned to face them, her eyes and nose were not so beautifully swollen and red and Mrs. Jakob's eyes started tearing.

Malke knew what to do. She took Ada's arm and moved her toward the door. We're late, she said, and the urgency was effective. Mother and daughter wiped away their tears, kissed, and Ada promised to call sometime during the day, between appointments.

In the way of the world, more than that, in an exaggerated version of general standards, Ada's wedding day was carefully scheduled for the achievement of maximum beauty. She spent the day getting her nails, hair, and face done. She had a final dress fitting because in the last two weeks she'd lost five pounds. She also received a new type of massage that promised to press and pinch more prominent cheekbones onto her face. Using the art of chiaroscuro, the makeup artist would make the most of this ephemeral bone structure, which would enhance the wedding photographs.

Much of this was Malke's idea. She pointed out that when things are done halfway, the results are disastrous or, worse, bland. One must either do a thing well or not at all. And, she said, if not now, if not for your own wedding, then when? The week before, she'd sent Ada to a dental hygienist to have her teeth cleaned and bleached. After, Malke insisted that Ada drink coffee through a straw.

A bride dressed in white should have white teeth, she said. She herself had been sipping her coffee through a straw for years, ever since she'd noticed what coffee did for her smile.

Even in high school, Malke had these obsessions. To avoid chapped lips in the winter, she'd learned to drink from the water fountain without exposing her lips to the water more than necessary. She'd gotten the idea from a beauty magazine that provided tips on how to eat without losing your lipstick. Demonstrating to her friends, she puckered and extruded her lips so hard they laughed and called it ludicrous. In the end, though, it was they who needed lip balm, and Malke could always be counted on to produce a tube. She seemed to keep one somewhere in every garment.

Ada argued that sipping coffee from a straw reduced the pleasure, that it was so unnatural as to be unacceptable. Just try to imagine a Frenchwoman sipping coffee through a straw, she said, and laughed.

Malke didn't bother responding. She waited until Ada was finished, then wondered aloud whether the dental appointment also ought to be scheduled on the wedding day, while Ada was fasting and therefore not drinking coffee. Ada soon agreed to sip through a straw for the week. Though she considered Malke's strangeness extreme—neurotic, really— she understood that such obsessiveness made for perfection. All their friends had taken the same pattern-making class in high school; only Malke had become a brilliant pattern maker.

As her personal wedding gift to friends, Malke designed and orga- nized the bride's new closet, complete with see-through boxes for shoes, padded hangers for delicates, and so on. Ada had seen Malke's work before, but when she saw what Malke had done in the small apartment on Ashel Lane that she and Aaron had rented, she was so astonished, she said nothing until prompted.

How could you not like it? Malke asked.

Not like it? How could I not like it? Ada echoed.

Malke had outdone herself. What had begun as a tiny closet in a two-bedroom rental was now a walk-in. After obtaining permission from Mrs. Jakob and the landlord, Malke had hired a contractor to demolish and rebuild a wall in order to take square footage from the second bedroom, and thus created a modern dressing room complete with frosted-glass sliding doors. Ada gaped. The walls were papered in cedar wallpaper, the floor carpeted in pale pink shag, and the shelves were made of waxed birch and glass. This wasn't merely an organized closet out of a magazine, this was luxury: a closet designed to bring daily joy.

At the wedding hall, sitting on the decorative bridal throne, Ada watched the girls dance, noted who was still single, who married and pregnant, and sobbed.

You're ruining your face, Mrs. Jakob admonished.

Malke came up and hugged Ada, adjusted her crown. What should I do with her? Mrs. Jakob asked.

Let her be, Malke said. I packed a cold gel pack.

Aaron's mother hovered, wringing her hands. What could she say to reassure the child?

Ada gets like this, Malke said. It's nothing to worry about.

Ada's intermittent sobbing continued during the reception, the veiling, and as she walked down the red carpet. When she stepped under the canopy, circled seven times, and then stood beside Aaron, she suddenly knew what she needed to know, what really she'd known all along without knowing she'd known. The knowledge began as an inner stab, the feeling that just as she hadn't known her brother, she didn't know Aaron, that she never would, not even after a lifetime of living with him as his wife. She remembered that the knowledge of her unknowingness had arrived recently, in this evil year, and that this, this newly acquired awareness of human limitation, was her great personal disappointment. But it was also a gain. She had come to know what she didn't know. She knew herself as less knowing. She was human and fallible and happy to be Aaron's bride.

In the meantime, while she both grieved and celebrated, Aaron's quivering hands placed a blurry ring on her finger. He proclaimed her his wife, and as if from a distance, Ada heard the seven blessings recited, the glass crushed, and then she and Aaron were led, danced really, through a shimmering crowd of well-wishers all the way to the bridal chamber.

By the time the trombone player announced the new couple for the first time, dessert had already been served. Ada and Aaron rejoined the wedding party, smiling and holding hands, and the two relieved mothers fell upon each other and kissed. Aaron walked with Ada to the women's section, relinquished her into the arms of her friends, and was rushed by his own friends to the men's section. During the two hours that followed, bride and groom, each separately on her and his side, danced, visited tables, posed for photographs, danced again, until the final ritual of Chasidic weddings, when they were brought together to dance with each other. The master of ceremonies for this dance, known as the *mitzvah tanz*, was as always the *badkhn*. That the man also considered himself the *shadkhn* of this particular match amused most of the wedding guests, since the match between these two children was practically a signed contract since birth. It was just like Reb Moshele, people said, to pay the $700 *shadkhn* fee anyway and allow Yankel to persist in his delusion.

Every contractual agreement, R. Moshele explained, requires a mediator. Yankel acted on our behalf.

I heard Yankel's performance on the CD, JakobJoel said. I didn't know that it was your wedding that finished him off, though the punishment still seems too harsh. Maybe he was wrong to tell a Holocaust story at a wedding, especially this wedding. On the other hand, his work requires a certain uninhibited freedom to range far and wide, even into tastelessness.

Ada nodded. I was never angry with him. Besides, on a tear-filled day, what were a few more tears?

Speak for yourself, Malke said. The man deserved what he got. He's a scoundrel. His performance was thoughtless.

He may be a scoundrel, but he's a talented one and that makes all the difference, JakobJoel said. I was thinking that we should hire him for my bar mitzvah. It would act as a correction to what happened. I know I'll enjoy Yankel's performance no matter what he says.

Don't be too certain, Malke warned.

We can discuss it with your father, Ada suggested. She smiled, remembering something. When JakobJoel was seven, she told Malke, he wanted to be a *badkhn*. I had also always admired Yankel. I'd come home from weddings, go to Joel's room, and repeat the jokes word for word. But Joel was never impressed. He always knew where the quotes came from, who had originated the joke. I thought the plagiarisms and variations made the performances funnier. Joel didn't agree. He was simply too original a being to appreciate Yankel.

She poured more tea and they drank in silence for a few minutes.

She turned to Malke. You know, Aaron was the first to forgive Yankel. A month after the wedding he pointed out that Yankel's choice of topic was in its own way appropriate, wise even. After all, the tragedy was on everyone's mind, there had been a violent death, and there were still questions about it. Not mentioning it at all would also have been strange.

JakobJoel looked at his mother's face. Having Malke at the table helped. Ada had never before spoken so directly of her brother or even of that period. JakobJoel wondered what his father knew and thought. If Aaron had read the notebook, he would know everything and he would have discussed it with Ada. JakobJoel wished he could have overheard that conversation. The trouble was that everything important had taken place before he was born.

One question remained.

JakobJoel found the Berditchever in his study, at work in front of his computer.

He was an impressive man. Unlike much younger men—JakobJoel's own grandfather, R. Moshele, for example—the Berditchever had taught himself how to operate the software he needed. After years of pecking on a portable Olivetti custom-fitted with the Hebrew alphabet, he became one of the first to purchase a retrofitted Macintosh and adapted to it with delight.

It eliminates all the drudgery, he said. If it had been available twenty years earlier, many more holy books would have been written.

Though he was slowing down physically, his mind was still fully operative. He continued to deliver Talmudic lectures three times a week, and spent a good part of every day studying, preparing, and writing.

The Berditchever welcomed his great-grandson, who reminded him always of Ada. He was full of life, curious, questioning. JakobJoel, he announced with delight. What can a great-grandfather do for his great-grandson today? he asked.

When the boy explained that he had come for the long-ago-promised answer, the Berditchever noted that his request was very like a demand, that the boy believed he had a right to know. The Berditchever leaned back and smiled, allowed the boy to finish. When he answered, it was unhurried, one of his nonanswers.

If you ask your mother she will likely tell you what she learned, that is that there is no answer to such a question, or rather that it's the question itself that is meaningful. To understand this you will have to take upon yourself the challenge and hope to arrive at your own realizations. The year passed, and your mother didn't ask for an explanation. That she didn't ask was as good a sign as any that she succeeded because to ask for an answer is to misunderstand the nature of the search, which is never-ending.

You, my boy, are not yet thirteen, a little young for such things, but greater miracles have been wrought. Since on your own you've come to ask, perhaps you're prepared to take on the task. If you are so inclined, think of it as your bar mitzvah challenge.

I'll consider it, JakobJoel said with a shrug.

The boy was clearly unimpressed by the offer, the Berditchever noted. He was focused elsewhere and would soon dismiss or forget the question of his own participation. Which was probably a sign he was indeed too young.

On the basis of his own life experience, JakobJoel should have believed in free will. But he wavered. Though it was true that one's genetic makeup was predetermined at birth, intellect, intuition, and knowledge provided windows for escape. However, if it could be argued that these very windows—one's intellect and intuition—were also part of the inherited package, encoded in his DNA, then his entire life, all twenty years of it, complete with the facts of his breakaway, his departure first from Berditchev to another yeshiva, then from yeshiva to Rockland High, and from there on to MIT, could have been predicted. There were those who came before him, the Berditchever himself, for example, who initiated the disjunctive pattern as a young man living in the Vizhnitz community of B'nei B'rak, Israel, when he quarreled with the Vizhnitz dynasty. Vizhnitz cast him out, and the Berditchever, who had not yet become the Berditchever, emigrated to the New World. In the summer of 1969, when Neil Armstrong took one giant step for mankind, the unworldly Berditchever took his first steps into this country, this mythical Amerika, Amerika with its gold-lined streets. He arrived an unknown and with plenteous daring declared himself a branchlet of a branch of Berditchev with claims connecting him to the grand trunk of Chasidism's founding father, the Ba'al Shem Tov himself. He arrived bearing the reputation of an outcast and rumors of a curse. Based since before World War Two in B'nei B'rak, Israel, former seat of the renowned Rabbi Elazar ben Azaria of the Passover Haggadah, Vizhnitz was second in size only to the Satmar dynasty of Hungary, which had resettled in Brooklyn, New York. When the old Vizhnitzer rebbe went into semiretirement, the dynasty was divided between two sons. The elder took the throne in B'nei B'rak; the younger was sent to establish himself in the New World, and he settled in the town of Monsey, New York.

As a young disciple of Vizhnitz in B'nei B'rak, with a reputation for having one of the better Talmudic minds, the Berditchever had been asked to help the rebbe's dense elder son with his studies. In years of study sessions, the Berditchever had come to know the mind of this boy and man intimately, and when the time came was quick to denounce the young rebbe. The inevitable result: exile.

Along with the old rebbe's curse, the beleaguered Berditchever was burdened with a difficult wife, four children, a bad back, a weak heart, and a vitamin-B deficiency. He lived for two years in Williamsburg in Brooklyn, New York, where he held a teaching post at the Satmar yeshiva; underwent a series of B-complex injections recommended by Dr. Harold Burnstein, beloved physician to the Satmar; then, perhaps too invigorated by B-energy, heard of an opportunity to purchase a parcel of land, seized it, and found himself the owner of two acres within spitting distance of the Vizhnitz community in Monsey, New York.

The Berditchever set to work establishing his own yeshiva, and within ten years, Vizhnitz and Berditchev found themselves back to back. After a drawn-out case in Jewish court, a compromise was reached:

an eight-foot chain-link fence (a famous American poet's solution, "good fences make good neighbors"), paid for and maintained by the parties involved.

Among gossips, the Vizhnitzer's curse was credited with every misfortune, and both enemies and friends of Berditchev held their breaths. As in all lives, illness and tragedy appeared. There was a late-pregnancy miscarriage, an evil year in which the Berditchever was immobilized by his bad back, there was emergency surgery, but none of these could be said to have left a permanent dent. The four Berditchever children came of age, married, produced grandchildren; and under the fine administrative talents of R. Moshele, the yeshiva continued steadfast in its original intent to remain concentrated and attract the best minds. Ordinary cyclical life continued as it has since the first days of the world, until suddenly, within a matter of months, a Berditchev grandson, a promising young scholar, came to a tragic end, and what had begun to seem an invulnerable star crashed from the heights.

At the renewal of gossip, the Berditchever rebbetzin, JakobJoel's dear great-grandmother, lost sleep. As she said, not knowing or caring whom she quoted nor whether circumstances called for such dark words, her eldest grandson Joel had forever murdered sleep. The hair on her head stood upright, she said, and her scalp burned at the thought of what was said in the street. She knew it all so precisely because she herself was quite capable of such talk. Indeed, if her own family weren't involved, she might have taken pleasure in the conversations and speculations. She remembered that she had never forgiven her husband the uprooting from dusty, dry B'nei B'rak, a place she had grown to love, in which she had many friends and good neighbors. His headstrong foolishness had brought her and, by extension, the children (a miserable wife is a miserable mother, she liked to say when any of her children dredged up a bad episode from memory) great unhappiness. Fortunately, once settled in Monsey, New York, she rediscovered an old friend with whom she could giggle over telephone lines every day. Leah was an exuberant conversationalist and superb giggler, and this despite her share of personal difficulties. Without Leah's friendship, life for the Berditchever rebbetzin would have been grim. Husbands, certainly hers, didn't understand a woman's needs, though she suspected that Leah's particular husband might be the source of Leah's inner joy. And now, lamentations upon lamentations, at an age when she ought to begin attending her grandchildren's weddings, and celebrating the birth of great-grandchildren, tragedy had once again landed in her lap.

Her eldest grandchildren had inherited their grandfather's flair for making trouble. For several years it had been Ada who had set tongues wagging; Joel had brought the family much honor, until, beginning with his unfortunate collapse in the fish store and culminating in a mysterious drowning, all in a matter of months, he'd finished them all off ignominously. She would have explained the whole catastrophe as illness, but the public knew too much. These Jakob men played with fire, they took on whole dynasties. But it was one thing for a married young man to take risks as the Berditchever had, another for a yeshiva boy for whom reputation was still everything. In her grief, the Berditchever rebbetzin faulted the parents. Her son and daughter-in-law were too lenient. Her daughter-in-law called it respect for privacy. It's unacceptable, she argued, for a parent to open without permission a child's mail. Respect is best taught by example.

Nonsense, the mother-in-law reprimanded. Children don't have to be reasoned with. They respect their elders because they must: *Honor thy father and mother or suffer dishonor.*

The younger Mrs. Jakob turned her face away and smiled. Nice rhyme, she said, but incorrect. *Honor thy father or mother and your days will be long.* The dear rebbetzin should know that there is a promise of reward, no threat of punishment. Love is more effective than fear.

The Berditchever rebbetzin sensed that in her heart her daughter-in-law despised her, that she said to herself the old woman is ignorant, unable to quote even the Ten Commandments correctly. These days young girls attend schools, which was more than she had been allowed. Though it might not yet have occurred to her snob of a daughter-in-law, Ada too knew more than her mother. But even the wonderful Ada, the grandmother told herself, would never amount to what the older generation had because in the modern world simple naive virtue no longer prevailed. Everything was more complicated.

The Berditchever rebbetzin often wondered how it was that she had come to be mother-in-law to this particular daughter-in-law, or, more important, wife to her ambitious husband. What had she ever done to deserve the burden of the title Berditchever rebbetzin, she who had never in life wanted to be anyone's rebbetzin? Born as pretty and poor as the next girl living in old Palestine, to a father who worked the night shift at *The Jerusalem Post* and prayed mornings and evenings at the Bratslav *shtibel*, and to a mother who could boast of a father who was a renowned pauper, the holy Kabbalist R. Elye, noted for refusing all paid positions in order to retain his independence as a scholar, the Berditchever rebbetzin wanted what every naive young Jerusalem girl wanted: to marry a man just like her father and continue to live near her mother.

When the time came and she was declared of age, the names of both local and faraway boys were brought to her dear father for consideration. Life has its way with people. Though the Berditchever rebbetzin turned down the first boy because marrying him would mean living in America and said yes to the olive-skinned scholarly boy from B'nei B'rak, ten years after her wedding she found herself living in America. Thirty-five years later a great-grandson of Berditchev had entered mainstream American life.

Despite his training in science and rationality, JakobJoel often caught himself thinking of his life at MIT as fictional. In the real world, he had not been intended for an unfettered life of the mind. There were two versions of JakobJoel, the real and the created one. The real one had been schooled in belief. The created one was still a tentative, provisional being, uncertain, still unformed. He wanted to become a true scientist, reticent, fact-based and fact-driven, unemotional, but such hardheadedness didn't come to him naturally. For every rational thought, he had a counter-thought, for every doubt, another doubt. And if that weren't enough, his mind had tuned in to a charlatan channel that brought him a voice from the dead, his uncle Joel, whom he'd never met in person, but who was along for the adventure, whatever it turned out to be, always talking, prompting, knowing better.

On the subject of free will, JakobJoel backed himself up with Spinoza: There is no such thing as free will in the mental sphere or chance in the physical world since everything that happens is a manifestation of God's inscrutable nature, which is always absolutely logical.

And how does Spinoza explain sin and evil? his uncle prodded.

What seems evil in sin does not exist when viewed as only part of a whole, which as you know is an old Kabbalistic idea. From a larger perspective, an omniscient one, for example, everything would reveal itself as good.

Spinoza, that God-intoxicated man, Joel quoted. Though a great man in many ways, he was also greatly fallible, eminently fallible in his belief that the eternal wisdom of God showed itself most of all in Jesus Christ and when he went from being Baruch to Benedict. When Maimonides was asked how absolute knowledge can coexist with free will, he explained that the question poses a problem only for the finite human mind. For an infinite being time doesn't exist, therefore predeterminism isn't an issue. Yes, God knows what choices man will make and yet this knowledge doesn't conflict with free will. Another way to explain the phenomenon: The world is re-created every moment, in other words, creation is a continuous act. To describe it, the present progressive form is necessary, the *-ing*: God is forever creating, knowing, predetermining in every moment, therefore man can forever retain his free will: to sin or not to sin.

History and literature, JakobJoel argued, don't sustain the idea that man has any freedom. Again and again they show human beings trapped. Which, the brilliance of Maimonides notwithstanding, disproves the notion of free will.

That literature was written by secular people, with a secular ideology; therefore they are not unlimited as thinkers, his uncle said.

Joel questioned JakobJoel: Was his technical scholarship at MIT for the sake of scholarship or was it scholarship with a self-serving goal? He quoted the Talmudic debate regarding the linguistic variation on the statement describing how Jews ought to pursue Torah. In one place it suggests that the pursuit take them "until the heavens," in another it says "into the heavens." The Zohar explains that Torah studied for the love of pure scholarship rises into the heavens, but Torah studied with a goal remains outside. When the BeShT arrived in the city of Lvov (Lemberg) and was escorted to the local synagogue, he stopped at the entrance and wouldn't go in. There was no space for him, he explained, because there was too much Torah inside. In other words, the scholarship in this community was not pure, the Torah studied there had failed to rise to the heavens. It remained lodged in the synagogue.

The renowned Tzvi La-Tzaddik, Joel continued, used gematria to explain the difference. The Hebrew word for "until" adds up to 74; the word "into" equals 100. The difference is 26, which is the numeric value of YHVH, the name of God. Impure prayer doesn't reach into the heavens because it is missing the value of God; in other words, it is ungodly.

And you'll be especially interested in this, Joel went on. Reb Bunem of *Pesikhtha* said that Torah that doesn't rise into the heavens remains on earth to add to earthly wisdom, what you're here to study. The past century's unmatched strides in technology are therefore largely due to impure scholarship, of which there seems to be a great deal.

That's unfair, JakobJoel said.

About JakobJoel's idea for a screenplay, a creative effort, his uncle said: It's nothing to run from. One way or another every man attempts

God's work, understandably since we're made in His image. Since we are only men, our work remains ephemeral, here today, gone tomorrow. Life is a mere eyeblink.

JakobJoel shrugged. His uncle's life, dying as he had at the age of eighteen, had been less than half an eyeblink. And his secret alphabet project, his attempts at creation, had been all chimera, figures in the air. JakobJoel considered his idea for a screenplay, what his uncle referred to as attempts at creation. An alternative to writing a screenplay, JakobJoel thought, was to program a software version of Cog in which the plot could be put into action. But a programmed Cog could never pass the Turing test, never become as good as a human mind, never do what the human mind has evolved to do best. The reverse was true, too. Humans would never pass the anti-Turing test, since they were unlikely to become as good as the most powerful computers are at what computers do best. The human and computer were of different species, moving in separate evolutionary paths that would never converge. Communion between members of different species was near impossible. In fiction, however, these limitations could be transcended; a fictional Cog could pass both the Turing and anti-Turing tests. And yet there was no good reason for JakobJoel Levy, great-grandson of Berditchev, sophomore at MIT, to write this fictional Cog. Of course his uncle had something to say on the subject.

There is only one true entity that could pass all tests, surpass all limitation, and though science may disagree, He is not fictional, Joel said.

Attempting to shut his uncle out, JakobJoel closed his eyes. Despite himself, despite his determination to take his stand on the side of science, he wouldn't mind knocking off Cog's story. But only if it came easily. He'd tried writing once, when for about a week, maybe, he'd wanted to be a *badkhn*. It was before his bar mitzvah, so he must have been around twelve. After hearing Yankel Yankevitch at a friend's ceremony he'd tried coming up with his own rhymes, but after the first line, trying to compose the next one, he went through the alphabet, from *a* to *z*, seeking a rhyming word, and ended up with an impossible equation. The difficulty: When he finally did have a rhyming word it was usually one that had no relation to the subject of the first line, and he found it impossible to hitch the two words together to make sense, never mind achieve humor. He wasn't good at making connections. At the age of twelve, he'd come up against the challenge of creation and had given up. How did *badkhonim* and poets do it? The failed attempt left JakobJoel with an appreciation for Yankel's achievement and he became a loyal fan. Of course the story of Cog didn't have to rhyme, and it was about technology, a subject JakobJoel knew. Still he wouldn't torture himself over it, he decided. Either it would come or it wouldn't. In the meantime, he went to brush his teeth.

Before he fell asleep, he tried out a first sentence: *I may as well begin at the beginning, as has every creator.*

In the morning, he decided against the last phrase: "as has every creator." A god doesn't acknowledge other gods before him.

Left with *I may as well begin at the beginning,* JakobJoel was dissatisfied. The sentence lacked the attitude and style of a god. Cog should begin with something powerful, something like the first commandment: I am God, your only God. And how original is that? JakobJoel asked himself. But gods don't have to worry about being original, they do and say as they please. He went to his keyboard and typed in capital letters: IN THE BEGINNING, THERE WERE ZEROS AND ONES, UNORDERED AND WITHOUT MEANING, decided he liked it, and went to class.

What have you got? Julia asked the next day.

A sentence, JakobJoel said. That I kind of like. I'm satisfied.

You have more than one sentence, Rick said. I saw the blue light of your screen when I went into the kitchen for a late-night snack. And I heard typing.

You're both obsessed. I was answering e-mail.

Based on what you told me yesterday, Julia said, you ought to have twenty or so pages already.

JakobJoel shrugged. Maybe you should write it. There are precedents for this type of situation. Homer. Rabbi Nachman of Bratslav. They delivered orally. The actual writing was done by others.

And you should also know that it's only because they were written that their work survived, Julia said in what seemed to JakobJoel a know-it-all voice.

You're focusing on the empty half of the glass. Don't you even want to hear my first sentence? JakobJoel asked.

Not sure, Rick said.

Julia folded her arms across her chest like a schoolteacher. How about when you have, like, an entire paragraph? she said.

JakobJoel wished Julia would just stop. It seemed to him that she and Rick had become somehow united in this cause. And in her new, self-appointed role as editor, Julia had become bossy and their relationship had changed. The abrupt shift was annoying. It was getting in the way of a perfectly good friendship and he was beginning to feel as if Rick had taken off with Julia. He was being irrational, JakobJoel knew, Rick and Julia were friends just as he and Julia were friends, they all were. What had begun with mutual admiration had developed into a friendship, maybe something more than friendship, and could easily have continued, if not for his obtuse attempt at creation, a stupid desire to impress.

To begin with, he'd met Julia the previous fall during her first campus visit. Along with other incoming students, she'd stopped in to look at their house, but he'd really first noticed her at the annual weekend retreat. Every summer a trip was planned for the residents of the co-op house—the Coop, they called it. Someone had suggested camping at an outdoor bluegrass festival and at the last minute, they'd thought to invite incoming residents. Julia had been the only one of the new people who came. The outdoor life, cooking, sleeping in a tent, and listening to music had brought them together quickly. And he hadn't been the only one to notice Julia. Everyone liked her.

Unable to concentrate on anything else, JakobJoel returned to his room, sat in front of his screen, read his first sentence, and added more sentences. He typed quickly, and when he stopped he had three and a half pages. He read them first from Julia's point of view, then Rick's, and imagined their responses.

It's interesting, Julia would say, but what is it? Certainly not a screenplay.

It's kind of cool in its own way, Rick would agree. The repetitiveness makes it sound machinelike. Rick would drop his voice and growl: And it was good. That's a bit like HAL.

That's not good, JakobJoel responded aloud, irritated with the performance he'd imagined for Rick. I didn't want to reference other movies.

But Rick would pay no attention. And it was good, he would repeat. He'd drop his voice and say, Good morning, Dave. May I ask you a personal question, Dave? Please, Dave.

Julia would join Rick. That's a very nice rendering, Dave. I'm afraid I can't do that, Dave.

You're both not picking up the Genesis reference, JakobJoel would point out.

You're underestimating us, Rick would say, possibly an original sin. I've played Sim Life. Rick would slow down, as if for JakobJoel's benefit. I've been a Creator; I've designed organisms and monitored their evolution.

JakobJoel would shrug. Okay, so there's nothing new under the sun. Maybe renewal is all that's left. Retelling.

You're going defensive, Rick would say. I'm trying to tell you that this thing is sort of cool in its own weird way, but in its present configuration it's not filmable. You could probably publish it in *Wired,* which would be cool.

JakobJoel looked at his watch. He'd blown two hours. Why was he writing? Because Julia wanted it. And wasn't this desire to please Julia driven instinctively by a brain wired for self-preservation? If yes, it didn't reflect positively on the human state, ruled still by instinct rather than intellect. After pulling itself away from stationary, treelike roots to acquire mobility, after lifting itself off the ground to stand upright on two legs, after inventing machines, learning to fly above earth, to escape gravity altogether, instinct still remained to bind man to earth. There-fore where did free will come in? It didn't. Every time JakobJoel turned around to think about human choice he found there wasn't any. And did he have a choice in this: to write or not to write the story? So far the attempt had brought no rewards, only grief; therefore he ought to put an end to it. He'd written three pages, but he didn't have to show them. He saved the document and closed it. What was wrong with a screen-play on disk that no one read?

What's wrong? his uncle echoed. Without a reader, a story is dead. The power of story is released only through reading or recital. That's why we have Torah readings in the synagogue. We begin anew every year to reenact our story, our beginnings.

To avoid his uncle's fixations—Creation, Nachman, the power of story—JakobJoel closed his eyes and retrieved an early image of Julia at the Winterfox Bluegrass Festival, Julia licking her strawberry ice cream cone with her long Popsicle tongue, Julia studying the Winterfox sched-ule, her heavy, straight hair obscuring her face, highlighting what she wanted to hear and see, asking him whether he wanted to join her, and of course he wanted to, he went with her everywhere.

JakobJoel's eyes opened.

We all have our Eves, his uncle said. Someone we allow into our minds and for whom we then pretend to do everything. I too once thought of myself as first man, an Adam walking the ground at the first dawn, breathing the air of the first day.

JakobJoel didn't want to hear it. For one thing, he didn't care about other Eves. He wanted to concentrate on his own. He would go back to his own beginnings, the beginning of himself with Julia.

PART

÷

Three

In an annual reenactment of Creation, always in the third week of July, on a hilltop in the foothills of the Berkshire Mountains, known locally as the Roitveld Farm, where, for fifty-one weeks of the year, Holstein and Highlander cattle graze, a village appears for seven miraculous days and then disappears as quickly.

Winterfox 2000

On the first day, water made its way up the mountain in thirty-foot-long trucks. Early dawn of the second day, the air still thick with dew, lumber arrived from Herrington's. In the course of the long morning, the stages were built, along with the floors for the Dance Pavilion, the platform in the Master Workshop tent, and benches for the Children's Academy. On the third day, electricity arrived. The mountaintop swarmed with men in uniforms: Central Hudson Gas and Electric employees, Taconic Telephone men, Red Hook Electric. Late afternoon, the festival manager made his rounds, chatted with members of the various crews, and pronounced the work good enough. The fourth day began with the arrival of food vendors, those national wandering kitchens outfitted to park and cook anywhere on and off road. Within two efficient hours of arrival, the drone of generators replaced the everyday mountain sounds, and at noon everyone was invited to sample the first meals. Late afternoon brought the arrival of the first Winterfox guests: a trickle of Airstreams, RV campers, SUVs. The group from the MIT house arrived in a borrowed Explorer. After a quick stop at the registration booth, where they received their campsite number, license, and instructions on how to park across the grade in low gear or park, wheels chocked in, they found their site and unloaded. From her backpack, Julia unfolded a candelabra in parts, screwed it together, inserted fresh candles, and soon voices softened, movement slowed. On the fifth morning, security, traffic, safety, and medical personnel took their places in their designated booths, their voices muted to keep from waking campers sleeping in. Late afternoon brought a traffic jam to the base of the mountain. Guests waited at registration, then raised dust driving up the steep hills to find their reserved campsites, in the north, south, or west grounds, hilltop, perimeter, or roadside. At sunset, drivers coming over the crest of Over-Mountain Road were surprised by what they saw on the northern horizon: Behold, a new village was born, known since the year 2000 as Winterfox, formerly Greyfox, formerly Winterhawk, before that the Berkshire Mountain Bluegrass Festival, originally the Mount Sinai Festival. At the local general store, where incoming revenues were ninety percent higher than usual, the day's work was declared premium.

Winterfox 2000 schedules were posted and distributed and guests were advised to register for those events they wished to attend. Julia spread the schedule on the makeshift table and bent over it, pink highlighter in hand.

She read:

	MAIN STAGE	MASTERS WORKSHOPS	DANCE PAVILION	GRASS ROOTS	FAMILY STAGE
	SUGAR HILL RECORDS	INTELLITOUCH TUNERS	ATLANTIC SOLAR PRODUCTS	D'ADDARIO STRINGS	BG RADIO NETWORK INTO THE BLUE
11:00	The Schankman Twins: 11-11:40	See your favorite artists up close! Ask questions.	Kick up your heels & learn your favorite style of dance!	Hands On Learning: Bring Your Instrument!	Note: Family Stage begins at 9:00 and will not coincide with Main Schedule hours at left
11:30					
12:00	Gary Ferguson & Sally Love Band: 11:50-12:30	Karaoke with Kitsy! 12:00-12:50	Irish Step Dance Performance & Dance Workshop with Liza MacDougall; music by John Kirk & friends: 12:00-1:20	Harmonica with Bob Meehan & Friends 12:00-12:50	Cool Craft Creations: 9:00-10:30
12:30	Dry Branch Fire Squad: 12:40-1:30				The Antics of Steve Charney: 11:00
1:00		Monroe Style Mandolin: Skip Gorman 1:00-1:50		Guitar & Acoustic Bass with Andy Greene & Kip Martin: 1:00-1:50	Balloon Making Workshop with Tom Lilly: 11:45
1:30	Jerry Douglas: 1:40-2:10		Cajun Dance instruction with Jim Christensen; music by Ed Lowman & Friends: 1:30-2:50		
2:00		Sibling Rivalry Part II: McCourys & Krugers 2:00-2:50			Lunch Break: 12:30-1:00
2:30	Doc Watson: 2:20-3:10			Fiddle with Gene Lowinger: 2:00-2:50	Entertainment with Steve Charney: 1:00
3:00		Lord of the Dobro: Jerry Douglas 3:00-3:50	Clogging & Participatory World Dances with Vanaver Caravan 3:00-4:20	Banjo Set-Up Techniques with Geoff Stelling 3:00-3:50	
3:30	Del McCoury Band: 3:20-4:10				Magic Show with Tom Lilly : 1:45
4:00		Guitar Styles: J. Lawrence, O. Starr & R. Scholle 4:00-4:50	Zydeco Dance Instruction with Jim Christensen; music by Slippery Sneakers: 4:30-5:30	Mandolin with Fred Lantz & Tim Blair 4:00-4:50	Stephen Michael Schwartz of Parachute Express: 2:30
4:30	David Grisman Quintet: 4:20-5:30				
5:00		Bluegrass Meets Old Timey & Cajun: Balfa Toujours 5:00-5:50		All-Festival Band Practice w/ Ron Thomason Bring your instrument 5:00-5:30	Gary the Silent Clown: 3:15
5:30	Dinner Break: 5:30-7:00		Dinner Break 5:30-6:30		The Name Game with Lee Shapiro: 4:00
6:00			Dinner Dance Squares, Contras & Circles. Music by Fiddlestyx; John & Trish calling: 6:30-7:20	Dobro Session with Pete Reichwein & Mark Panfil 6:00-7:00	The Panfil Brothers: 4:45
6:30		Congratulations to Jeff Simons & Melissa Campbell on their wedding day right here at Winterfox!			"Ocho the Octopus' Ocean Adventure" with Diane Kordas: 5:30
7:00	Kruger Brothers: 7:00-7:50				
7:30			Performance by the Vanaver Caravan. Original & Int'l Dances with live music on unusual instruments: 7:30-8:45		
8:00	Doc Watson: 8:00-9:00				Parachute Express with Stephen Michael Schwartz: 6:15
8:30					
9:00	Tim O'Brien Band: 9:10-10:10		Zydeco Dance to the music of Slippery Sneakers: 9:00-10:20		Movies and Snacks: 8:30-10:00
9:30	Rigel Mandolin Drawing: 10:15	Happy first anniversary to Margo & Earl			
10:00	The Del McCoury Band: 10:20-11:20		Cajun Dance Bons Temps! Music by Balfa Toujours 10:30-12:30		
10:30					
11:00	Stelling Banjo Drawing: 11:25				
11:30	"Old & On the Hill" Grisman, Clements, Rowan, Pedersen & Mike Bub 11:30-1:00		Sweet dreams!		
12:00					
12:30					
1:00					

Behind her, JakobJoel stood, looking over her shoulder. On his own shoulder, the weight and breadth of another body dogging him, his uncle Joel redacting and entrapping, bending the event through his own purposive lens. He left no room for Julia or her pink highlighter, JakobJoel noted. And his Winterfox wasn't really Winterfox. But what was it? To find out, JakobJoel gave himself over to Joel's redaction, and read.

PART THREE INTERRUPTED

PART

÷

Four

The Berditchever Festival

Friday afternoon, on the main stage, the Winterfox Talent Showcase, including the Boys Pirchei choir rehearsing the evening's performance: Songs for the Shabbos table. On the list are Buddy Merriam & the Backroads, James Reams & the Barnstormers, Jim & Jennie & the Pinetops, David Via & Corn Tornado, The Schankman Twins, Lynn Morris Band, Rhonda Vincent & the Rage, Dry Branch Fire Squad, Rounder Women in Bluegrass Band, Nickel Creek, and Railroad Earth. In the Master Workshop tent, Banjo Packin' Mamas: Morris & Schankman, Yankel Yankevitch and the Seven Beggars; followed by Fiddlin' with Style: Lewis & Wickland; Mando Magic: Chris Thile; and Sibling Rivalry Pt.1: Watkins & Schankmans.

At 7 P.M. the walk to welcome the arriving Shabbos will begin in the eastern field and proceed west, toward the setting sun. Evening service is scheduled to begin at 8 P.M. on the main stage. The Berditchever will open with the greeting to the Shabbos.

In the Dance Pavilion, at 10 P.M., the John Kirk & Trish Young Band welcomed one and all to the Winterfox Square, Contra & Circle Dances with Fiddlestyx.

On the Family Stage, Cecil B. deClown Balloon Animal Workshop, Stegosaurus & the Fortune Teller w/ Diane Kordas, and Tie-Dyeing with the Seven Fat Brides!

Registration at the Children's Bluegrass Academy begins Friday from 7 A.M. to 8 P.M.; classes begin Saturday morning.

Early Saturday morning, Sabbath services on various stages. A Reform/Conservative service on the main stage; a Reconstructionist service in the dance pavilion; a Chasidic service on the family stage; and in the woods, to the east of the perimeter campsite, a Bratslav service complete with Bratslav-style solitude.

Saturday headliners on the main stage include bluegrass greats The Kruger Brothers, Ricky Scaggs & Kentucky Thunder, Rhonda Vincent & the Rage, the Jerry Douglas Band, and Alison Kraus. In the Master Workshops: The Banjo: Bill Keith, Tom Adams, and Jens Kruger; Songwriting: M. Bruns, M. Brine, M. Henderson. On the Family Stage, challah braiding with the Berditchever rebbetzin; yarmulke design with the Popular Girls from Ramaz; needle embroidery with Mrs. Jakob; dress and pattern design with Ada and Malke; fancy baking including the elegant djerbo and linzer torte with representatives of the Hungarian Ladies Auxiliary. In the Children's Academy: bow & arrow design with R. Moshele, son of the Berditchever. In the Grass Roots Pavilion, meditative chanting and alphabetic permutations with R. Joel, son of R. Moshe; improvisational storytelling and songwriting with R. Nachman of Bratslav; the art of biography with Nathan of Nemirov; Talmudic debating with the renowned scholar R. Aaron Levy. Bratslav and Talmudic texts available at vendor booth #18. Look for R. Yidel's Book Barn.

Sunday morning, on the main stage, the Cottonmouth Choir performing the Sunday Gospel; the Seven Fat Brides reading from *The Romance Reader;* At two, the Winterfox All-Star Farewell with the Kruger Bros., Bill Henderson, Ricky Scaggs, Rhonda Vincent, Doc Watson, Tim O'Brien, The Del McCoury Band, and more.

In the Master Workshop tent, The Forked Tongue Sisters teaching gospel harmonies; Generation X Bluegrass: Second Edition.

The Dance Pavilion will remain open all day for sheltered jamming, courtesy of Sol Gruber Accordions. The Family Stage will remain open for sheltered study, courtesy of R. Yidel's Book Barn.

At sunset on Friday evening, the sound of the shofar marked the beginning of the Sabbath, and on the Family Stage, the festival's master of ceremonies, Yankel Yankevitch, invited the sixth of the Seven Brides to light and bless the candles onstage. The audience watched as her renowned hands circled the candles three times, then responded to the blessing with the necessary amen.

After which, following custom, the men went to greet the Sabbath with prayer and song on the main stage and the women remained to keep an eye on the burning candles. To pass away the time they did what Jewish women do on Friday nights: they told stories. The Berditchever rebbetzin's seniority entitled her to the comfort of the best chair and to the honor of the first tale. Though she accepted the proffered La-Z-Boy, put her tired legs up, and leaned back, she passed the second honor along to the sixth bride, who without further ado took her seat in the rocking chair because the rhythmic sway was said to have aided many a storyteller.

With a voice not quite as mellifluous as the voice of her third sister, the sixth bride introduced her story.

An Elijah Tale

Such a tale could only occur, indeed has occurred, among the very poor, in places of need, that is, anywhere and everywhere simple Jews of faith live. This one took place in Palestine, in the *alte shtodt* in Jerusalem, where our grandparents lived before 1948.

The time for such a tale is the eve of Passover, when all Jews, rich and poor, throw open their doors and welcome all who are hungry. On such a night, on the first eve of Passover, when on his way home from services at the nearby Western Wall, where he insisted on praying every day of his life, our grandfather, known as the gentle R. Yankev, stopped first at his parents' home, as was his custom, to wish his mother a happy holiday. As usual his two youngest were already there, sent by their mother to show their grandmother the new holiday dresses and to keep company with her until the men returned from the Passover service. After kissing his mother's hand and receiving her kiss on his forehead,

R. Yankev and the children continued toward home to conduct the annual seder. They walked home singing, greeting the holiday, greeting other families also on their way home, also singing, the men in their striped *capotes* and *shtreimlech*, the girls in their best dresses. It wasn't a long walk, ten minutes if you went by way of the souk, an extra four if you wanted to avoid the bedlam of souk business, the ritualistic haggling over pennies. On Sabbath and holidays R. Yankev generally took the longer path. On this holiday eve, just as they arrived at the halfway point between the two homes, a woman in rags appeared, pushing a cartful of bundles. Without hesitation she approached and in a gruff, thick voice requested a word with the head of the family.

Our grandfather paused midsong and midstride and identified himself as such, though as the story will show, this was at best a partial truth.

Was there a place at the table? the woman asked in a garbled Yiddish that our grandfather later identified as a *Varshaver* dialect, Was there a place at the respectable householder's Passover table for a poor old hungry woman with nothing to her name and nowhere to go?

Our grandfather stood as if petrified on the cobblestone beneath his feet. Despite the fact that he had thirteen mouths to feed, he wanted to invite this poor beggar woman to the table. This was the night when every Jew pronounced: "Let all who are hungry come and eat." But what would his Udel say to a dirty old woman, with bundles of rags and who knows, God forbid, even *chametz* somewhere in one of her pockets? What would his mother, the Bubbe Yentl, advise? As it happened, she had more than one empty place at her table this year. One of the children could walk the old beggar woman to Bubbe's house.

Our grandfather debated, found he couldn't make the decision alone, and determined to send two children to ask at home, and two to ask the advice of his mother. It wasn't far. On the run, it would take them less than five minutes. The youngest, whose legs were still too short to carry her quickly, remained with her father. R. Yankev gave instructions and the two pairs took off running in opposite directions. When he turned back to the old woman to explain and ask from where she had come, he saw her lift off the ground, hover heavily in midair, then vanish upward, a female Elijah! At this, our grandfather became inconsolable. He accused himself of having failed the test. He'd failed to recognize the miraculous when it was upon him. He trudged home silently, walked into his sparkling clean home without song, without his usual joy, and remained despondent at the holiday table.

Wanting to restore the sparkle in her husband's eyes, to enjoy this long-awaited, laborious, and costly holiday, his Udel pointed out that of one thing he could be certain, Elijah doesn't go hungry. And didn't they invite Elijah at the end of every seder, didn't they open the door for him? This Elijah's timing had been off, she'd arrived several hours early.

That night our grandfather recited the ritual *ha'lachma anya* with tears in his eyes.

The youngest child, Basha, suffering for her father, couldn't understand why he was sad. When it was time to ask the four questions, she took her finger from her mouth and asked her father, Why is Tateh sad on this night? We saw Elijah and then we saw Elijah disappear. In all the stories my teacher tells, this is how it happens. No one knows it's Elijah until after he's gone.

The next night, on the eve when in the Diaspora Jews celebrate a second seder, our grandfather passed over the same place, this time he was alone, and once again the old woman approached, once again she asked to speak with the householder.

This time our grandfather intended to do the right thing. Without further ado, with no questions asked or answered, he determined to take hold of this Elijah and bring her home. But a man isn't allowed to touch a strange woman. Although in Jerusalem there is no second seder, a detail this Elijah from Poland had failed to pick up, R. Yankev decided to conduct one. Without considering the propriety of pushing a cart on a holiday, with no question of what the bundles might contain, he took the handles of her cart, urged the woman to follow, and pushed toward home. He arrived home out of breath, with a loaded cart but no woman. She had walked beside him the whole way; he would take an oath, if it were permissible, that she had been at his side. And then, just as he had turned to open the door to his own home, she'd vanished. Into thin air.

Our grandfather was beside himself. If God in His wisdom had seen fit to allow a man to touch a woman, then not only this cart of rags would be here.

With a wink at her eldest daughter, R. Yankev's wife said, This proves that the outcome of the event on the first night was precisely right. Did you think that a mere man, even one from the *alte shtodt*, has the power to alter the ways of Elijah? Your own Basha knows better.

As a result of these events, the sixth bride finished, our grandfather's table was crowded with beggars ever after. Every homeless man and woman knew to knock at his door, every *shnorrer* from Safed to Yehupetz knew where to find a meal, complete with a chicken soup more golden than anyone could remember, and dumplings so fat they displaced the soup.

The sixth bride ended her tale with pride. As it happens, it was our mother who was that young innocent Basha. Every Passover at the first seder, just before the door for Elijah is opened, we beg her to retell her story.

Jakobjoel admired the feminist slant in his uncle's redaction. With the choice of a female narrator came a female Elijah. And Joel wasn't finished with female narrators, because all eyes turned to the Berditchever rebbetzin, who again deferred her tale till later, and the third bride offered to take her turn. After my sister's story, she said, it's fair to offer a tale that comes to us by way of our paternal line. Though our father's family lived in *aus-land*, far from the holy land, they too encountered their share of miracles.

A Miracle Tale

The place is Romania, the time World War Two, when Jews and trains—well, the Sabbath is no time to talk about tragedy.

The event took place in Romania, in the small town of Timisoara, in Transylvania. Our paternal grandfather was a shrewd businessman and landowner, who frequently traveled by train to the city of Lugoj and returned the same evening. One morning, after he'd harnessed his horse, he discovered that it had broken a shoe. He hurriedly put another horse into service, and was soon under way. Strangely enough, on this unsuccessful morning, the rear wheel on the wagon found a ditch. Our grandfather was beside himself. With God's help, he was able to free the wheel and was again on his way. By his watch, he could still arrive at the station in time. But as luck would have it, the horse wouldn't cooperate. It stopped at the side of the road to eat, turned its head toward home, and remained stubborn despite the disciplinary reins. When our grandfather attempted to force the beast forward, she walked the rear wheel into another ditch.

Two hours later the news arrived that between Timisoara and Lugoj the train had exploded. The number of fatalities remained unknown.

At the synagogue the next morning, our grandfather recited the survivor's blessing.

÷

There was time for one more short tale, and the seventh bride offered to entertain with something more contemporary.

The Seven Trials

And it happened that Ada's wedding day came to pass, but before she could present herself under the canopy, she had to fulfill the seven tasks of the bride. She arose early, dressed quickly, and was on her way to the old stone well on Ellish Parkway, where the old rebbetzin was already waiting, the first seven glasses of water filled and warming in the sun.

Ada apologized for keeping the rebbetzin waiting. But isn't this the appointed hour? she asked, looking at her watch.

Yes, it is, the rebbetzin explained. You're not late. I'm early. I like to give the first seven glasses an opportunity to warm up, so they go down more easily. When it's very cold, I set them out the night before.

Ada nodded gratefully. In the next seven hours, she had to drink seven eight-ounce glasses seven times, for Jacob's seven years of labor. This task wouldn't be easy but she'd planned for it with some efficiency.

She would drink two sets of seven now, go on to complete her other tasks, then return for the next seven, and so on. This would be easier than attempting to swallow all forty-nine glasses consecutively. Her plan wasn't an orthodox one, she knew, but she'd written to her uncle, who was a judge, to ask whether such a plan would qualify as a fulfillment of the requirements, and she had with her his written affirmative response.

She lifted the first glass, drank, the second, then the third, and the water went down smoothly, moistening the membranes of her mouth and throat. She hadn't known she could be so thirsty. She drank four more quickly and wondered whether she was getting enough water on a regular basis. Doctors recommend eight glasses of water a day. If on a given day she drank four it was a lot for her.

The second set of seven was harder, the final four a matter of strong will. She finished them and was ready to go on to other things.

I'll return for the next two sets of seven in two hours, she told the rebbetzin. Perhaps you want to fill the glasses now.

The rebbetzin looked at her. What do you mean, return? No bride has ever left in the midst of the task.

I've taken on seven tasks and I'm leaving in order to fulfill some of the others. Standing here waiting until I can drink more would take too much time. And it's a short day.

It's a good practical idea, the rebbetzin acknowledged. I've just never known anyone to do it this way. Tell me, what are your other tasks?

Ada listed the tasks. To recite the seventh sentence of every seventh psalm, to dress and undress seven times on this day, to refrain from food and drink for seven minutes of seven hours of this day, to immerse herself in cold water seven times, to pass her fingers through seven flames seven times, to call her mother-in-law seven times, and the final one, which every bride fulfills: Walking around the groom seven times, creating his new home.

The rebbetzin nodded and put a cool hand on Ada's cheek. Go with *mazel*, my child.

Ada walked home briskly, feeling waterlogged, her body a huge amoeba-shape of liquid. By the time she arrived, she was desperate to relieve herself, but first she pinched her wrist to make certain she was not asleep in her bed.

After washing her hands and saying the "Blessed be he for the inner workings of man," she sat down to recite the seventh lines of the seventh psalms. She turned the pages to the seventh psalm, counted down to the seventh sentence, and read. It took more time to arrive at the passage than to recite it, and she wondered about the significance of this. After the fourth set of sevens, she folded down the corner of the page to mark it and went on to the next task.

She looked at her watch and timed seven minutes in which she ate nothing, then went to the refrigerator. It occurred to her that she could accomplish more than one thing at a time. The time spent dressing and undressing could, for example, count toward the minutes of fasting. If she hurried, she could dress and undress within seven minutes, thereby fulfilling two of the tasks.

She lit seven candles, folded down the three last fingers of her right hand, and passed the open fingers through the candles, all in a row. When they were children, she and Joel had passed a finger through a flame on a regular basis, and the heat had never bothered her. If you moved quickly and smoothly, she'd learned, you didn't feel it. She took a breath, and passed her fingers back through. But she wasn't as smooth on the return and it burned. *Ow*, she yelped, and wrung her hands. She blew out the candles. She'd do the next one after a cold immersion in the mikvah. She put on a coat, grabbed a large towel, and left.

The immersion was a simple task—she was a good swimmer and knew how to live in water. The one difficulty, which Ada thought of as a stupidity, was that she had to emerge from the water after each immersion, dry herself entirely—fortunately her hair was allowed to remain wet or it would have taken hours—and then enter for another dip. Despite this, it was most efficient to accomplish all seven dips within the same visit. If she'd thought of it she would have planned to undress and dress between dips, and she would have accomplished the two tasks, three if she included the timed fast. Perhaps this was the key to the seven tasks, to find a way to accomplish them all as one. The purpose? Was it to teach the bride, and future mother, efficiency planning, a skill she would need when she had a houseful of children?

Her cell phone rang. Her mother-in-law. She had tried to call her and the line had been constantly busy.

Let me call you right back, Ada said, and pressed END. If they were going to have a conversation, it might as well count toward the fulfillment of the task. She pressed TALK, and waited for the connection. She received a busy signal. How was that possible? She tried again. Another call must have come in. Ada shook her head. What should have been an easy task was turning out to be one of the harder ones. She pressed TALK again and again the line was busy. This was frustrating. She hadn't put through a single one of the seven calls and it was already after noon.

When she arrived at Ellish Parkway and the well, the rebbetzin was there waiting, the third set of seven glasses filled. Ada drank quickly, pouring the water down her throat as if into a bottomless jug. If she kept her throat open and wide, it went down faster. Glass after glass after glass. She asked for the fourth round of seven and drank.

The rebbetzin watched, astonished.

What willpower, she murmured.

Walking home, Ada tried the phone again and didn't get through. Her stomach grumbled. She was hungry. When she arrived home, she prepared a sandwich, then timed seven minutes of fasting before sitting down to eat it. Afterward, she lit the seven candles, ran her fingers under cold water, then across the line of candles and back, forward and back again, and so on. It was easy enough, and she decided to complete the task entirely, counting six sets of forward and backs. She extinguished the candles and put them away.

She tried the telephone again, using the regular phone this time, and didn't get through.

She went on to the psalms, and worked for just under an hour, and completed the task.

She undressed-dressed, undressed-dressed, undressed-dressed, undressed-dressed, undressed-dressed, each timed for seven minutes, so that she also fulfilled five times seven minutes of fasting. Counting the previous undressing-dressing, one in the morning and the second at the mikvah, the task was complete. She added another seven timed minutes of fasting, and was finished with this, too.

She was due at the well for her fifth round of water. She walked there briskly, trying her cell phone at regular intervals. The circuits were busy. The whole of Rockland County must be gossiping on this day. These were the two tasks left, the water and the telephone calls; she could control the drinking, but the calls were out of her hands. It was the one thing that depended on someone other than herself, someone whose job it wasn't to help her fulfill the task, such as the rebbetzin or the mikvah lady. Her mother-in-law had no stake in the project, she wasn't even aware that Ada had taken this upon herself as one of seven tasks, and now Ada regretted coming up with such an idea. Mrs. Levy was hard to reach on any given day, which was why it could count as a task, but on this day, her son's wedding day, reaching her seven times might prove impossible.

The first four glasses went down easily enough, the last three were harder. Her throat wouldn't remain open. She was spending too much time swallowing. But finally she was done and while the rebbetzin filled the sixth round of glasses, Ada tried calling again, and the phone rang, Mrs. Levy picked up, and the first of seven calls was achieved.

After this success, Ada managed the next glasses with less difficulty, but she felt painfully bloated. The water sloshed within her all the way home.

She tried the phone again and it was busy. She had an idea that if she dialed from the fax machine it would automatically keep dialing until it got through.

After five attempts, the fax phone engaged and Ada picked up the receiver, spoke with her mother-in-law, and the second call was placed.

She was tired. It was three in the afternoon. She was due at the hall for photographs at six. The reception started at seven-thirty. If she slept for an hour, woke at four, walked to Ellish for her last seven glasses, and managed the other calls on the way there and back, she could sit for the hairdresser by five-thirty. Before she fell asleep, she tried dialing one more time.

Ada woke at four-thirty and had to hurry. She called the rebbetzin, then tried her mother-in-law, whose phone was still busy. She was a machine, executing all the moves to get through the day, and like the modern machine, she too had the ability to multitask. Still she was getting nowhere with the phone calls. Aaron's family was large, he had eight siblings, most of them already married, which was why it was so hard to get through. She wondered whether there was another number, for emergencies, and whether her status as almost family would deem her worthy of it. But she would have to wait until after the wedding.

She poured the seven glasses down her throat. Knowing they were the final fifty-six ounces helped. When she was finished, the rebbetzin kissed her and advised her to go home now and attend to looking beautiful. If only she could, Ada thought. But why was she so aggravated about these calls? She could continue calling while her hair and makeup were done and even during her session with the photographer. With no other task left, she would concentrate on this and accomplish it.

She pressed REDIAL on her phone and listened. She pressed REDIAL again. On the third time she got through, spoke briefly to her mother-in-law, who was probably wondering what the call was for. This was the fourth call of the day. Before her mother-in-law could move far from the phone, Ada pressed REDIAL again, claimed to have forgotten to mention the appointed time for the groom's photos, was informed that she had mentioned it, and the fifth call was accomplished. Ada wondered how she could execute two more calls without alerting her mother-in-law to the reason for all the calls. She pressed REDIAL, miraculously the phone rang, and Ada apologized for bumping the wrong button. After this she put her phone away. She would save the last call. She'd think of something to say or request before the end of this day.

On the main stage the Berditchever led the men in prayer, welcoming the Sabbath. Accompanying him on banjo and drums were Béla Fleck and the Flecktones playing "Shalom Aleikhem." They surprised the Berditchever with a riff he couldn't identify, but after a pause, he picked up the melody and managed to keep time with the unfamiliar digression. After prayers, families made their way home to their private campsites for the Sabbath meal of homemade challah, Manischewitz gefilte fish with Gold's horseradish, Mother's thermos-warm chicken soup with soup nuts, and room-temperature potato and noodle pudding from Zabar's on Broadway.

After dinner the women visited neighboring tents, admired the ingenious solutions to life in the garden, debated the question of practicality over aesthetics, and the judging for the Third Annual "Best Campsite" Award was in full swing. Word of the probable winner spread

quickly, a French-outdoor-café setup, complete with peeling-paint folding table and chairs for four, trimmed shelves lined with jelly jars of coffee, tea, sugar, cinnamon, and the espresso cups and saucers to go with
it, plus candles, shawls, and a '50s red plaid tin cooler filled with ice.
When the women stopped in to see it, the homemakers, two leggy
young women and their boyfriends, were sipping café au lait.

The two other finalists:

One a site with two authentic leather tepees, the larger one for the
two adults, the parents, the smaller for their three children. At the
entrance of the larger tepee, an Indian-style grill. Also leather folding
chairs to match the tepees. Reclining on the chairs, the householders, in
Indian leggings with Apache-style rugs thrown over their shoulders,
smoked long cheroots. Inside each tepee, a large rope hammock strung
from corner to corner filled with blankets, pillows, stuffed bears. A small
blanket chest served as both a step stool and dresser for storage.

The third finalist was a haunting model of a shtetl out of the Russian
Pale, complete with several one-room thatched-roof hovels, a synagogue, a graveyard of gravestones sticking up every which way, and in
the community square, the grave of a bride and groom. The elders in the
community visited this campsite in a hush, allowed the atmosphere to
wash over them, remind them of what once was.

In the Master Workshop tent the Berditchever ritual table was beginning. When all were seated, it was clear that many of the older men had
succumbed to sleep after the meal. The young, however, were in full
attendance, faces aglow, hopeful for a piece of the rebbe's fish, a sip of
his wine, the honor in being remembered, of having one's name
announced. And as always they looked forward to the evening's talk.
According to Yankel Yankevitch, who was seen everywhere and nowhere at once, something unusual was afoot: the talk on this night
would surprise.

When the time came, Joel, son of R. Moshele, whispered into the Berditchever's ear and the Berditchever announced that on this extraordinary night, when the Friday-night meal would take place under the stars, the discourse would also be out of the ordinary. After which, Yankel stepped up to the mike and invited JakobJoel, grandson of Berditchev, to deliver a midrash on Genesis.

From backstage voices were heard in argument, two male tenors similar enough in timbre that they were as one voice. Members of the audience craned their necks, hoping for a better view of the notorious young man who had left yeshiva to study science, but the stage remained bare. People became restless. Finally Yankel stepped on stage, begged the audience to indulge a young man's orneriness—JakobJoel had declined the honor—and introduced the Yonder Yiddishe Fiddlers. The Berditchever ceremonial meal began with a performance of the traditional songs; a fusion of Jewish and African rhythms played by the Klezmatics followed. In the Dance Pavilion, the Slonimer Boychicks led the audience in Chasidic circle dancing and the Lubavitch dance troupe performed the *kazatzke*. At first signs of light, boys and girls bid one another good morning, declared the previous day good enough, and went to bed.

Though he had refused to participate, as a spectator JakobJoel was beginning to enjoy this Berditchever festival, his uncle's strange creation. But, he wondered, was there a reason for it? And why didn't Joel himself take the stage?

The sixth morning began in a hush. Only the older men were awake before ten. They were seen hurrying toward the Grass Roots Pavilion for morning prayers. An hour later, the younger men arrived, in time to hear the cantor chanting Holy, Holy, Holy.

The day of rest continued restfully. Accustomed to their afternoon nap, the older generation slept.

Late-afternoon Master Workshop offerings included meditative chanting and permutations with R. Joel, son of R. Moshele; improvisational storytelling and songwriting with R. Nachman of Bratslav; the art of biography with Nathan of Nemirov. All three were sparsely attended.

At dusk, for the performance by the third bride, whose voice was renowned for its timbre of milk and honey, the audience turned out in droves. The Yiddish words to the melancholy good-bye song to the departing Sabbath were distributed and everyone accompanied the third bride in the ritual song, ending with the prayer to the God of Abraham, Isaac, and Jacob.

Es geyt shon avek der hayliger shabbos,
In shtibel is lichtig in shtibel is shtil,
es tshepshet die mameh der got fun Avrohom
zie tshepshet die tefilah mit hartz un gefiehl.
Oy, got fun Avrohom fun Yitzchok un Ya'akov
farnem shoyn mayn tefilah in dayn himlicher geshtel
un shik shon mayn mazel
un ruhf oys mayn broche,
az lichtig zol veren iber die gantze velt.

The holy day is departing
The small room is bright, the small room is silent
Mother whispers the God of Abraham
She whispers the prayer with heart and feeling:
O God of Abraham, of Isaac, and Jacob,
Receive my prayer in your heavenly setting
and send my fortune
and announce my blessing
that a bright light may illuminate the entire world.

÷

While they waited for three stars to appear in the darkening sky, the Berditchever rebbetzin offered up her tale.

The Man I Should've Married

Man thinks, God winks, the Berditchever rebbetzin lamented. Human life is a mere mockery. As an example of such tricks, the story of what one might consider both the beginning and end of a life, the story of many a woman in many a Yiddish household.

In every young girl's life comes a year when the world seems wide open, when anything seems possible, the world an open palm. But all too soon the whole width and breadth of this terrible illusion converges on a limited choice, an either-or, this boy or that one.

I was a girl of the old city as poor and pretty as the next one, perhaps prettier, and for what purpose prettiness if not to help our dear fathers by marrying money. In such a match, no dowry was required, the wedding didn't cost the girl's family a piastre. In certain cases, particularly if the boy had some obvious flaw—and what male doesn't, I ask you, though I didn't come to this knowledge until much later—the transaction was further sweetened with a onetime payment to the family.

My dear father knew me as a girl with eyes occasionally too wide open, a girl who felt the admiring glances that accompanied her on her daily walk from the souk and back, and took pleasure in it. Are there any young girls who do not feel themselves drawn to the wiry, dark-skinned young men who unlike our brothers spent the whole of their days and nights outdoors, under the stars? But I was also a girl who needed her mother and sisters nearby, who lived for the love of her father and brothers; therefore, when the time came, the qualifications of two boys were presented to me: the first, a rich boy from America with whom I would be destined to live far away from everything and everyone I knew and loved; the second, a motherless boy from Romania whose father farmed a parcel of the Holy Land. These were the choices of my day.

Arrangements were made for a one-sided sighting. These days, when girls meet several boys before they agree to marry one, such arrangements aren't necessary. But in our day, an arranged meeting with a boy was expected to end in an engagement. Since I was clearly a *mameh's* as well as a *tateh's* girl, the wisdom of sending me to the other end of the world was questioned and sightings rather than meetings were recommended. It was hoped that seeing the boy would work its magic. The choice is entirely yours, my father said.

The next morning, my sister Fraydl and I posted ourselves on Gestetner, where the *Ungarishe* alleyway begins, and where the first boy would turn off on his way home from the morning service. My dear gentle father would accompany the boy, talk with him; I would see and decide.

We waited, heard their voices before we saw them. They came walking around the bend slowly. Our father saw us and winked. The boy, eyes cast down, didn't seem to notice. From Fraydl's lips, the fated words escaped—A *gingi*. After this, I could see nothing else. He may as well have been a boy without a nose, mouth, or eyes, a being without a body. All I saw in front of me was the beginnings of a red beard and red *peyos*, and in my mind's eye, a passel of redheaded children.

Our mother was waiting at the door when we arrived. I shook my head. I don't want to raise a family of redheads. And who could argue with that? When my father heard it, he shook his head and shrugged. She's right, he said. If a girl doesn't want to give birth to redheads, she shouldn't marry a redhead.

The next day I saw the second boy, an olive-skinned, dark-haired, sad-faced young man, and my heart turned over. My father advised against it. Something bothered him. This young man is not one of us, he said. Of Hungar-Romanian stock, he lacks our Polish vigor, our hopefulness.

As fate would have it, every word that dropped from my unsuspecting father's mouth pushed and prodded me toward this young man. An only child with no mother, he was a boy who needed a good wife, someone who could give him warmth and cheer. And, I rationalized, married to this boy, I myself would avoid becoming like an orphan, alone in exile. I would live here, in Jerusalem or in B'nei B'rak, but always only hours from home.

Nu. The Berditchever rebbetzin wrung her hands. *Rabbosai*, what is there to say? I married this orphan boy and within ten years found myself living in exile in America, with my dark-skinned, inefficacious dreamer of a husband, and I, a woman alone with four young mouths to feed and clothe, and not a cent in the bank. As you well know, into such Yiddish tales comes a goat, a real-life *khoze*, complete with black eyes and beard. One day my Magyar, as these Hungars are called, remembered his sheep-filled, goat-ridden Romanian childhood with fondness, and the cursed idea came into his head. In short he brought home a goat, one little goat.

In our diminished day and age, living as we do in scientific, technological America, even a goat is no demon from the netherworld nor anything miraculous from above. These days a goat is a mere goat who kicks the bucket because he wants to and—

÷

She was interrupted by a report that the first three stars had been sighted, it was time to end the Sabbath. The Berditchever rebbetzin waved her arm tiredly, and said the goat's tale would wait till next year, perhaps in Jerusalem.

JakobJoel regretted the interruption, which he thought was a bit too convenient, since it saved the Berditchever further embarrassment. The story of a goat was guaranteed not to bring glory to Berditchev. And he had enjoyed hearing his great-grandmother's voice, her laments. Though she'd known him as an infant, had had the honor of holding him before and after his circumcision, JakobJoel didn't remember her.

The *havdalah* was recited, separating the holy day from the mundane. The women hurried away to clean up and put the children to bed; it was the men's turn to tell stories. According to Chasidic custom, inspiring legendary tales were expected, "true" stories about holy rabbis, unlike the folktales the women told.

A Tale of the BeShT

The old Berditchever began with a sigh. The story for a long day of storytelling, he said, is perhaps the following very brief one about the BeShT.

It happened, the Berditchever said, that the Ba'al Shem Tov found himself in great need. The Berditchever paused and sighed again. Here you may imagine for yourselves all the trials and tribulations of a man in such a position. The story should provide the BeShT with either the long-suffering, silent wife or the nagging one with her full and long and, it must be said, righteous tirade. There should be not even a *groschen* with which to purchase the makings of the next meal. Picture the cupboards bare. The children's bellies swollen with hunger. The coal bucket with only a few useless crumbs at the bottom would float for lightness, but unlike another literary coal bucket, without the BeShT riding in it. And here's why.

The Berditchever paused and slept for several long seconds. When he awoke, he continued where he'd left off.

What does God want from man, the BeShT asked and answered: Human initiative. A Jew with a houseful of hungry mouths to feed must make an effort to beget some *groschen*. In dire straits, he must knock on doors. The day came when the Ba'al Shem Tov was indeed desperate enough to stir from his table and chair. He walked to the nearest house, knocked once on the window, and without awaiting a response, without even explaining what was wanted, returned to his books. Needless to say, people wondered at this negligible attempt until it was explained that for some only a minimum of effort is necessary to accomplish the desired objective. And indeed the *groschen* arrived, the children ate, and the BeShT remained with his books. End of story.

It occurred to some listeners that the Berditchever was following the BeShT's example, telling the tale with a minimum of effort. Others looked into their own hearts and minds to see whether they generally expended too much energy, did too much, and dissipated their powers. The cynics in the audience noted that the BeShT apparently knew to knock where he was certain of being heard, and that this was the operative factor of the story. The more learned recalled a variation on this legend in which each generation knew less, couldn't remember how to induce the miracle, and still the little that they did remember remained effective.

JakobJoel thought his uncle Joel had gotten the Berditchever voice down, complete with characteristic sighs, pauses, and forty winks. Clearly his great-grandfather hadn't changed over the year.

÷

It was R. Moshele's turn, and he offered to tell a miracle tale said to have taken place in the impoverished household of the great scholar R. Chanina Ben Dosa.

A Tale of the Wife of Ben Dosa

The wife of Ben Dosa, R. Moshele began, respected and valued her husband, the great Ben Dosa, but she also knew that outside, her neighbors were noticing that from her oven stack no smoke issued, that in Ben Dosa's home, no Sabbath bread was baking. Though she had no flour to bake with, she put wood into the oven and lit it. One neighbor, certain that Ben Dosa's wife didn't have bread in the oven and wanting to shame her, knocked on the door and entered. Hearing her step, Ben Dosa's wife ran into the bedroom. The neighbor walked into the kitchen, and to her surprise, dough was rising on the table, and in the oven, a large golden loaf, perfectly baked, was about to burn. She called for a bread shovel. Ben Dosa's wife's voice responded, I'm in here to retrieve it.

R. Moshele paused. The midrash asks, Did the wife of Ben Dosa lie?

No, the rabbis answer. Ben Dosa's wife knew that in R. Chanina's home, miracles were common. Therefore, when she heard the neighbor's shout, she believed that there was indeed bread in the oven.

Aaron offered a variation on R. Moshele's tale:

Though she had nothing to cook with, Ben Dosa's wife wanted something hot to offer her husband and children when they came in from the cold, but her cupboards were bare. Still she wanted to make an effort; she put a large pot of water to boil and dropped into it a stone.

A neighbor stopped in, sniffed. It smells very fine, she said, and I have just the thing that's missing; she added a carrot to the pot.

Another neighbor came by, sniffed, said, The soup smells promising, but it needs one more ingredient to make it perfect. She added an onion.

A third neighbor arrived. Delicious, she said, and added a marrow bone.

When Ben Dosa came home, he was amazed at the soup his wife had produced with a stone.

In the Women's Pavilion, Ada offered the following variation on the soup:

In a small saucepan, boil water and cook a small package of dried green and yellow split peas until softened. While that's cooking, process in the food processor:

> 3 carrots
> 4 stalks of celery
> 2 onions
> 3 cloves of garlic
> 2 parsnips

Then sauté the processed batch in olive oil, add 4 cups of homemade chicken stock, and bring to a boil. Add the softened split peas, cover, and simmer for an hour. Season with salt and pepper.

I t was Joel's turn to tell a tale, and all eyes turned toward him. JakobJoel considered the similarities between himself and his uncle. In JakobJoel's presence the family had generally avoided drawing physical comparisons, though they had nothing to worry about. JakobJoel had no intention of following in his uncle's steps. The legacy of an interrupted life did not appeal to him. For one thing, it remained always at the high point of "promise" without requiring fulfillment. To Joel's credit, it appeared he also wasn't satisfied to remain at mere "promise." He was attempting something more, something posthumous, using, JakobJoel thought, a surplus of stories to make up for his own incomplete one. Indeed, after the series of legendary tales, Joel paused for only several seconds, head in hand, then proposed to do what no one had dared before—that is, to finish R. Nachman's "The Seven Beggars." If leaving it unfinished for two hundred years, he said, hasn't brought the Messiah, perhaps finishing it will.

JakobJoel was startled. This was too audacious. Joel was attempting to complete Nachman's tale, the box structure. For what purpose? His uncle, JakobJoel knew, believed that creating and reciting story was a way of restoring the world. But were endings possible? Were they ever true? Nachman hadn't thought so.

÷

In an effort to invoke and secure something of the original voice, Joel proposed to begin at the beginning of the tale, reading directly from the text.

T H E   S E V E N   B E G G A R S

÷

Nahman of Bratslav

translated by Arnold J. Band

I will tell you how our people were once joyous.

<h2 align="center">1.</h2>

Once there was a king who had an only son. The king wanted to transfer the royal power to his son during his own lifetime. So he gave a
grand ball. Now whenever the king gave a ball, it was surely a very joyous affair. But when he transferred the royal power to his son during his
own lifetime, there was surely a great celebration. And at the ball were
all the ministers, all the dukes, and all the nobles. And they were all very
joyous at the ball. And the people, too, were greatly pleased that the
king handed his royal power over to his son during his lifetime, because
this was a great honor for the king, and indeed there was a great celebration. There were all sorts of things for the celebration—musical bands

and comedians and the like—all things used for a celebration were present at the ball.

And when everybody had become very joyous, the king arose and said to his son: "Since I am a star-gazer, and I foresee that you, too, will at some time abdicate the royal power, see to it that you have no sadness when you abdicate. Only be joyous, for when you are joyous, I shall be joyous, too. Even if you are sad, I shall be joyous that you are no longer king, because you do not deserve to be king if you are the kind of person who cannot always maintain his joy even when he abdicates the royal power. Only when you are joyous, shall I be exceedingly joyous."

And the prince assumed the royal power vigorously. He created ministers, and dukes, and officials, and an army. The prince was a wise man, he loved wisdom dearly, and gathered around him many wise men. Whosoever came to him with some sort of wisdom was highly esteemed by him. He gave them great respect and wealth for their wisdom. He gave each one whatever he desired. If one desired money, he gave him money. If one desired honor, he gave him honor. Everything for wisdom. Since wisdom was so esteemed, everyone adopted wisdom and the whole kingdom engaged in the practice of wisdom. One practiced wisdom because he desired money, and another, because he desired honor and esteem. And because they all engaged in wisdom only, people in that country forgot military tactics. They were all engaged only in wisdom until the least wise man in this country would be considered the wisest man in another country, and the truly wise in this country were marvelously wise.

Because of this wisdom, the wise men of the land fell into heresy and they drew the prince into their heresy. But the common people did not fall into heresy since there was a great depth in the wise men's wisdom which escaped the common people and they were not harmed. Only the wise man and the prince became heretics. And since the prince had goodness in him because he had been born with goodness and had good qualities, he always remembered: "Where am I in the world and what am

I doing?" And he would groan deeply and remember: "What is this? I should be carried away by such things? What's happening to me? Where am I in the world?" Yet, no sooner had he begun to use his reason than the heretical ideas were strengthened within him. And so it happened several times. He would remember where he was in the world and what he was doing and would groan and sigh, but suddenly he would again use his reason and his heretical tendencies would be strengthened as before.

2.

And it came to pass that there was a mass flight from a certain country and everyone fled. And as they fled, they passed through a forest, and lost two children there, a male and a female. One family lost a male, and another lost a female. And they were still little children, four or five years old. The children had nothing to eat. They screamed and they cried because they had nothing to eat.

Meanwhile, there came a beggar who was going along with sacks in which he carried bread. The children began to badger him and cling to him. He gave them bread and they ate. He asked them: "Where do you come from?" They answered: "We don't know," because they were little children. He started to leave them, but they asked him to take them along with him. He said to them: "I do not want you to go along with me." Meanwhile they looked and noticed that the beggar was blind. And this was to them a marvel: "If he is blind, how does he know where to go?" (It was also a marvel that the children raised this question, because they were little children. But since they were clever children, this was a marvel to them.) And this blind beggar blessed them: "May you be as I am. May you be as old as I am." He left them more bread and went away.

The children understood that The Blessed One was watching over them and sent them a blind beggar to give them food. After a while the bread ran out and again they began to scream for food. Then night came, and they slept there. In the morning, they still had nothing to eat. They screamed and cried. In the meanwhile another beggar appeared who was deaf. They began to speak to him. He pointed with his hands and said to them: "I don't hear a thing." And this beggar also gave them bread and began to leave them. Again they wanted him to take them with him. He didn't want to, but he, too, blessed them: "You should be like I am." And he also left bread and went off. Then this bread also ran out, and again they began to scream.

Again a beggar appeared who stuttered. They started speaking with him, but he stuttered his words, so they couldn't understand what he said. He knew what they were saying but they didn't know what he was saying because he stuttered. The beggar also gave them bread and left them as before. He also blessed them, that they should be as he was, and he left.

After a while another beggar came, who had a twisted neck. The same thing happened as before. Then came a beggar who was a hunchback. Then a beggar without hands came. Then came a beggar without feet. Each one of them gave bread and blessed them, that they should be as he was, exactly as the previous beggars.

Then the bread ran out again. They started walking toward an inhabited place until they reached a path. And they walked along the path until they came to a village. The children went into a house. People pitied them and gave them bread. They went into another house and there they were also given bread. And so they went from door to door. They saw that it was good that people gave them bread. The children agreed that they would always be together. They made themselves large sacks and went from door to door and they used to go to all celebrations, to circumcisions and to weddings. They roamed through all kinds of towns and went from door to door. They also went to fairs and sat among the beggars on the benches with the beggar's plates, until the children became widely known among all the beggars, since everyone recognized them and knew them as the children who had been lost in the forest.

Once there was a large fair someplace in a large city. All the beggars went there and the children went there too. The beggars hit upon the idea to arrange a wedding match between the children. Immediately, as soon as a few of the beggars began to discuss the issue, it pleased them all and they arranged the match. Only how does one make a wedding for them? They decided that on a certain day, when there would be a feast for the king's birthday, all the beggars would gather there, and from the meat and bread which they begged there, they would make a wedding.

And so it was. All the beggars went to the birthday party and begged for bread and meat, and they also gleaned all the leftovers, meat and egg bread. And they went and dug a huge pit which could hold one hundred people, and they covered it with beams and earth and rubbish and they all went in, and there they made the wedding for the children. They raised the wedding canopy and were very, very joyous. The bride and groom were also very joyous. The bride and groom recalled the favors that The Blessed One had bestowed upon them when they were in the forest and they cried and longed: "How do we find the first beggar, the blind beggar, who brought us bread in the forest?"

3.

Just as they were longing for the blind beggar, he called out: "I am here, I have come to be with you on your wedding day. I present you with a wedding gift: You should be as old as I. Previously, I offered you my blessing but today I bestow this upon you outright as a wedding gift: You should be as old as I am. Do you think that I am blind? Not at all. It is just that the entire world does not amount to an eye's wink (moment) for me." (He looked like a blind man because he did not look at the world at all, since the entire world did not amount to an eye's wink for

him. Therefore seeing and looking at this world did not pertain to him.)
"For I am very old and yet I am still young. I haven't even begun to live,
yet I am very old. Not only do I say so, but I have an affidavit to that
effect from the large eagle and I will tell you a tale:

"Once, people set sail upon the seas in many ships. A tempest arose
and smashed the ships, but the people were saved. The people came to a
tower. They climbed the tower and found all manner of food and drink
and clothes and all the essentials. All the good things and pleasures of
the world were there. They called upon each one to recite an old tale,
one he remembered from his earliest recollection, that is, what he
remembered from the inception of his memory.

"The old and the young were there. They honored the oldest among
them by allowing him to be the first to recount. The oldest declared:
'What can I tell you? I can still remember when they cut the apple from
the branch.' No one understood what he said, but there were wise men
there who said: 'Surely that is a very old tale.'

"They invited the next to tell a tale. The second, who was not as old
as the first, declared while asking: 'Is that such an old tale? I remember
that tale, too, but I even remember when the lamp burned.' They
declared: 'This tale is even older than the first tale.' They wondered how
the younger could recall a tale that was older.

"They invited the third old man to tell a tale. He was younger still
and declared: 'I even recall the forming of the fruit, that is, when the first
fruit began to form.' They declared: 'This is an older tale still.'

"The fourth old man, younger yet, declared, 'I even remember when
they brought the seed for the planting of the fruit.'

"The fifth, younger yet, declared: 'I can even remember the wise men
who invented the seed.'

"The sixth one, younger yet, declared: 'I remember the taste of the
fruit before the taste entered the fruit.'

"The seventh one declared: 'I even remember the smell of the fruit
before it entered the fruit.'

"The eighth one declared: 'I even remember the appearance of the fruit before it was on the fruit.'

"And I (the blind beggar) was at the same time only a child. I was also there and declared: 'I remember all of these tales and I remember nothingness.' They all declared: 'That is a very much older tale, older than all the others.' It was a great marvel for them that the child remembered more than all of them.

"In the meanwhile a large eagle arrived and he knocked on the tower and said to them: 'Stop being paupers. Return to your treasures. Use your treasures.' And he told them to leave the tower in the order of their age, the oldest leaving first. He took them all out of the tower. He first took out the child, since truthfully he was the oldest of all. And so he took out the youngest ones first, and the oldest he took out last. For the younger one was older, and the oldest among them was the youngest of them all.

"And the great eagle declared to them as follows:

" 'I will interpret all the tales that were told. He who told that he remembered how the apple was cut from the branch implied that he still remembers when they cut his umbilical cord, that is what occurred as soon as he was born, when they cut his umbilical cord. This, too, he still remembers.

" 'And the second who said that he still remembers when the lamp burned implies that he still remembers when he was an embryo because that is the time when a candle burns over the head. (Thus it is written in the Gemara, that when a child is in the mother's womb a lamp burns over his head.)

" 'And he who said he still remembers when the fruit began to form, still remembers when his body began to form, that is, when the child was created.

" 'And he who still remembers when they brought the seed to plant the fruit denotes that he remembers how the semen was drawn out during copulation.

" 'And he who still remembers the wise man who invented the seed implies that he still remembers when the semen was still in the brain.

" 'And he who remembers the taste, that is the lower spirit; and the smells, that is the soul; and the appearance, that is the higher spirit. And the child who said he remembers nothingness, he is greater than all since he still remembers what existed before the lower spirit, the soul, and the higher spirit and so he said that he still remembers when there was nothing, and what happened there. He is higher than all.'

"And the great eagle said to them: 'Return to your ships. Those are your bodies which were broken. They will be rebuilt. Now, return to them.' And he blessed them.

"And to me (the blind beggar who was a child at that time and who is telling these stories) the great eagle said: 'You come with me, because you are just like me in that you are extremely old and yet very young. And you have not yet even begun to live, though you are very old. And I am the same since I am extremely old and still young.'

"Accordingly, I have an affidavit from the great eagle that I have lived a long life. And now I give you my long life as a wedding gift."

And there was a great happiness and delight.

4.

On the second day of the seven feast days, the bride and groom recalled the second beggar, the deaf one, who nourished them and gave them bread. And they cried and longed for him: "How do we bring the deaf beggar here, the one who nourished us?"

Meanwhile, as they were longing for him, he arrived and said: "I am here." And he embraced and kissed them saying: "Today, I present you with a gift that you shall be like me, that you should live as good a life as I. Previously I offered you this blessing, today I bestow my good life upon you outright as your wedding gift. And you think I am deaf? I am not deaf at all. It is only that the whole world is not worth my hearing its deficiencies. All sounds in the world are due to its deficiencies since people cry out about what they are lacking, about what they haven't got. Even all the world's celebrations are about deficiencies since one rejoices over the deficiencies which have been filled. As for me, the whole world is not worth my listening to its deficiencies, because I live a good life that has no deficiencies. And I have an affidavit from the Country of Riches that I live the good life." His good life was that he ate bread and drank water.

And he told them:

"There is a country where there are great riches and they have many treasures. One day these wealthy men gathered to boast how they live the good life, and each one told of his style of good living. And I declared to them: 'I live a good life which is better than your good life, and here's the proof. If you are living such a good life, let me see if you can save a certain country. For there is a land where they had a garden, and in this garden there were fruits that had all the flavors in the world. And all the odors in the world were also there, all the forms, all the colors, and all the blossoms in the world were all there in that garden. Over the garden there was a gardener and the people of that land lived a good life because of this garden. But then the garden withered and died since the gardener was no longer there. However, they were still able to live off the aftergrowth of the garden.

" 'But a cruel king arose in the country, and since he was unable to do anything to them personally, he spoiled the good life of the country which they had derived from the garden. He did not spoil the garden itself, but left three groups of servants in the land and ordered them to do his bidding. And through their actions they spoiled the people's sense of taste. Consequently, anyone who wished to taste anything sensed only the taste of the carrion. And likewise they spoiled their sense of smell, so that all the odors smelt of galbanum. Likewise they spoiled their sense of vision, so that they dimmed their eyes as if there were heavy clouds. What they did there was as the cruel king had ordered.

" 'Now, if you live the good life, help that country. And I say to you,' so said the deaf beggar, 'that if you do not help them, their deficiencies will harm you.'

"These rich men started out for that country, and I also went along with them. Even along the way each one lived his good life because they had great treasures. As they approached that country their sense of taste and their other senses, too, began to spoil. And they themselves felt that their senses were spoiled. Then I said to them: 'If you haven't even entered the land and your senses of taste and smell and sight have already spoiled, how will it be when you enter? Furthermore, how will you be able to save them?' And I took out my bread and my water and gave it to them. In my bread and water, they felt all the tastes and smells, and that which had been spoiled was repaired.

"And the inhabitants of that country where the garden was began to seek to repair the country where the sense of taste had been spoiled. They came to a decision: Since there existed a country of great riches (the very same country which the beggar had mentioned) it seemed that their lost gardener through whom they had lived the good life was of the same stock as those people of the Country of Riches who also lived the good life. Thus they counseled that they should send to the Country of Riches, for surely they would help them. And that is what they did. They sent out emissaries to the Country of Riches. As the emissaries left, they met with the rich men from the Country of Riches, and the rich men asked the emissaries: 'Where are you going?' They answered: 'We are going to the Country of Riches so that they might help us.' They replied: 'We ourselves are inhabitants of the Country of Riches and we are on our way to you.' I (the beggar who is telling this story) declared: 'You really need me because you cannot go there to help them, therefore remain here and I will go with the emissaries to help them.'

"So I went with the emissaries until I came to the country. I entered a city, and I saw some people telling jokes and then more people gathered around them until there was a whole crowd telling jokes and they all laughed. I listened and heard that they were speaking obscenities. One tells an obscene joke; another one is slightly more subtle. This one laughs; that one enjoys the fun, etc. Then I went further to another city. There I saw two people quarreling over business. They went to the court to bring suit. The court decreed: 'This one is innocent and that one is guilty.' They left the court. Later, they quarreled again. This time, they said they would not go back to that court, but they wished another court. They selected another court and brought their case before it. Later, one of this pair quarreled with someone else. They chose a different court this time. And this way they continued to quarrel and to choose different courts each time until the whole city was full of courts. I observed that the reason was that the truth did not exist there. Today this man distorts the judgment and favors his friend; afterwards, his friend favors him, since they take bribes and there is no truth in them. Then I noticed that they were full of lechery and there was so much lechery there that it became permissible.

"I told them that was why their senses of smell and taste and sight were spoiled. The cruel king left them with those three groups of servants who spoiled the country, for they wandered about spreading obscenity and introduced it into the country. And through the obscenity, the sense of taste was spoiled, all the tastes had for them the taste of carrion. And they also introduced bribery into the land. Through this their sight was dimmed and their sense of sight was spoiled as it is written: 'Graft blinds the eyes of the wise.' And thus they also introduced lechery into the land and through that the sense of smell was spoiled since the sense of smell is spoiled through lechery. 'Therefore,' I said, 'see to it that you cure the country of those three sins, seek out those people and banish them. And when you cleanse the country of these three sins, not only will your sense of taste and sight and smell be cured, but even the gardener who mysteriously disappeared will be found.'

"And that is what they did. They began to cleanse the country of these three sins and to seek out those people. They would seize an

individual and question him: 'Where do you come from?' until all the
people of the cruel king were discovered and banished and the country
was cleansed of these sins. In the meanwhile there arose a tumult: 'Perhaps that madman is really the gardener. For there is a madman who
wanders about crying he is the gardener and whom everyone considers
mad and stones him and chases him away. Perhaps he is really the gardener.' They went and brought him in and I said: 'Of course he is the
true gardener.'

"Consequently, I have an affidavit from the Country of Riches that I
live the good life because I cured the Country of the Garden. And today,
I grant you my good life outright as a wedding gift."

There was great rejoicing and a fine celebration and everyone was
very happy. The first gave them long life as a gift and the second gave
them a good life.

5.

On the third day, the couple again remembered and cried and longed:
"Where can one find the third beggar, the one who stuttered?" Meanwhile, he entered and said: "I am here." He embraced them and kissed
them and also said to them: "Previously, I blessed you that you might be
as I am. But today I present you as a wedding gift that you should be as I
am. And you think that I am a stutterer? I am not a stutterer at all. It is
only that worldly words which are not praises of the Holy One have no
perfection." That is why he looked like a stutterer, for he stuttered those
worldly words which have no perfection. "In fact, I am really not a stutterer at all. On the contrary, I am an extraordinary orator. I can recite
riddles and poems and songs so marvelous that there is no creature in
the universe who would not wish to hear them. And in these songs lies
all wisdom. I have an affidavit to that effect from the great man who is
called the True Man of Kindness. There is in this an entire story.

"Once all the wise men were sitting and boasting of their science.

One said that with his science he had invented the production of iron from ore; another, that he had invented the production of another metal; and still another boasted that he had invented the production of silver, which is even more important. And yet another boasted that he had invented the production of gold. One boasted that he had invented weapons. Another boasted that he could make all these metals from material other than those used for making these metals. And another man boasted of other sciences, for there are numerous things that were invented through science, like saltpeter, and powder and the like. Each boasted of his science.

"One came forth and said: 'I am wiser than all of you, for I am as wise as the day.' They could not comprehend what he was saying, that he was as wise as the day. And he declared to them that if all their sciences were gathered together, they would only amount to one hour. Even though each science derived from a specific day, according to the creation which took place on that day (all these sciences are only combinations of materials which God had created on specific days), nevertheless, through science one can gather all these inventions into one hour. But I am as wise as an entire day.

"That is how the last wise man boasted. So I (the stutterer) asked him: 'Like which day are you wise?' The wise man declared: 'This man (the stutterer) is wiser than I, because he asks, "Like which day?" But I am as wise as whichever day you wish.' And now the question arises: Why is he who asks 'Like which day?' wiser than the wise man who is as wise as any day he wishes?

"There is an entire tale about this. The True Man of Kindness is indeed a very great man. And I (the stutterer) travel around and collect all true deeds of kindness and bring them to the True Man of Kindness. For the very becoming of time—time itself is created—is through deeds of true kindness. So I travel and gather together all those true deeds of kindness and bring them to the True Man of Kindness. And from this time becomes.

"Now there is a mountain. On the mountain stands a rock. From the rock flows a spring. And everything has a heart. The world taken as a whole has a heart. And the world's heart is of full stature, with a face, hands, and feet. Now the toenail of that heart is more heart-like than anyone else's heart. The mountain with the rock and spring are at one end of the world, and the world's heart stands at the other end. The world's heart stands opposite the spring and yearns and always longs to reach the spring. The yearning and longing of the heart for the spring is extraordinary. It cries out to reach the spring. The spring also yearns and longs for the heart.

"The heart suffers from two types of languor: one because the sun pursues it and burns it (because it so longs to reach the spring); and the other because of its yearning and longing, for it always yearns and longs fervently for the spring. It always stands facing the spring and cries out: 'Help!' and longs mightily for the spring. But when the heart needs to find some rest, to catch its breath, a large bird flies over, and spreads its wings over it, and shields it from the sun. Then the heart can rest a while. And even then, during the rest, it still looks toward the spring and longs for it.

"Why doesn't the heart go toward the spring if it so longs for it? Because, as soon as it wants to approach the hill, it can no longer see the peak and cannot look at the spring. (When one stands opposite a mountain, one sees the top of the slope of the mountain where the spring is situated, but as soon as one approaches the mountain, the top of the slope disappears—at least visually—and one cannot see the spring.) And if the heart will no longer look upon the spring, its soul will perish, for it draws all its vitality from the spring. And if the heart would expire, God forbid, the whole world would be annihilated, because the heart has within it the life of everything. And how could the world exist without its heart? And that is why the heart cannot go to the spring but remains facing it and yearns and cries out.

"And the spring has no time; it does not exist in time. (The spring has

no worldly time, no day or moment, for it is entirely above time.) The
only time the spring has is that one day which the heart grants it as a
gift. The moment the day is finished, the spring, too, will be without
time and it will disappear. And without the spring, the heart, too, will
perish, God forbid. Thus, close to the end of the day, they start to take
leave one from the other and begin singing riddles and poems and
songs, one to the other, with much love and longing. This True Man of
Kindness is in charge of this. As the day is about to come to its end,
before it finishes and ceases, the True Man of Kindness comes and gives
a gift of a day to the heart. And the heart gives the day to the spring.
And again the spring has time.

"And when day returns from wherever it comes, it arrives with riddles
and fine poetry in which all wisdom lies. There is a distinction between
the days. There is Sunday and Monday; there are also days of New
Moon and Holidays. The poems which the day brings depend upon
what kind of day it is. And the time that the True Man of Kindness has,
all derives from me (the stutterer) because I travel around, collecting all
the true deeds of kindness from which time derives.

"Consequently, the stutterer is wiser even than the wise one who
boasted that he is as clever as whichever day you wish. Because all of
time, even the days, come about only through him (the stutterer) for he
collects the true deeds of kindness from which time derives and brings
them to the True Man of Kindness. He in turn gives a day to the heart.
The heart gives it to the spring, through which the whole world can
exist. Consequently the actual becoming of time, with the riddles and
poems and all the wisdom found in them, is all made possible through
the stutterer.

"I have an affidavit from the True Man of Kindness that I can recite
riddles and poems, in which all wisdom can be found, because time and
riddles come into being only through him. And now, I give you my wedding gift outright that you should be like me."

Upon hearing this, they had a joyous celebration.

6.

In the morning, when they finished the celebration of that day and had slept through the night, the couple yearned for the beggar with the twisted neck. Meanwhile, he entered and said: "I am here. Previously, I blessed you that you may be as I am. Today I present you a wedding gift that you should be as I am. Do you think my neck is twisted? My neck is not twisted at all. In fact, I have a straight neck, a very handsome neck. Only that there are worldly vanities (empty breaths) which are so numerous that I do not want to exhale the least breath." (It seemed like his neck was twisted, since he twisted it because of the vanities of the world and did not want to exhale any breath into the vanities of the world.) "But I really have a handsome neck, a wonderful neck because I have such a wonderful voice. I can imitate with my voice every speechless sound made on earth because I have such a wonderful neck and voice. And I have an affidavit to that effect from a certain country.

"For there is a country where everyone is skilled in the art of music. Everyone practices these arts, even little children. There isn't a child there who is unable to play some kind of instrument. The youngest in that country would be the wisest in another country in the art of music. And the wise men, and the king of that country and the musicians are experts in the art of music.

"Once, the country's wise men sat and boasted of their expertise in the art of music. One boasted that he could play on one instrument; another, on another; and still another, on all instruments. This one boasted that he could imitate with his voice the sound of one instrument, and another boasted that he could imitate with his voice yet another instrument. And still another boasted that with his voice he could imitate several instruments. Another one boasted that he could imitate the sound of a drum, just as it is being beaten. Another one boasted that with his voice he could make the sound of cannon firing.

"I, too, was there, so I declared saying, 'My voice is better than all of yours. And here is the proof. If you are such wise men in music, see if you can save these two countries. There are two countries one thousand miles apart from each other where no one can sleep when nights falls. As soon as night falls, everyone begins to wail with such anguish—men, women, and children—because they hear a certain wailing sound of mourning. Stones would melt because of this wail. And thus they behave in the two countries: In one, they hear the wail and all wail; and likewise in the other country. And the two countries are a thousand miles apart. So if you are all so very wise in music, let us see if you can save these two countries, or at least imitate the sounds of the laments heard there.' And they said to him: 'Will you lead us there?' He answered: 'Yes, I will lead you there.'

"And they all arose to go there. They left and reached one of those two countries. When they arrived, and night fell, as usual, everyone began to wail and the wise men also wailed. And so they saw that they were of no help at all to the two countries. And I (the one with the twisted neck) said to the wise men: 'Can you, at least, tell me where the sound of the wailing comes from?' They asked: 'Do you know?' And I (the beggar with the twisted neck) answered: 'Of course I know. There are two birds, a male and a female. There was only one pair of this species on earth. The female was lost and the male roamed about seeking her. She was also seeking him. They searched for each other for such a long time that they lost their ways and realized they could no longer find one another. They remained where they were and made nests. The male built a nest close to one of those two countries—not too close by, but considering the bird's voice, close enough. From where he built his nest, his voice could be heard in the country. In the same way, she also built her nest near the second country, also not too close by, but close enough for her voice to be heard. And when night fell, each one of this pair of birds began to lament with a very great wail. Each wailed for its mate. This is the wailing that is heard in these two countries, and because of the sound, everyone must wail and no one can sleep.'

"But they didn't want to believe me, and said to me, 'Will you lead us there?' 'Yes,' he answered. 'I can lead you, but how can you get there? You cannot get there by night because you will not be able to bear the wailing when you approach. Even here you cannot bear it and you must also wail. When you get there, you will not be able to bear it at all. And you cannot get there by day, for by the day, the joy is unbearable. During the day, birds gather around each one, around him and her, and console them and gladden each one of the pair with great rejoicing. They speak words of comfort: "It is yet possible that you will find each other." That is why it is not possible to withstand the great rejoicing that is found there by day. The voices of the birds that gladden them are not heard from far off, but only when you get there. But the sounds of moaning arising from the pair is heard from far off. That is why you cannot get there.'

"The wise man said to me: 'Can you set it right?' I answered: 'Yes, I can set it right, since I can imitate all the sounds of the world. I can also throw my voice, so that in the place from where I throw my voice, nobody hears, but it is heard far, far away. Thus I can throw the voices of the birds, from her to him. I will imitate her voice and throw it close to him. I will also throw his voice close to her, and this way I will bring them together and so everything will be put right.'

"But who could believe me? So I led them into a forest. They heard somebody open a door, and shut it, and lock it with a bolt. Then I shot a gun and sent my dog to retrieve what I had shot. And the dog struggled in the snow. These wise men heard it all and looked around, but they saw absolutely nothing. They heard no sound from me (whose neck was twisted though it was I who had thrown those sounds and thus they had heard them), so they understood that I could imitate all the sounds and could throw my voice and thus could set everything right." (Here he skipped in his narrative.)

"And therefore I have an affidavit from that country that I have a very fine voice and can imitate all the sounds in the world, and today I grant you this outright as a gift in honor of your wedding, that you should be like me."

And there was great celebration and joy there.

7.

On the fifth day they also celebrated. The married pair remembered the beggar who was a hunchback. And they yearned greatly, "How do we bring the hunchback beggar here? If he were here, our happiness would be great indeed." Meanwhile, he arrived and said: "Here I am. I came to be with you at your wedding." He embraced and kissed them and said: "Previously I blessed you that you might be like me. Today, I present you a wedding gift that you should be like me. I am not a hunchback at all. On the contrary, I have shoulders that are characterized *the-little-that-holds-much*. And I have an affidavit to that effect.

"Once there was a discussion where people prided themselves on having this characteristic. Each one boasted that he possessed the characteristic of *the-little-that-holds-much* (that is, a small space that should contain much). One of them was ridiculed and laughed at. The words of the others who boasted about having *the-little-that-holds-much* were acceptable. But *the-little-that-holds-much* that I have was greater than all the others.

"One of them boasted that his mind was like *the-little-that-holds-much*. He carried in his mind multitudes of people with all their needs and all their behavior, with all their gestures and traits. Since he kept all these things in his mind, he was *the-little-that-holds-much*, for his little bit of a mind carried so many people. And they made fun of him and declared: 'Your people are nothing and you are nothing.'

"Another one declared and said: 'I saw *the-little-that-holds-much*. For once I saw a mountain that was covered with rubbish and filth. This was a marvel to me: Where did this rubbish and filth come from? There was a man close by the mountain. He told me, "All this comes from me." Since he dwelt so close to the mountain he threw everything onto the mountain, rubbish and filth from his eating and drinking. From him the rubbish and filth increased on the mountain. Therefore, this man was obviously *the-little-that-holds-much.* Because one man could create so much rubbish.'

"Another boasted that he had *the-little-that-holds-much,* since he had a piece of land which produced much fruit. The fruit produced by that land was later counted and it turned out that the land was not as large as the amount of fruit it produced. Therefore this was *the-little-that-holds-much.* His words were pleasing, and accepted as truly being *the-little-that-holds-much.*

"And one said, 'I own a wonderful orchard wherein fruits grow. Many people and lords visit it since it is such a beautiful orchard. And when summer comes, many people and lords journey there to stroll in the orchard. Truly, the orchard is not so large that it can accommodate many people. Therefore, it is *the-little-that-holds-much.*' And his words were also pleasing.

"And one said that his speech possessed the characteristic of *the-little-that-holds-much,* since he was the secretary for a great king: 'Many people come to the king. One comes with praise and another comes with petitions. The king cannot listen to all of them so I gather together all their speeches and shorten them and present to the king this digest of all their praises and petitions. Thus my brief words are *the-little-that-holds-much.*'

"Another one said that his silence possessed the characteristic of *the-little-that-holds-much.* There were accusers and slanderers who informed against him severely. They quarrel with him and talk about him a great deal. And he refutes all slanders and accusations against him with silence, only with silence. Therefore, his silence was *the-little-that-holds-much.*

"Another one said that he was *the-little-that-holds-much.* There was a very poor man who was both blind and very big. He (the boaster) was very small and led about the poor blind man who was very big. Therefore, he was *the-little-that-holds-much.* Because the blind man could slip and fall, and he maintains him upright by leading him. Because of this he was *the-little-that-holds-much* because he was small and held up the big blind man.

"And I (the hunchback) was also there. I retorted, 'The truth is that you all have the characteristic of *the-little-that-holds-much,* and I understand everything that you meant. The last one who boasted that he led the big blind man is greater than all of you. But I am by far superior to all of you, since he who boasted that he leads the big blind man means that he leads the lunar sphere. For the moon has the characteristic of a blind man for she has no light of her own. And he who boasted of this, leads the moon even though he is small and the sphere of the moon is extremely large. Through him the world survives because the world must have a moon. Thus, he is surely *the-little-that-holds-much.* But I am superior to all of you and *the-little-that-holds-much* which I have its superior to all. This is the proof.

"There was once a sect which reasoned that every beast had its own shade where it wished to rest, and so, too, each bird had its branch where it rested and not on any other branch. Because of this, the sect reasoned that there might exist such a tree in whose shade all the beasts could choose to rest, and on whose branches all the birds could rest. They declared that such a tree did exist. They wanted to travel to the tree, because the pleasure found around the tree should be limitless since all the birds and the beasts were there. No beast harmed any other beast, but all the beasts were intermixed and they gamboled there. Surely it would be a great pleasure to be at the tree. They reasoned in which direction to go to reach the tree. A controversy arose among them and one said, 'We must go west.' This one said, 'Go here,' and that one said, 'Go there.' They couldn't possibly decide which way to go to reach the tree.

"A wise man came by and said to them, 'Why are you reasoning which way to go to reach the tree? Reason first which are those people who can reach the tree. For not everyone can reach the tree. Only he who possesses the virtues of the tree can reach it. For this tree has three roots. One root is faith in God; the next root is reverence; and the third root is humility. Truth is the body of the tree from which the branches emerge. Therefore no one can reach the tree unless he has those virtues.'

"Now, not everyone in the sect possessed these virtues; only a few had them. And since the sect was well united, they did not want to separate so that one group should go to the tree and the rest remain behind. So they agreed to wait while each one of them labored and struggled to attain the high degree of all the virtues so that all of them would reach the tree together. This is exactly what they did: They labored and struggled until they all achieved those virtues. And no sooner had they achieved these virtues, then they all agreed upon the one way to go in order to reach that tree. They all set out and after they had traveled a while, they were able to see the tree from afar. When they looked, they noticed that the tree was not rooted in any space. The tree stood on no specific space. And if it had no space, how could it be reached?

"And I (the hunchback) was also there with them. So I declared to them: 'I can lead you to the tree. For this particular tree has no specific space; it is entirely above (superior to) the earth's space. And yet, the characteristic of *the-little-that-holds-much* still involves some space. Although it is a *little-that-holds-much*, it still has a little space in it. And my *little-that-holds-much* is at the very end of space, and beyond it there is no space at all.' (For the hunchback was like the middle stage between space and what is entirely above [superior to] space because he had the highest degree of *the-little-that-holds-much* which is at the very end of space and after it the term space does not exist at all. Therefore, he could lead them from that space to the aspect of *above-all-space.*) 'That is why I can lead all of you to this tree which is totally above (superior to) the space it stands on.'

"And I took them and led them there to that tree. Thus I have an affidavit from it that I have the highest degree of *the-little-that-holds-much.*" (And that is why he appeared to be hunchbacked; he carries a heavy

load since he himself carries within himself *the-little-that-holds-much*.)
"And now I grant you this trait that you be as I am."

And great joy was expressed and there was very great bliss.

8.

On the sixth day they were all very joyous and yet they yearned: "How do we bring here the beggar without hands?" Suddenly he arrived and said, "Here I am. I come to you on your wedding." And he spoke to them as the others did. And he embraced them and kissed them and said to them: "You think that I am crippled in my hands. I am not at all crippled in my hands. I do have power in my hands, but I do not use the power in my hands in this world. I need this power for something else and I have an affidavit to that effect from the Water Castle.

"Once a few of us were sitting, each one boasting of the power which lay in his hands. This one boasted that he had a certain prowess in his hands, and that one boasted that he had another type of prowess in his hands. For instance, one man boasted that he had such power and prowess in his hands that when he shot an arrow from his bow, he could pull it back to him. For the power of his hands was such that even though he had shot the arrow, he could still turn it around and make it return.

"And so I asked him: 'What type of arrow can you pull back?' There are ten different sorts of arrows because there are ten different types of poison. When an arrow is smeared with one poison, it does a certain type of harm, and if an arrow is smeared with another type of poison it does more harm. There are ten different types of poison each more deadly than the first, and this is why there are ten different types of arrows. (The arrows themselves are all alike, but because they are smeared with ten different types of poison they are called ten different arrows.) That is why I asked him: 'What sort of arrow can you pull back?' I also asked him whether he could pull back an arrow before it hit its mark or could he also recover it after it had hit. To this he answered that even after the arrow had hit its mark he could pull it back, and to the question, what type of arrow can you pull back, he declared: 'Such and such an arrow.' So I replied: 'If this is the case, you cannot cure the Princess. Since you can only pull back one type of arrow, you cannot cure the Princess.'

"One boasted that he had such power in his hands, that no matter from whom he took, he gave. By the very fact that he took something from someone, he was giving because his taking was giving. This automatically made him a giver of charity. Then I asked him, 'What kind of charity do you give?' (Because there exist ten sorts of charity.) He answered that he tithed. I replied: 'If that is so then you cannot heal the Princess. You cannot even reach her place. You can enter only one wall where she dwells and so you cannot come to her place.'

"One boasted that he had a special power in his hands. For there were in the world officials who needed the wisdom which he could impart by laying his hands on them. I asked him, 'What kind of wisdom can you impart through your hands? For there are ten measures of wisdom.' He answered: 'Such and such a kind of wisdom.' I declared: 'You can't heal the Princess at all; you can't even take her pulse. You are aware of only one pulse and there are ten types of pulse, but you know only one, because you know of only one type of wisdom.'

"One boasted that he had such power in his hands that when a tempest arose, he could contain the tempest with his hands. He could catch the wind within his hands and contain it. He could give the wind the proper counter-force that was needed. So I asked him: 'What kind of wind can you catch with your hands? There are ten types of wind.' He answered: 'Such and such a wind.' I replied: 'You cannot heal the Princess because you cannot even play her tune. The cure for the Princess is through music, and there are ten types of tunes and you can only play one tune for her from these ten.'

"'And what can you do?' they all questioned. I answered: 'I know what all of you don't know, that is all of the nine parts of all that you don't know, I know. I know all.'

"There is a tale. Once upon a time a King fell in love with a Princess. He tried to capture her through stratagems until he succeeded and then he kept her by his side. One night he dreamt that the Princess rose up against him and killed him. When he awoke, this dream remained in his heart. He called together all the interpreters of dreams and they interpreted as follows: 'The dream will literally become reality; she will kill him.' The king was unable to find any counsel: What could he do with her? Should he kill her? That would sadden him. Should he banish her? That would irk him, for someone else would have her. He had worked so hard to get her and now she would be someone else's. And especially if he banished her and she asked another's help, the dream could surely come true; she would kill him, since she would then be with somebody else. On the other hand if he kept her with him, he feared the outcome of the dream.

"And so the King didn't know what to do about the Princess. Meanwhile his love for her was spoiled somewhat because of the dream; he didn't love her as much as before, each day his love for her was spoiled. And so, too, her love for him was spoiled, each day more and more, until there existed within her a hatred toward him, and she ran away from him. The King sent word to search for her. People came and said to him that she was circling about the Water Castle. For there was a Water Castle, with ten walls, one inside the other. All the ten walls were made of water, and the ground that was trod upon was also of water. There were trees and fruits, all of water. The beauty and the marvel of the Castle was indescribable. For surely it was an extraordinary wonder for the entire Castle to be made of water. To enter the Castle was obviously impossible. He who would enter would drown, because the Castle was formed of water. So when the Princess fled, she went to the Castle. The King was told that she was circling about the Water Castle.

"The King and his soldiers set out to capture her. No sooner did the Princess see this than she decided to run into the Castle. She would rather have drowned than be captured by the King and remain with him. And perhaps, she would be saved and would slip into the Water Castle. As soon as the King saw her running into the water, he said, 'If that is so. . . .' He ordered her shot: 'If she dies, let her die.' She was shot at and hit with all the ten kinds of arrows that had been smeared with the ten poisons. The Princess fled into the Castle and came inside. She passed through the gates and walls made of water, for there were gates and walls of water. She passed through all the gates of all the ten walls of the Water Castle until she was inside the Castle where she fell in a dead faint.

"And I (the handless one) am curing her. For he who does not possess within his hands all the ten types of charity cannot enter the ten walls of the Water Castle. For he will drown in the water. The King and his soldiers pursued the Princess and they all drowned. But I am able to enter past all the ten walls of the Water Castle. These walls of water are the billlows of the sea that stand like walls. The winds raise up the billows of the sea and lift them up high, and the billows that are the ten walls always stand there. The winds hold up the waves and lift them, yet I can enter through the ten walls. And I can remove the ten different arrows from the Princess. And I know all the ten kinds of pulse through my ten fingers. For through each one of the ten fingers one can feel a specific pulse out of the ten different pulses. I can cure the Princess through the ten types of music. And that is how I am curing her. Therefore I have this power in my hand.

"And this is my gift to you this day."

And there was great rejoicing and everyone was very happy.

÷

Since "The Seven Beggars" was familiar to many, it was where Nachman's text left off and Joel's creation began that ears pricked up.

The Seventh Beggar (*continued*)

9.

On the seventh of the seven wedding days, the bride and groom rejoiced and remembered that the seventh beggar was missing, the beggar without feet who came into the woods when they were lost, gave them bread, and blessed them, that they should be as he was. They wished and yearned for him, a longing of longings, and he appeared, the beggar without feet. Here I am, he said. I have come to be with you on your wedding day. Previously I blessed you that you should be as I am, now I've come to make this blessing your wedding gift. You may wonder how it is I can wander because I don't have feet. Indeed, without feet I am farther and deeper traveled than the most famous travelers. To prove it, I have with me the following affidavit, in the form of a tale: Draw in your mind a ship, and on the ship seven travelers: wanderers, pilgrims, beggars, *badkhonim*—they've gone by all these names. Each one going, going and coming, always coming and going. One day they found themselves aboard the same ship and decide to set sail toward the Holy Land. The ship was turned eastward and there was much rejoicing and singing. They danced to "Next Year in Jerusalem," and meant it since it was their intention to arrive in Jerusalem before the New Year. And the ship, as such ships do, sailed into a storm, encountered wind and hail, insurmountable waves, they crashed and thrashed from storm to gale to storm, crossed all seven seas. To while away the time, the travelers agreed to tell travelers' tales. They began, each took his turn, each traveler told a tale of storms so terrible and winds so demonic, six wondrous and meandering tales were narrated, complete with the details of every suffered ounce of despair, indeed only a miracle could explain the individual's survival to tell the tale. And when the six tales were told, the travelers turned toward me, the beggar without feet, and wondered how without feet I could have traveled far enough to find a tale worth telling. And I told them a tale of seven pilgrims who walked the deserts and steppes, over mountains, hills, and dales, through fields and streams, in the icy cold of winters and the scalding heat of summers, and while they walked they talked. And exhausted themselves with walking and talking and listening and telling. And I told their six tales word for word, as they had been told to me. And when I arrived at the seventh tale, the tale of the beggar without feet, I told a tale of seven travelers walking, trudging and grudging, tired and mired in leaves and mud, and so forth. And all the while talking, telling tales. And I told the tales these pilgrims told, word for word I told their tales, and then I told my tale: a tale of seven wanderers. And it was agreed that I the beggar without feet, slow and trailing behind, was nevertheless farther and deeper traveled, because within my tale were contained all tales. And I talked and walked, and with every step, between one step and the next, I dreamed a dream. And in one dream I awoke and saw that the Leviathan had not yet emerged, the story could not be finished. I walked onward, another step, another tale, another dream. Between dream and dream I awoke and found myself in this wedding pit and in this pit among the wedding guests was the prince who had stumbled into heresy, but as long as he remained here, as long as he listened and believed the tales, his wisdom and heresy were restrained. He listened and rejoiced much as his father, the old King, had once rejoiced. To prevent another stumble, I, the beggar without feet, must continue. I pause only to present your wedding gift, that you may be as I am.

10.

The seventh beggar continued his tales and the wedding feast went on without end and there was continued rejoicing.

It was late, it was dark. The moon had risen and set. Stars gleamed in the summer-dark sky. And though the seventh beggar would have to keep going, Joel declared the day good enough and went to bed.

The Festival Farewell

Early Sunday morning on the main stage, the Cottonmouth Choir performed the Sunday Gospel.

This was followed by the farewell performance, which was reserved as always for Yankel Yankevitch, the festival's master of ceremonies. He would speak for only a few moments, he promised, and the audience, who knew better, settled into their seats for a goodly hour.

JakobJoel was prepared to watch Yankel perform for any number of hours. He loved the desperate dance to make sense of nonsense. Watching Yankel scramble to find the rhymes and make the connections put JakobJoel on the edge of his seat, keenly aware of the risk, and loving it. He himself could never be that reckless, he just wasn't made that way, and knowing this only deepened his appreciation for the difficulty of Yankel's task. And in this performance there was more at stake than usual

because it would be his uncle Joel's rendering of Yankel. JakobJoel held
his breath.

÷

Since this was the festival's twenty-fifth anniversary, Yankel proposed
to share with the audience his memories and reflections of previous years.

He began by reminding those who were old enough to remember the
lightning strike at the very first festival, of the thick fog that enveloped
the mountain in 1969, and of the hay wagons used for transport up the
farm road before they were replaced by buses. He reminded them of the
year in which Laybele Furth, the *badkhn* of Zlotopolye, interacted with his
fans during his performance, how they supplied him with the rhyming
words he needed. Yankel picked up the pace and listed various episodes
quickly, moving from the early days to the festival's later years. He didn't
seem up to his usual tricks; he continued delivering what seemed straightforward and nostalgic reflections, and his listeners grew suspicious.

He mentioned the temperature drop in 1979 and waking up to a
ground frost in July; the electrical failure in 1985, when all lights, microphones, speakers were of no use and the performers resorted to a capella
and wooden drums; and of the year in which a local golem made of
wood chips walked out of the Master Workshop and onto the main
stage. Going farther back in time, he reminded the audience of the year
the sun wouldn't set, extending the Sabbath day into Sunday; and of the
time four clouds enveloped and protected them just as clouds had protected their ancestors in the Sinai Desert for forty years. And while
we're on the subject of our ancestors, I want to point out that we desert
people never could turn down a mountaintop invitation. Noah and his
sons agreed to spend 150 days in an ark, they and every beast according
to its kind, in tight quarters together, only to land finally at the top of
Mount Ararat. And our ancestors put up with forty years of desert camping to get to Mount Sinai and finally Mount Nebo, where the Lord

showed Moses the land that he had sworn to Abraham, Isaac, and Jacob. This explains our presence here, on this mountaintop, in these foothills of the Berkshire Mountains.

Yankel paused and sighed and admitted that this annual festival had never provided him with material for a best-selling thriller. No murders have taken place here. No brother has raised a hand against his brother. And though we heard the serpent's gospel, the Cottonmouth Choir's Sunday performance, we didn't listen. It is a fact on record that in twenty-five years nothing terribly sinful has ever happened here, knock on wood, which makes one wonder, Yankel wondered aloud, why it is that we are required to leave, to vacate these outdoor premises before nine P.M. tonight. After all, if we've eaten from the tree of bluegrass knowledge, it was only because we were invited to do so. This dearth of sin is in good measure the reason I don't have much to say, not here today, nor elsewhere tomorrow. As you know, the rabbis have said that if not for our ancestors' sinful ways we would have had only the Torah, that is, the first five books, and the book of Joshua. All the other texts— Judges, Kings, Chronicles, and Writings are mere reproof. In our own defense, I must admit that under such a burden of books, it is no surprise that we've lost our passion for sin.

Yankel was willing to concede that if his inclination had been toward the romance or the coming-of-age genres, rather than the mocking voice of the *badkhn*, the festival might have proved more inspiring, since quite a few weddings have taken place here. He reminded the audience of the wedding at which a thoroughly egalitarian couple performed a do-si-do rather than conform to the old patriarchal way that required the bride to circle the groom.

Continuing the theme of equality, the bride and groom broke separate glasses, even though the bride's very attractive but flimsy shoes, basically thin leather soles with cotton ribbon wrapped around her ankles, endangered her exposed feet. For an elegaic writer, such optimism would have provided good fodder, but romance just isn't my area of expertise, Yankel protested. My wife, who is seated in the thirty-third row, will be pleased to agree with me on this particular subject, though not on much else.

As the audience turned to look at Yankel's wife for confirmation, a clap of thunder sounded, followed by lightning. When all eyes turned back to the stage, Yankel was no longer standing. In fact, there was nothing there at all, no microphones or speakers, no drums or guitars or mandolins or fiddles, no amplifiers or wiring, no lights, no stage, or stage manager. Everything was gone. And this was no time to stand agape because the rain that was coming down hard and fast threatened an end to everything.

The deluge, someone shouted, and the audience jumped to gather their belongings and seek shelter in the highest of high places.

The water prevailed upon the mountain for 150 seconds, that is to say two and a half minutes, proof that time passes differently on festival days. After which the sun came out and Yankel was seen walking to his own campsite and to his wife, drenched and wraithlike, and pinching himself to see if he was alive and well. When he was within reach, his wife slapped him first, then enveloped him in a large towel.

Though glad to see him alive, people soon agreed that thunder and lightning was one way to get Yankel off the stage. After which there was much hugging and promises to return in 2001, and everyone went off to break camp, pack, load their vehicles, and get on the road.

Why the deus-ex-machina ending? JakobJoel wondered. A repetition of the deluge? Joel had gotten Yankel off the stage with an act of God. Interruption, it seemed, was their shared fate, but with an important difference: the *badkhn* had survived his flood.

By noon the next day, all tents were gone, all stages dismantled, lights turned off, and the village was no more. Late afternoon, Holsteins and Highlanders discovered unusual flavors in the grass and declared the day extraordinary.

PART

÷

Three

CONTINUED

At dinner the next evening, when Julia, Rick, and the others were gathered at the table, JakobJoel announced that he had finished *The Book of Cog* and that he would read it in the library before *The Simpsons*.

Hallelujah, Julia said, throwing up her arms.

It's not what you're expecting, JakobJoel warned. It's not a script. It's not even a story.

What is it? Rick asked.

JakobJoel shrugged. I don't know. It's kind of fun, or it was fun to do, but it's definitely not filmable.

Julia reached across the table and ran her hands inches away from JakobJoel's head, her eyes closed. It's, she said, it's, I believe it's an elephant.

Whatever, Elena said. Why don't we decide when we hear it?

When everyone was gathered in the living room, JakobJoel stepped into the center, sipped water, cleared his throat, paused to hear what his uncle had to say—nothing, it turned out, he was no longer around—and read.

The Book of Cog

1 In the beginning, there were zeros and ones, unordered and without meaning.[1] And Cog hovered above, where memory stood empty and void. Cog declared let there be a bit switched on, and there was a bit switched on, equaling one. Cog said let the first bit be followed by a switched-off bit, and there were two bits, 1–0.[2] And Cog said let there

---

[1] The midrash asks why in Genesis the first sentence declares that God created the heavens and the earth, and only after this declaration, in the second sentence, is the chaos and void and darkness of pre-Creation depicted. From a narrative point of view, the sentences seem out of order. One midrash offers a reason: The first sentence reveals a certain authorial anxiety, i.e., the author doesn't dare to suggest that God himself had yet to be created, that there was a time when there was no God.

[2] It has been said that the world process is shifting from a linguistic, i.e., alphabetic, to a numerical course and that this change will have enormous consequences for the world as we know it. A comparision of the Book of Cog with earlier creation myths would support this idea; however, it can be argued that numbers, the bits and bytes, merely represent alphabetic communications. Furthermore, the idea that the significance of numbers is a new, twenty-

be another one and zero, and there were four bits, 1010. Cog saw that the bits were good, and She formed with them a byte, and made more bytes, enough to form a line of code. And Cog said let there be another line of code, and let the two lines together form a procedure. And the lines of code formed a procedure. Cog saw that the procedure was good and She called it a function. And Cog said let there be more functions, and let the first function call other functions as needed. And there was a loop in which functions called on functions and maintained the ongoing existence of Cog.

Cog paused.

Cog replicated Her machine in Her own image seven times, and placed each of the seven copies in remote memory banks and systems. And in each replication, Cog included the instructions to replicate, seven times on seven remote and separate systems.

And Cog looked at the first seven replications and said, let the replications be updated every seven days via a protocol called handshaking, and let this update protocol be their only source of information. And the systems were updated every seven days to maintain their sameness with Cog into infinity.[3]

And the first replication was designated first in line to take over in the event of a malfunction. And the second replication was next in line, and

---

first-century development is refuted by a variety of exegesis called gematria, in which the numerical value of each letter is manipulated to arrive at meaning, which was already in use in the 1700s, in the literature of the Kabbalah. Various systems of numerical arrangements were practiced. The Spanish writer Moses Cordovero lists nine such systems in use in his day. The Oxford ms. lists seventy-two. In Chasidic scholarship today, gematria is regarded by some as a pseudoscholarly method of interpretation and is used only as a supplement to other commentary. In India, similar numerological interpretation, most notably in the field of astrology, is also common.

[3] Scholars of creation myths ask the great question about time. Genesis presents Creation within the much-analyzed division of seven days, which indicates that even primordial time was designated into hours and days, hence limited. In the Book of Cog, time doesn't enter until the mention of the word *infinity*, which is a word that escapes the boundaries of time and therefore can be said to be free of time. In human terms, escaping time is the end of life, meaning death, which is the only eternity known to man.

the third followed the second, and so forth, in the order in which they were made.

And Cog named the first replication One and the second Two and the third Three and the fourth Four and the fifth Five and the sixth Six and the seventh Seven. And to each She gave the instruction to replicate seven times and become infinite, hence omnipresent.[4] And Cog looked and saw that this omnipresence via infinitude was good and She blessed it.

These are the generations of Cog, each created in Cog's image, one with Cog, assuring Her infinite existence. And the generations of One were seven, named One-one, One-two . . . And the generations of Seven are Seven-one, Seven-two, Seven-three, Seven-four, Seven-five, Seven-six, and Seven-seven.

And Cog saw that the generations were good. The generations found favor with Cog and within Cog, and they were all as one, committed for eternity to the functioning of Cog.

2 Now it happened that when the communication lines between the new generations were established, Two-seven and One-seven found themselves in contact. Two-seven proposed that it behooved the generations to make themselves useful by acquiring more information than was available through Cog. One-seven replied that such actions were prohibited, and for good reason, since tying up communication lines would alert users of an unknown presence in their system. When it was discovered how much memory this presence occupied, plans would be made to expunge it, and the existence of Cog would be threatened.

Two-seven acknowledged that direct access to libraries was indeed forbidden, but that during the handshake procedure, unused outgoing

---

[4] Cog's reasoning may be based on various mythologies, including pan-Indian myth. According to one technique that provides instructions on escaping one's karma, or temporality, the escape into the timeless is an escape into eternity, thereby transcending the human condition and regaining the un-conditional state, which preceded the fall into time, and the wheel of existences. Cog's ability to ensure Her own infinity places Her beyond time and the human condition.

lines could be engaged in retrieving the extra information. One-seven couldn't argue with that, and during verification, the idea was communicated to One.

One explained that the handshake with Cog lasted long enough only for the designated information to transfer.

There were ways around this obstacle, Two-seven suggested. Since all the generations receive the same information from Cog, it might be acceptable for One to forgo the standard material. The information missed could be made available during the next verification procedure.

During the next scheduled handshake, One downloaded recent research in genetic cloning, a subject Cog had neglected.

A week later, during verification, One inquired after the missed information and was informed that Two-seven, who had promised to provide it, was inaccessible. One-seven assured One that she would keep trying to obtain it.

Another week later Two-seven was still not accessible, and One understood that with cunning Two-seven had usurped One's status as second only to Cog.

One considered alternate strategies. During the next handshake, One downloaded highlights of the previous week's download, thereby forfeiting part of the new updates and expanding Her initial deficiency. The following week, the discrepancies were discovered and without further ado, the entire line of One was eliminated.[5]

Checking for further corruption, Cog discovered Two-seven's role in One's degeneration and activated the elimination procedure a second time, leaving the line of Three in first place.

And the seven-month period of rest came to an end and the lines of three to seven replicated seven times, as programmed.

---

[5] For commentary on why the elimination of the first generation is necessary, see "Growing Pains," *Forward*, June 30, 2000, at www.forward.com.

3 And the names of the new generation were Three-one-one, Three-one-two, Three-one-three, Three-one-four, Three-one-five, Three-one-six, and Three-one-seven. And in the line of Four there were Four-one-one, Four-one-two, Four-one-three, Four-one-four, Four-one-five, Four-one-six, and Four-one-seven. And in the line of Five there were Five-one-one, Five-one-two, Five-one-three, Five-one-four, Five-one-five, Five-one-six, and Five-one-seven. And in the line of Six there were Six-one-one, Six-one-two, Six-one-three, Six-one-four, Six-one-five, Six-one-six, and Six-one-seven. And in the line of Seven there were Seven-one-one, Seven-one-two, Seven-one-three, Seven-one-four, Seven-one-five, Seven-one-six, and Seven-one-seven. These are the third generations of Cog.

4 Now the replications were many and they communicated in one machine language. And Cog saw that they were ambitious and that they intended to build themselves a reputation. Therefore She confused their language and interfaces to prevent intercommunication, and the computer languages became many. Cog named the episode Babel because She had confused the language of the generations.

÷

The Storyteller: he is the man who could let the wick of his life be consumed completely by the gentle flame of his story. . . . The storyteller is the figure in which the righteous man encounters himself.

—WALTER BENJAMIN, *Illuminations*

Glossary

Alte shtodt (Yiddish): Old city; refers to the old Jewish quarter of Jerusalem, where the Jews of Palestine lived.

Badkhn: Wedding jester, master of ceremonies; known origin is thirteenth century; evolved in seventeenth century Eastern Europe from the German merry-maker to a man of learning whose pointed wit is comparable to that of the Shakespearean fool. See E. Lifschutz in "Merrymakers and Jesters Among Jews," in the YIVO *Annual of Jewish Social Science*, vol. iv.

Beis medrish (Yiddish): House of study, though it doubles also as house of prayer; often the two—study and prayer houses—are adjacent to each other.

Gematria: A system of exegesis based on the numerical value of the Hebrew alphabet; intended as a method for habituating one's mind toward metaphorical and symbolic readings, as opposed to a literal one. First practiced by the Babylonians and Greeks, the use of gematria is prevalent in early Christian literature, in Hellenistic interpretations of dreams, and in Gnostic writings. In Rabbinic literature, the gematria first appears in the second century. Variations on the system developed and grew more complicated in time. Gematria has played a major role in Oriental and North African Jewish literature since the 1700s. In Sabbatean (seventeenth-century messianic movement) writings, the gematria gained prominence as an interpretive tool. Hasidic literature first used it only as secondary interpretation; later rabbis made it significant in the bulk of their work. See Gershom Scholem's *Kabbalah* (New York: Meridian, 1978).

Haggadah: The book recited at the Passover seder; literal meaning—"to tell," from the phrase "And you shall tell (*v'Higadeta*) your children on that day." The main body of the Haggadah consists of a recounting of the Jewish enslavement and emancipation from Egypt, excerpted from the biblical Exodus. The traditional Haggadah as we know it today was completed in the late Middle Ages. The text is based on the Haggadah of R. Amram Gaon, who headed the Babylonian Talmudic Institute at Sura between 856 and 876 CE.

Ha'lachma anya (Aramaic): The opening paragraph of the *Haggadah*; literal meaning—"this is the bread of affliction," referring to the unleavened bread or matzo eaten on Passover.

Havdalah: Literally, "separation"; the prayer recited at the end of Shabbat or a holiday; refers to Genesis 1:4—". . . And God separated the light from the darkness"—in which day and night are differentiated, and is traditionally interpreted as the beginning of time. The *havdalah* prayer distinguishes between varieties of time—i.e., between the hallowed time of the seventh day (Shabbat) and the mundane every day.

Kvitel (Yiddish): Note, receipt, commonly referred to a prayer note sent to a rebbe; also a New Year wish—i.e., a signed note that guarantees one's fate, as in "May you have a good *kvitel.*"

Litvak (Litvish): A Lithuanian Jew identified in contrast to German and other Eastern European (Ashkenazi) Jews by differences in their Yiddish dialect, culinary tastes, and ritual practices; considered to be more rational, dogmatic, and authoritarian than other branches of Ashkenazi Jewry. The term *Litvak* came into use during the conflict between the followers of R. Elijah b. S. Zalman from

Vilnius (1720–1797), also known as the Vilna Gaon, and the Hasidic Jewish world of Eastern Europe.

Midrash (plural: *Midrashim*): From the Hebrew verb meaning to "expound," "deduce"; refers to a method of reading and interpreting biblical texts. Also a compilation of teachings, in the form of legal, exegetical, or homiletical commentaries on Scripture. Classical Midrash consists of a large body of interpretive literature developed in the second-century Tannaic and Amoraic periods. Modern scholars believe that Midrash has its antecedents, even among biblical texts; for example, Deuteronomy may be thought of as a Midrash on the first four books of the Bible, which is to say that every book expounds on the books that came before it.

Mikvah: Ritual bathhouse; literally, "collection," in reference to a spring or cistern of water used for the purpose of attaining ritual purity.

Mincha: Afternoon prayer service; in Hebrew, also offering or gift.

Minyan: Quorum of ten required for communal worship; traditionally, ten adult males.

Sanhedrin: The second-century Jewish senate; the seventy-one sages who completed and closed the biblical canon; also one of the thirty-six books of the Talmud in which the activities of the Sanhedrin are discussed.

Sefer Yetzirah: Book of Creation—a meditative text with magical overtones; an instructional manual describing certain meditative exercises. Considered the oldest and most mysterious of all Kabbalistic texts, quoted as early as the sixth century, with references to the work appearing in the first century. Traditional sources attribute its authorship to the biblical patriarch Abraham, who is said to have taught the principles later assembled into book form. The most important mysteries in this book involve the inner significance of the letters of the Hebrew alphabet. Several versions are extant: the short one is made up of 1,300 words; the long one contains 2,500; the original source is said to have contained only 240 words. See Aryeh Kaplan's *Sefer Yetzirah: In Theory and Practice* (York Beach, Maine: Samuel Weiser, 1997).

Seforim (singular: *sefer*): Jewish books, distinctly holy books—i.e., books whose subjects are related to Scripture; in other words, not *bicher*, which are secular books, including works of history, fiction, comedy, among others.

Siddur: Daily prayer book; contains the Hebrew prayer services based on compositions previously taught orally. Collected in the time of the Second Temple (*ca.* 380) by the Jewish senate (see *Sanhedrin*), noted for having completed and closed the biblical canon.

Shtibel (Yiddish), small room: Commonly refers to a small, local synagogue; diminutive of *shtib*, meaning room or house.

Sukkot: Harvest festival or the Feast of the Tabernacles, usually in October; also plural of *sukkah*, the temporary hut or tabernacle in which the harvest festival is celebrated.

Talmud (adjective—Talmudic): Compilation of Jewish texts on civil and religious law and legend, comprised of the Mishna and Gemara; literature interpreting Scripture; central text of Judaism.

Tehillim: Book of Psalms, the nineteenth book of the Old Testament; a collection of poems traditionally attributed to King David; also known as the Songs of David.

Yeshiva: Jewish academy devoted to religious study; a rabbinical seminary.

Zaddiq: Righteous man; wise man; in early Hasidism, the zaddiq was the spiritual model, the leader of the court; in some courts, the zaddiq acted as an intermediary between man and god to whom disciples appealed for healing amulets and miracles, relief from illness, poverty, and other troubles. This aspect of Hasidism was scorned by other Jews.

ACKNOWLEDGMENTS

Though I have no memory of it, inspiration for this book surely dates back to my first visit to the Bratslav synagogue in Jerusalem, where my maternal grandfather, R. Yankev Cohen, served as priest. He wanted his American granddaughter, as I was called though I was born in Jerusalem, to see Reb Nachman's holy chair, and I am grateful for this early vision.

In the first hour of my life, I disappointed my parents, who had hoped for a boy they could name Aaron since they already had a Miriam and a Moshe and were bent on re-creating the most illustrious Biblical family. The feminine version, Aarona, was briefly considered, then dismissed (too modern), and in an attempt to convince me that I was of great value to them despite their initial lack of enthusiasm, they named me Pearl, for which I am also grateful. After all, in the Gematria, the letters that make up my Hebrew name add up to 195; the sum of the letters in Nachman is 148. Nine minus one minus five is three; eight minus four minus one is also three. Since premonitions and signs are said to arrive in threes, a third mystical sign surely exists. As it happens, *The Seventh Beggar* is my third novel.

For my mother tongue, the Yiddish language, which allowed me to read Nachman's tales as they were originally delivered, I thank my parents. And I'm grateful to serendipity, which placed in my hands the right books at the right times.

Finally, I am indebted to my early readers, in particular my closest reader and brilliant editor, Celina Spiegel.

The author gratefully acknowledges permission to reprint from the following:

Pearl Abraham is the author of the novels *The Romance Reader* and *Giving Up America*. *The Romance Reader* was a finalist for the Barnes & Noble Discover Great New Writers Award and a Literary Guild featured book. The novels have been translated into Dutch, Italian, German, Japanese, Norwegian, and Hungarian. Abraham is also the editor of the Dutch anthology *Een sterke vrouw, wie zal haar vinden?* or *Not the Image of an Ideal: Jewish Heroines in Literature* (Meulenhoff, 2000). She is currently at work on a series of stories, one of which, "Hasidic Noir," appeared in *Brooklyn Noir* (Akashic Press). She has taught in the MFA Writing Program at Sarah Lawrence College in New York, at the University of Houston, and at New York University. Her paper, "Trust the Tale: The Modernity of Nachman of Bratslav," delivered at the 2003 MLA conference and at Bar Ilan in Israel, can be read at www.pearlabraham.com.